STAR WARS™

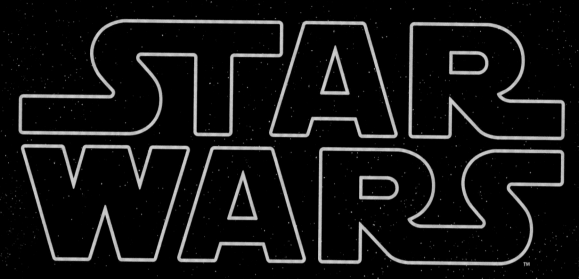

MUTINY AT MON CALA

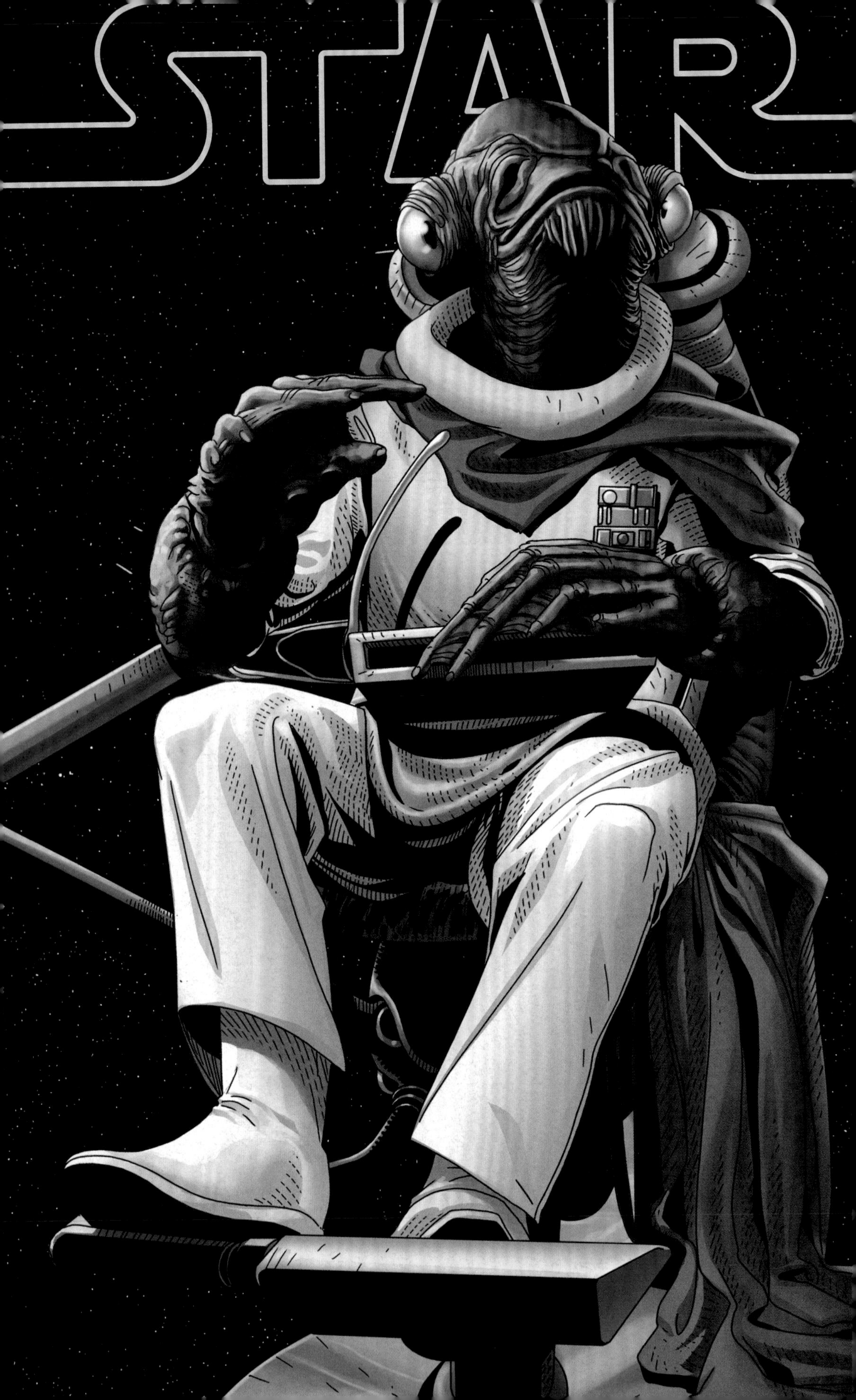
STAR

MUTINY AT MON CALA

Writer	**KIERON GILLEN**
Artist	**SALVADOR LARROCA**
Color Artist	**GURU-eFX**
Letterer	**VC's CLAYTON COWLES**
Cover Art	**DAVID MARQUEZ & MATTHEW WILSON**
Assistant Editor	**HEATHER ANTOS**
Editor	**JORDAN D. WHITE**
Editor in Chief	**C.B. CEBULSKI**
Chief Creative Officer	**JOE QUESADA**
President	**DAN BUCKLEY**

For Lucasfilm:

Assistant Editor	**NICK MARTINO**
Senior Editor	**ROBERT SIMPSON**
Executive Editor	**JENNIFER HEDDLE**
Creative Director	**MICHAEL SIGLAIN**
Lucasfilm Story Group	**JAMES WAUGH, LELAND CHEE, MATT MARTIN**

Collection Editor	**JENNIFER GRÜNWALD**
Assistant Editor	**CAITLIN O'CONNELL**
Associate Managing Editor	**KATERI WOODY**
Editor, Special Projects	**MARK D. BEAZLEY**
VP Production & Special Projects	**JEFF YOUNGQUIST**
SVP Print, Sales & Marketing	**DAVID GABRIEL**
Book Designer	**ADAM DEL RE**

STAR WARS VOL. 8: MUTINY AT MON CALA. Contains material originally published in magazine form as STAR WARS #44-49. First printing 2018. ISBN 978-1-302-91053-2. Published by MARVEL WORLDWIDE, INC., a subsidiary of MARVEL ENTERTAINMENT, LLC. OFFICE OF PUBLICATION: 135 West 50th Street, New York, NY 10020. STAR WARS and related text and illustrations are trademarks and/or copyrights, in the United States and other countries, of Lucasfilm Ltd. and/or its affiliates. © & TM Lucasfilm Ltd. No similarity between any of the names, characters, persons, and/or institutions in this magazine with those of any living or dead person or institution is intended, and any such similarity which may exist is purely coincidental. Marvel and its logos are TM Marvel Characters, Inc. Printed in Canada. DAN BUCKLEY, President, Marvel Entertainment; JOHN NEE, Publisher; JOE QUESADA, Chief Creative Officer; TOM BREVOORT, SVP of Publishing; DAVID BOGART, SVP of Business Affairs & Operations, Publishing & Partnership; DAVID GABRIEL, SVP of Sales & Marketing, Publishing; JEFF YOUNGQUIST, VP of Production & Special Projects; DAN CARR, Executive Director of Publishing Technology; ALEX MORALES, Director of Publishing Operations; DAN EDINGTON, Managing Editor; SUSAN CRESPI, Production Manager; STAN LEE, Chairman Emeritus. For information regarding advertising in Marvel Comics or on Marvel.com, please contact Vit DeBellis, Custom Solutions & Integrated Advertising Manager, at vdebellis@marvel.com. For Marvel subscription inquiries, please call 888-511-5480. **Manufactured between 6/1/2018 and 7/3/2018 by SOLISCO PRINTERS, SCOTT, QC, CANADA.**

10 9 8 7 6 5 4 3 2 1

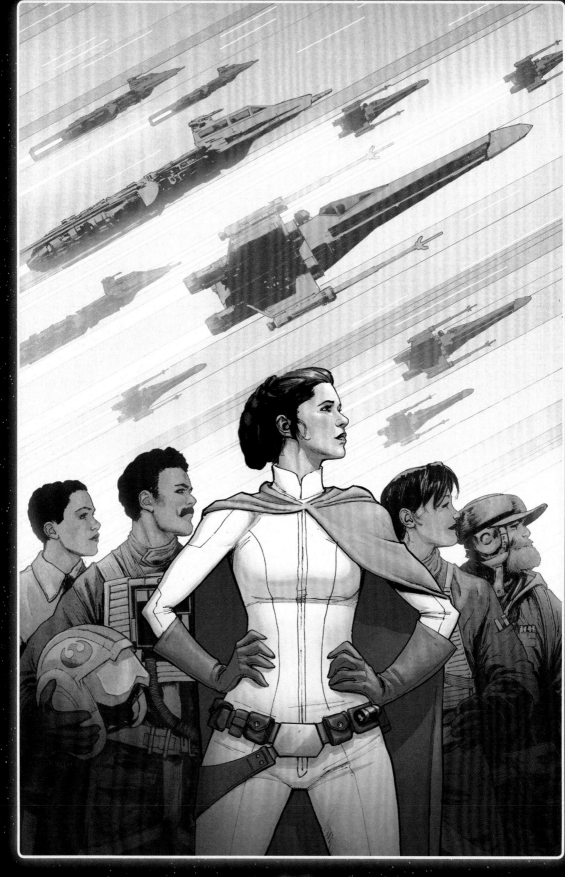

MUTINY AT MON CALA

It is a period of rebuilding in the galaxy. The Death Star has been destroyed as has the Imperial orbital drill on Jedha. A spark of hope has emerged among the Rebellion.

Recently, rebel leaders Princess Leia, Luke Skywalker, and Han Solo have been in search of a new base of operation as they continue the fight against the Galactic Empire's tyrannical reign.

New alliances are formed every day....

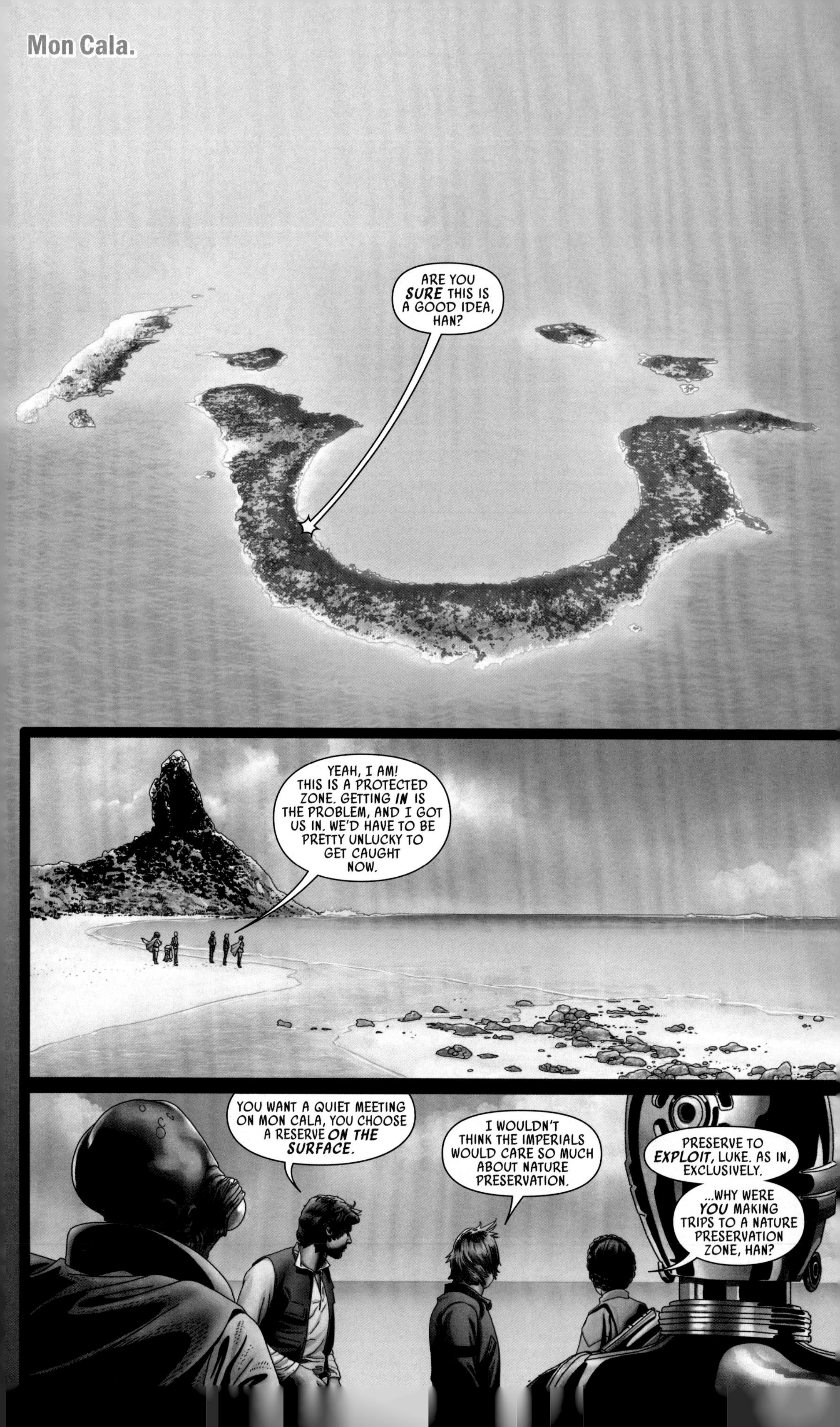
Mon Cala.
ARE YOU SURE THIS IS A GOOD IDEA, HAN?
YEAH, I AM! THIS IS A PROTECTED ZONE. GETTING IN IS THE PROBLEM, AND I GOT US IN. WE'D HAVE TO BE PRETTY UNLUCKY TO GET CAUGHT NOW.
YOU WANT A QUIET MEETING ON MON CALA, YOU CHOOSE A RESERVE ON THE SURFACE.
I WOULDN'T THINK THE IMPERIALS WOULD CARE SO MUCH ABOUT NATURE PRESERVATION.
PRESERVE TO EXPLOIT, LUKE. AS IN, EXCLUSIVELY.
...WHY WERE YOU MAKING TRIPS TO A NATURE PRESERVATION ZONE, HAN?

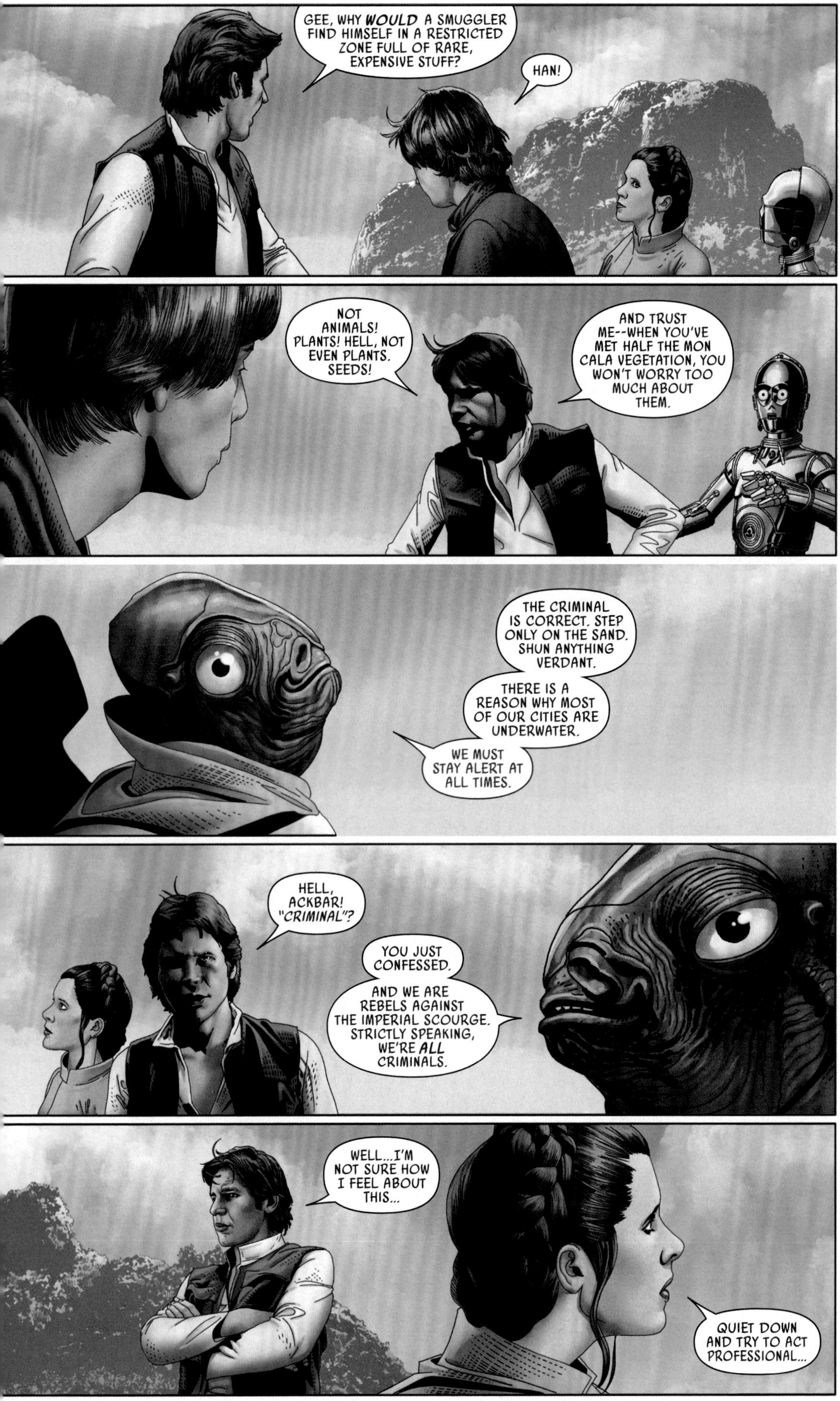
GEE, WHY WOULD A SMUGGLER FIND HIMSELF IN A RESTRICTED ZONE FULL OF RARE, EXPENSIVE STUFF?
HAN!
NOT ANIMALS! PLANTS! HELL, NOT EVEN PLANTS. SEEDS!
AND TRUST ME--WHEN YOU'VE MET HALF THE MON CALA VEGETATION, YOU WON'T WORRY TOO MUCH ABOUT THEM.
THE CRIMINAL IS CORRECT. STEP ONLY ON THE SAND. SHUN ANYTHING VERDANT.
THERE IS A REASON WHY MOST OF OUR CITIES ARE UNDERWATER.
WE MUST STAY ALERT AT ALL TIMES.
HELL, ACKBAR! "CRIMINAL"?
YOU JUST CONFESSED.
AND WE ARE REBELS AGAINST THE IMPERIAL SCOURGE. STRICTLY SPEAKING, WE'RE ALL CRIMINALS.
WELL...I'M NOT SURE HOW I FEEL ABOUT THIS...
QUIET DOWN AND TRY TO ACT PROFESSIONAL...

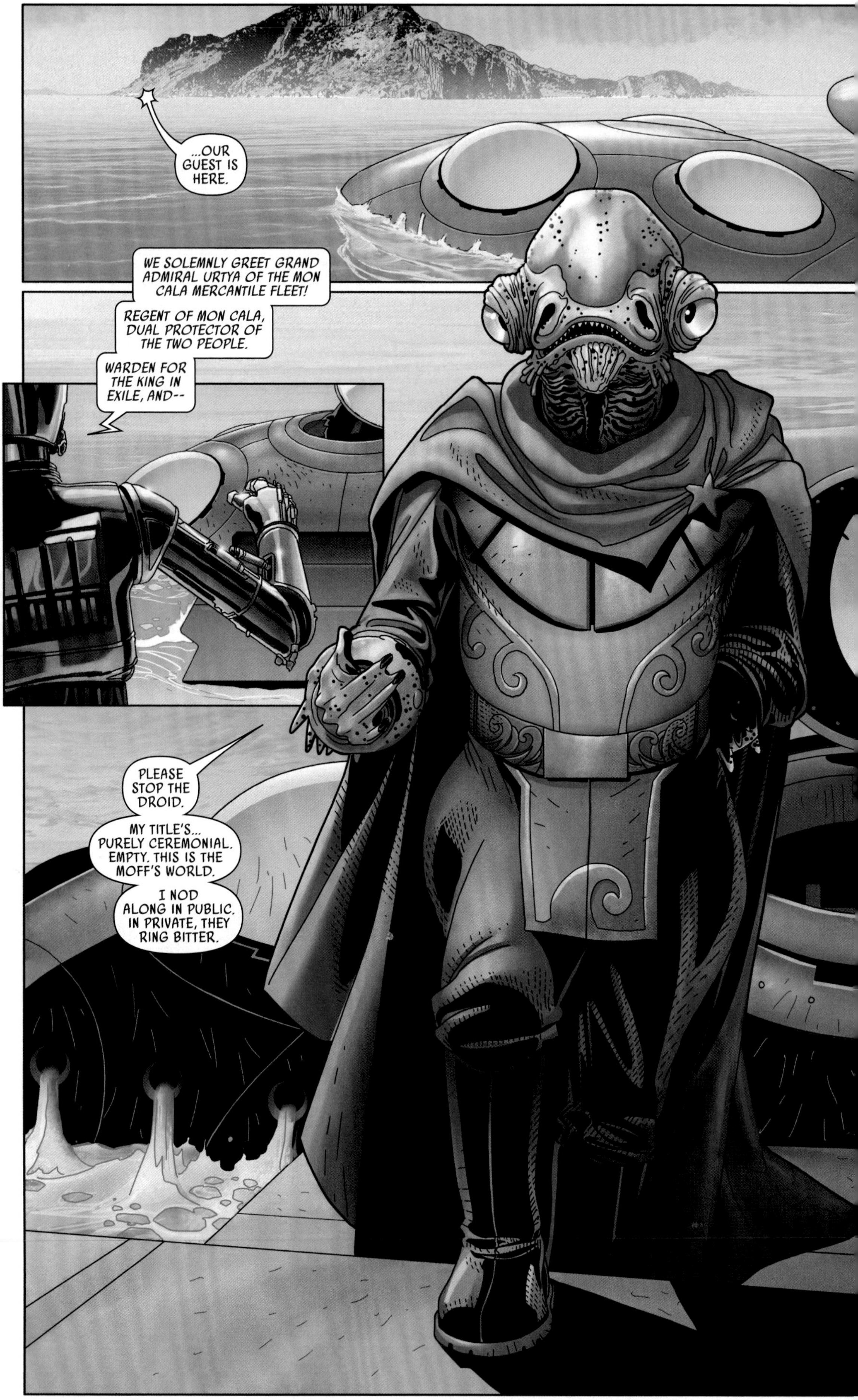
...OUR GUEST IS HERE.
WE SOLEMNLY GREET GRAND ADMIRAL URTYA OF THE MON CALA MERCANTILE FLEET!
REGENT OF MON CALA, DUAL PROTECTOR OF THE TWO PEOPLE.
WARDEN FOR THE KING IN EXILE, AND--
PLEASE STOP THE DROID.
MY TITLE'S... PURELY CEREMONIAL. EMPTY. THIS IS THE MOFF'S WORLD.
I NOD ALONG IN PUBLIC. IN PRIVATE, THEY RING BITTER.

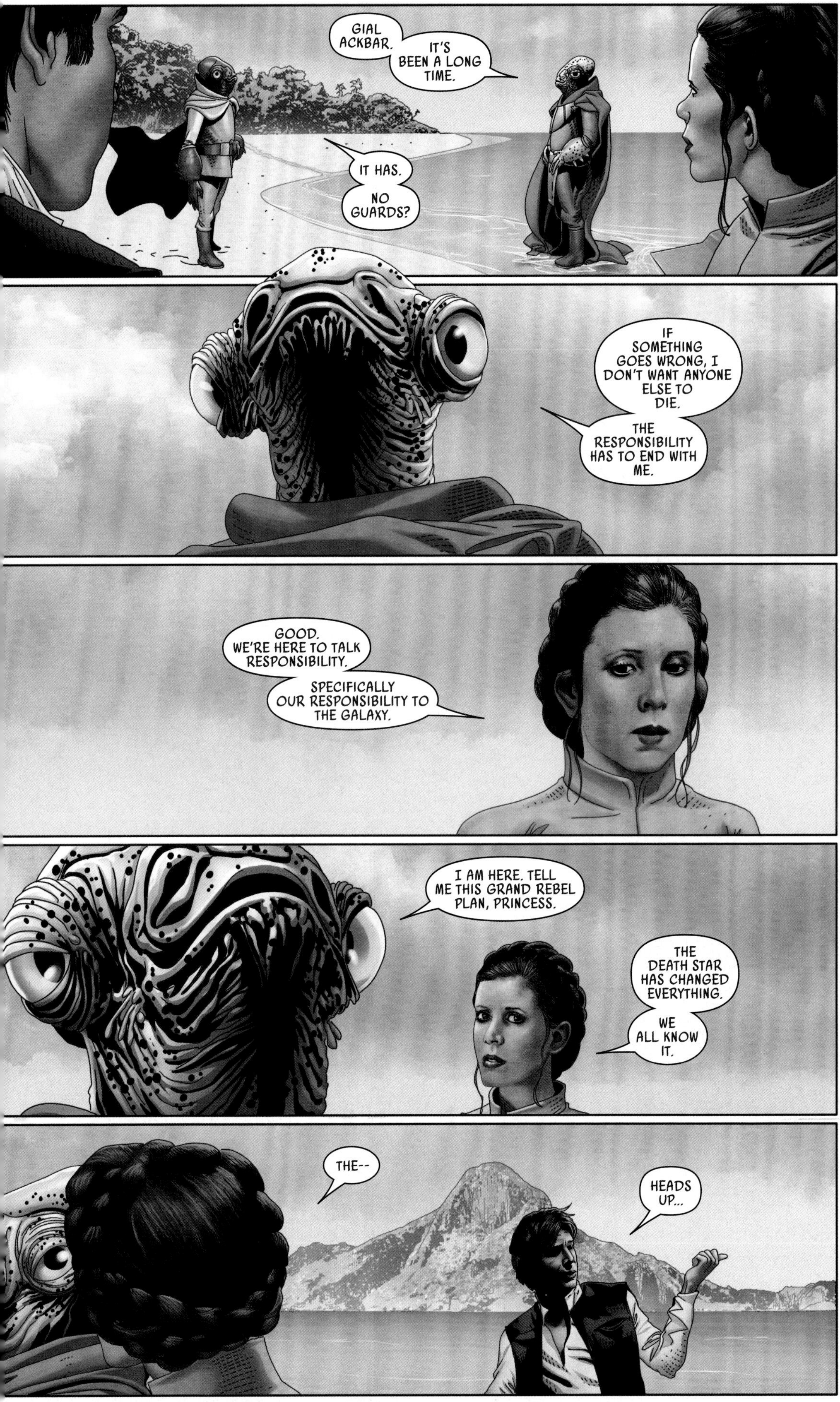
GIAL ACKBAR.
IT'S BEEN A LONG TIME.
IT HAS.
NO GUARDS?
IF SOMETHING GOES WRONG, I DON'T WANT ANYONE ELSE TO DIE.
THE RESPONSIBILITY HAS TO END WITH ME.
GOOD. WE'RE HERE TO TALK RESPONSIBILITY.
SPECIFICALLY OUR RESPONSIBILITY TO THE GALAXY.
I AM HERE. TELL ME THIS GRAND REBEL PLAN, PRINCESS.
THE DEATH STAR HAS CHANGED EVERYTHING.
WE ALL KNOW IT.
THE--
HEADS UP...

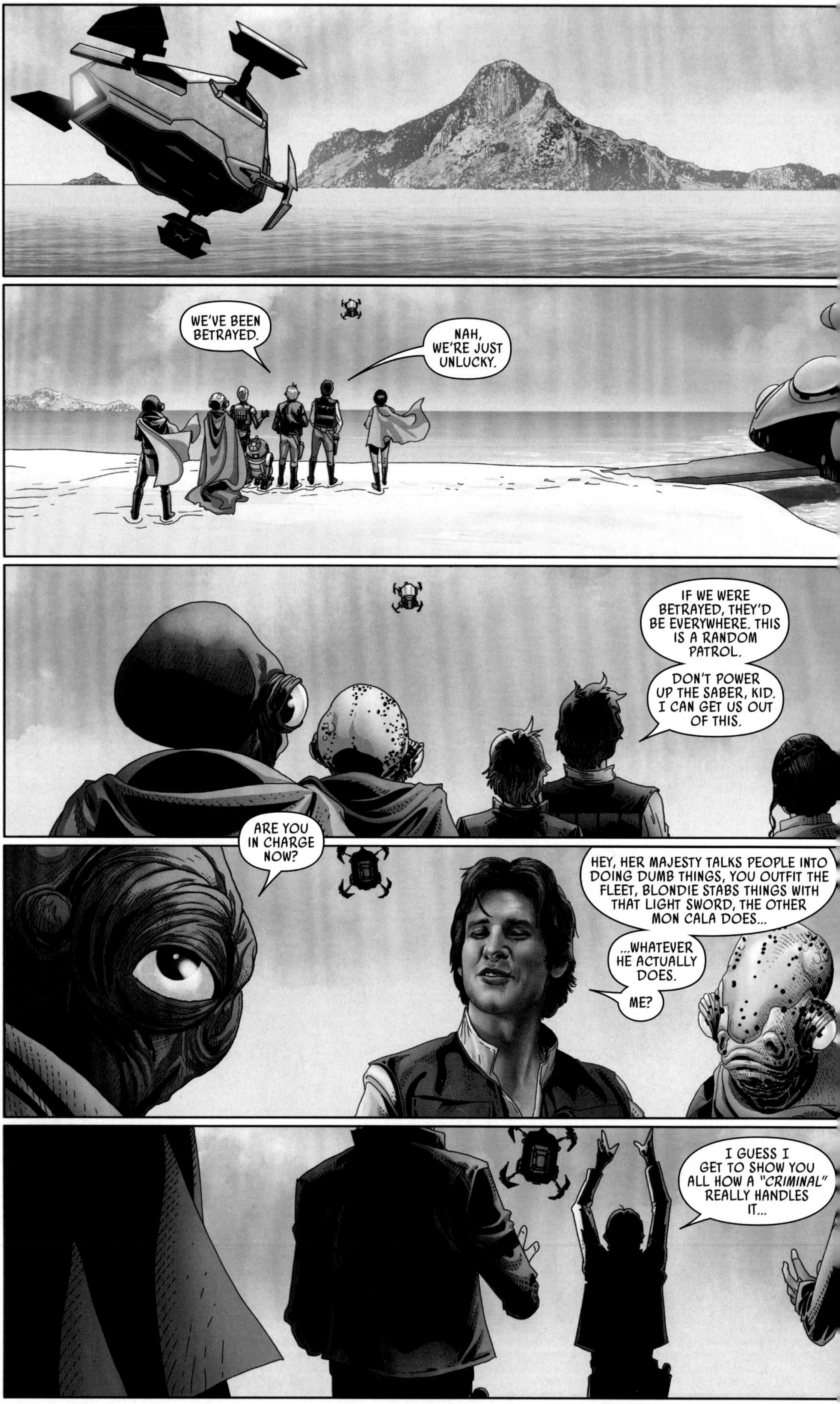
WE'VE BEEN BETRAYED.
NAH, WE'RE JUST UNLUCKY.
IF WE WERE BETRAYED, THEY'D BE EVERYWHERE. THIS IS A RANDOM PATROL.
DON'T POWER UP THE SABER, KID. I CAN GET US OUT OF THIS.
ARE YOU IN CHARGE NOW?
HEY, HER MAJESTY TALKS PEOPLE INTO DOING DUMB THINGS, YOU OUTFIT THE FLEET, BLONDIE STABS THINGS WITH THAT LIGHT SWORD, THE OTHER MON CALA DOES...
...WHATEVER HE ACTUALLY DOES.
ME?
I GUESS I GET TO SHOW YOU ALL HOW A "CRIMINAL" REALLY HANDLES IT...

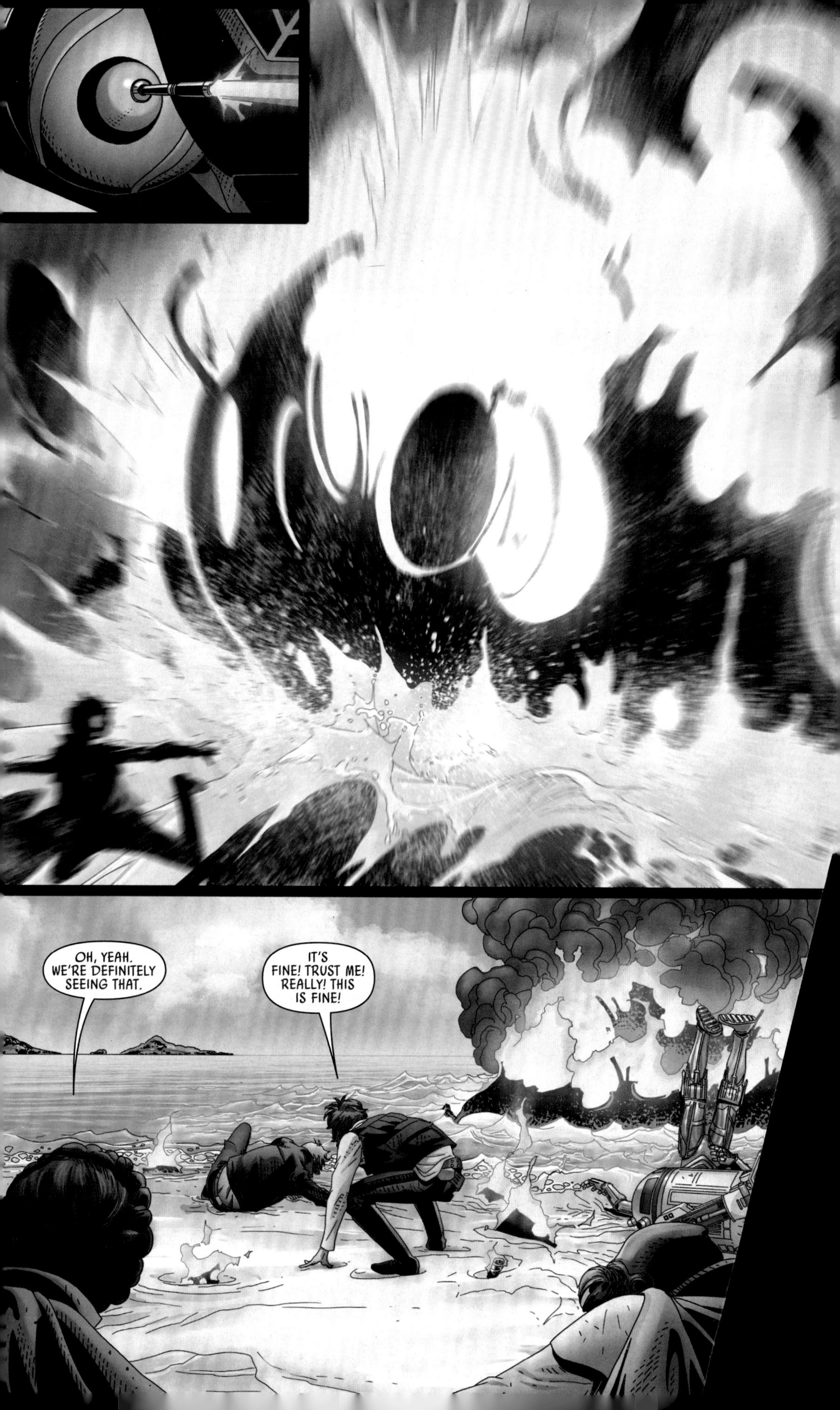
OH, YEAH. WE'RE DEFINITELY SEEING THAT.
IT'S FINE! TRUST ME! REALLY! THIS IS FINE!

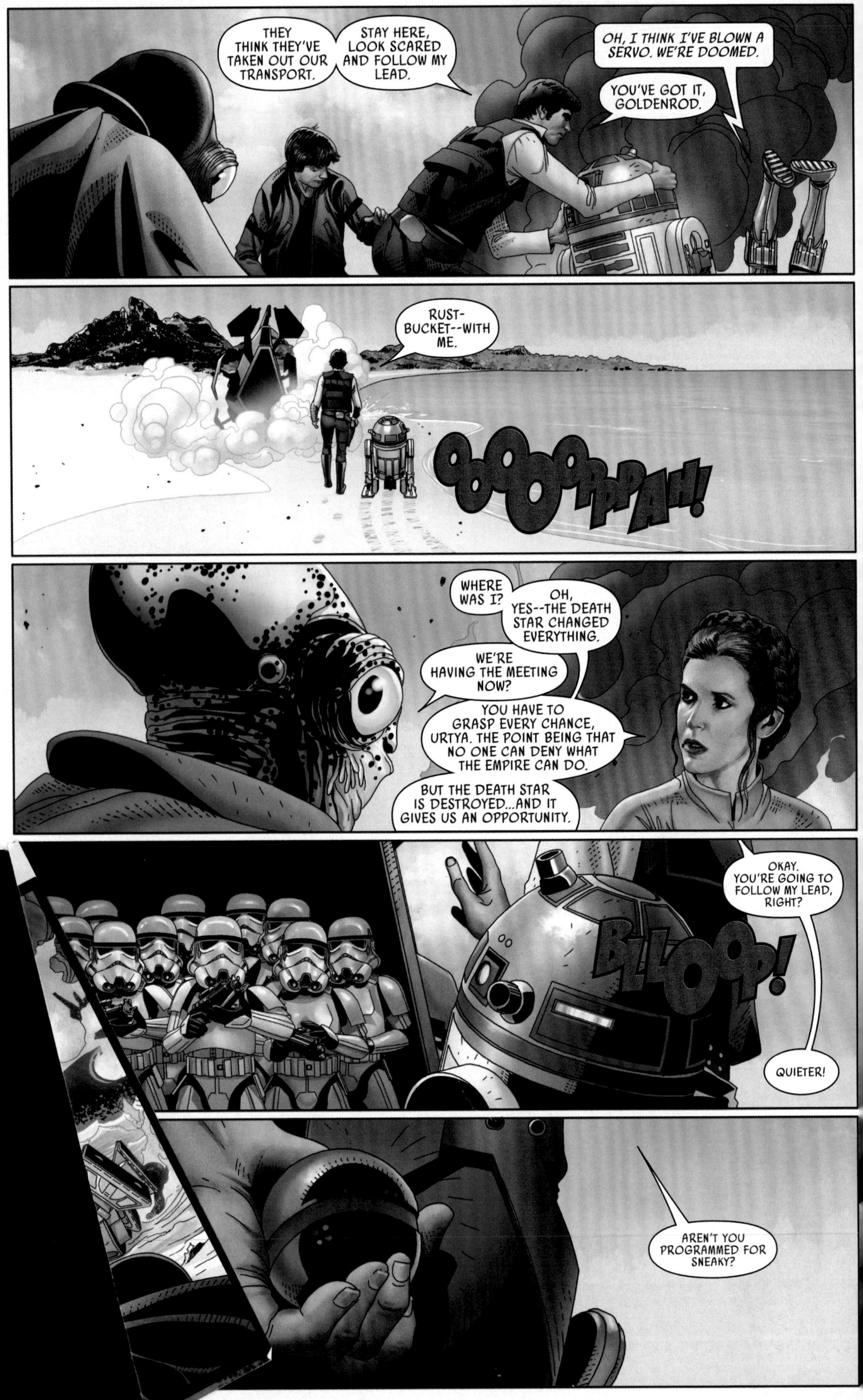
THEY THINK THEY'VE TAKEN OUT OUR TRANSPORT.
STAY HERE, LOOK SCARED AND FOLLOW MY LEAD.
OH, I THINK I'VE BLOWN A SERVO. WE'RE DOOMED.
YOU'VE GOT IT, GOLDENROD.
RUST-BUCKET--WITH ME.
OOOOOPPPAH!
WHERE WAS I?
OH, YES--THE DEATH STAR CHANGED EVERYTHING.
WE'RE HAVING THE MEETING NOW?
YOU HAVE TO GRASP EVERY CHANCE, URTYA. THE POINT BEING THAT NO ONE CAN DENY WHAT THE EMPIRE CAN DO.
BUT THE DEATH STAR IS DESTROYED...AND IT GIVES US AN OPPORTUNITY.
OKAY. YOU'RE GOING TO FOLLOW MY LEAD, RIGHT?
BLLOOP!
QUIETER!
AREN'T YOU PROGRAMMED FOR SNEAKY?

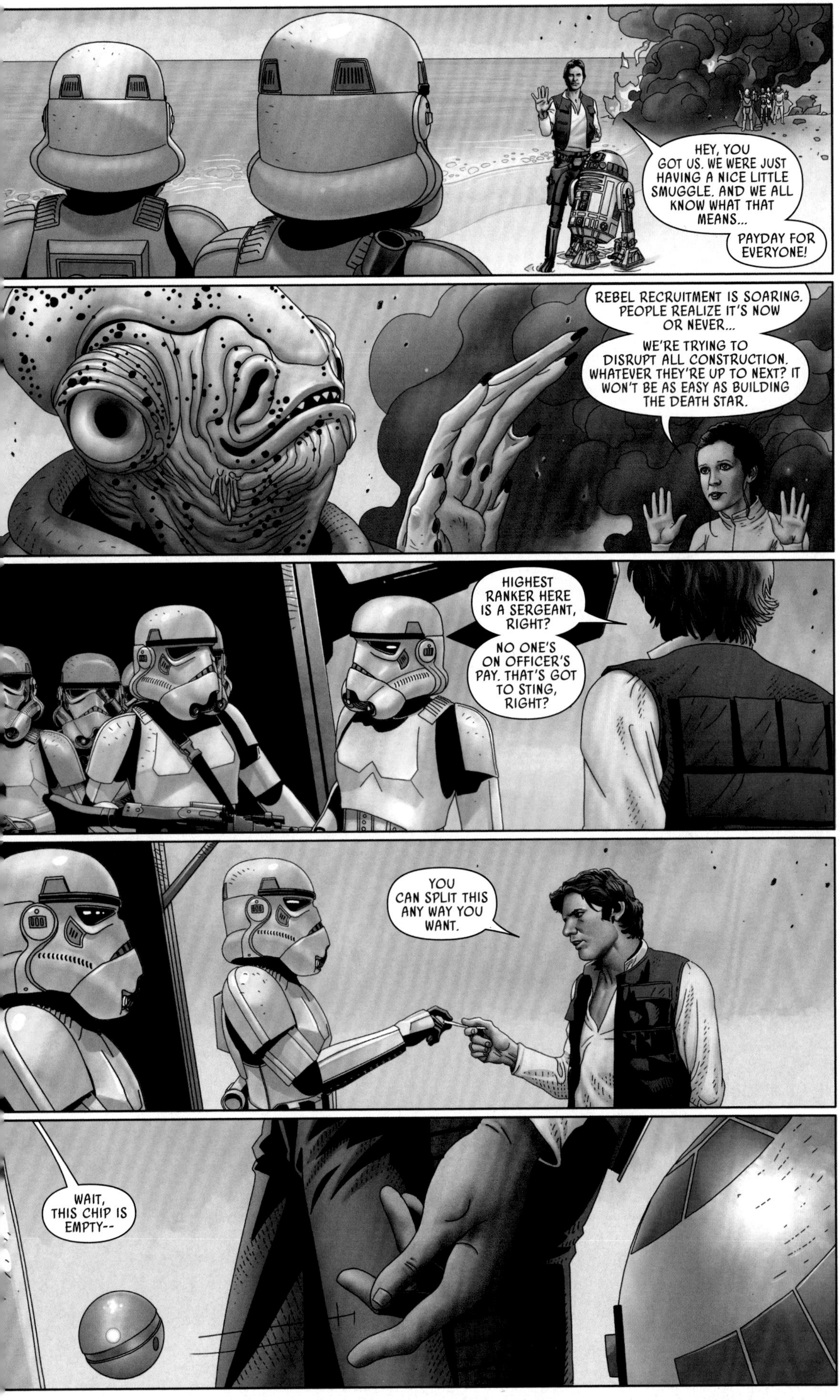

HEY, YOU GOT US. WE WERE JUST HAVING A NICE LITTLE SMUGGLE. AND WE ALL KNOW WHAT THAT MEANS...
PAYDAY FOR EVERYONE!
REBEL RECRUITMENT IS SOARING. PEOPLE REALIZE IT'S NOW OR NEVER...
WE'RE TRYING TO DISRUPT ALL CONSTRUCTION. WHATEVER THEY'RE UP TO NEXT? IT WON'T BE AS EASY AS BUILDING THE DEATH STAR.
HIGHEST RANKER HERE IS A SERGEANT, RIGHT?
NO ONE'S ON OFFICER'S PAY. THAT'S GOT TO STING, RIGHT?
YOU CAN SPLIT THIS ANY WAY YOU WANT.
WAIT, THIS CHIP IS EMPTY--

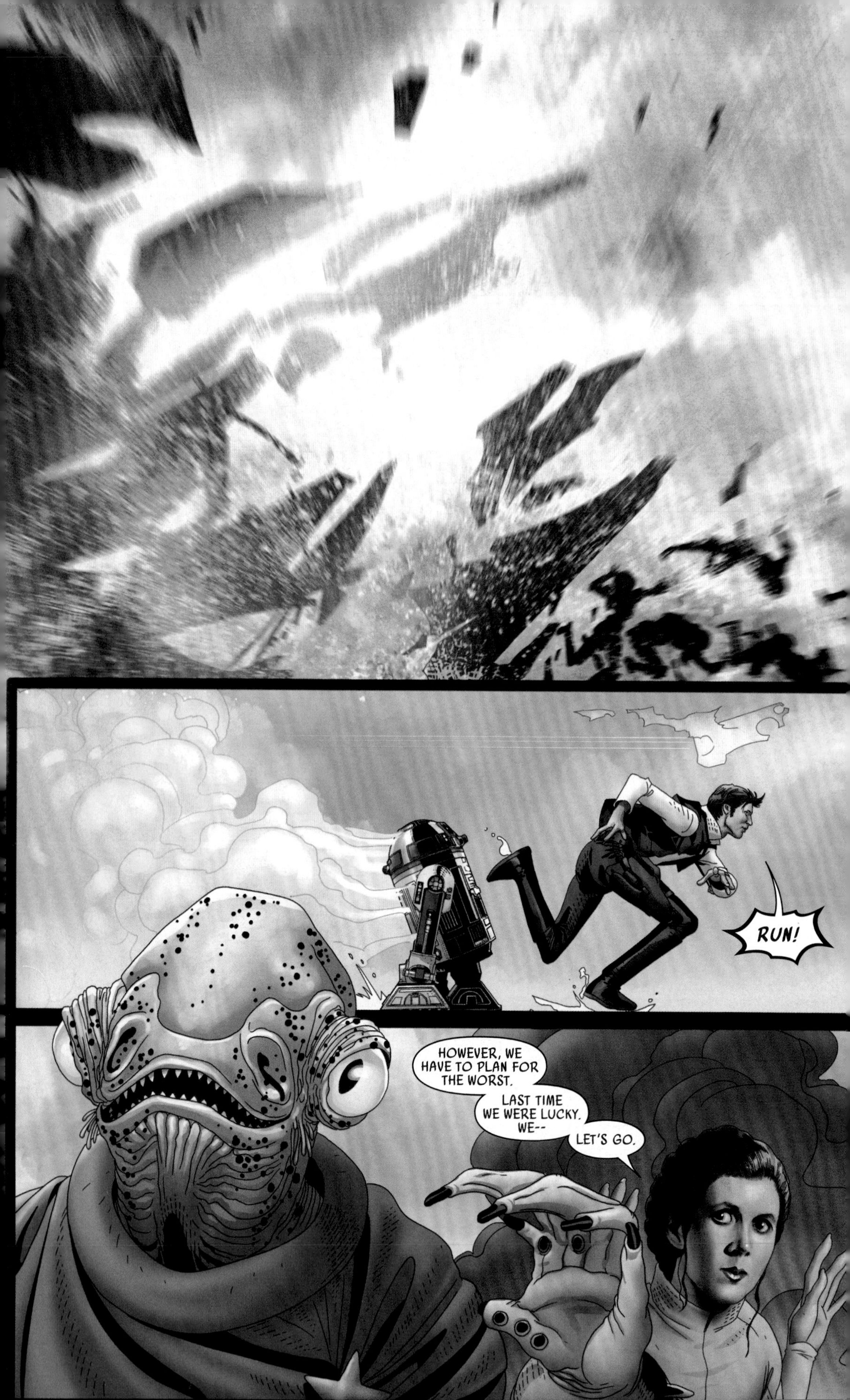
RUN!
HOWEVER, WE HAVE TO PLAN FOR THE WORST.
LAST TIME WE WERE LUCKY. WE--
LET'S GO.

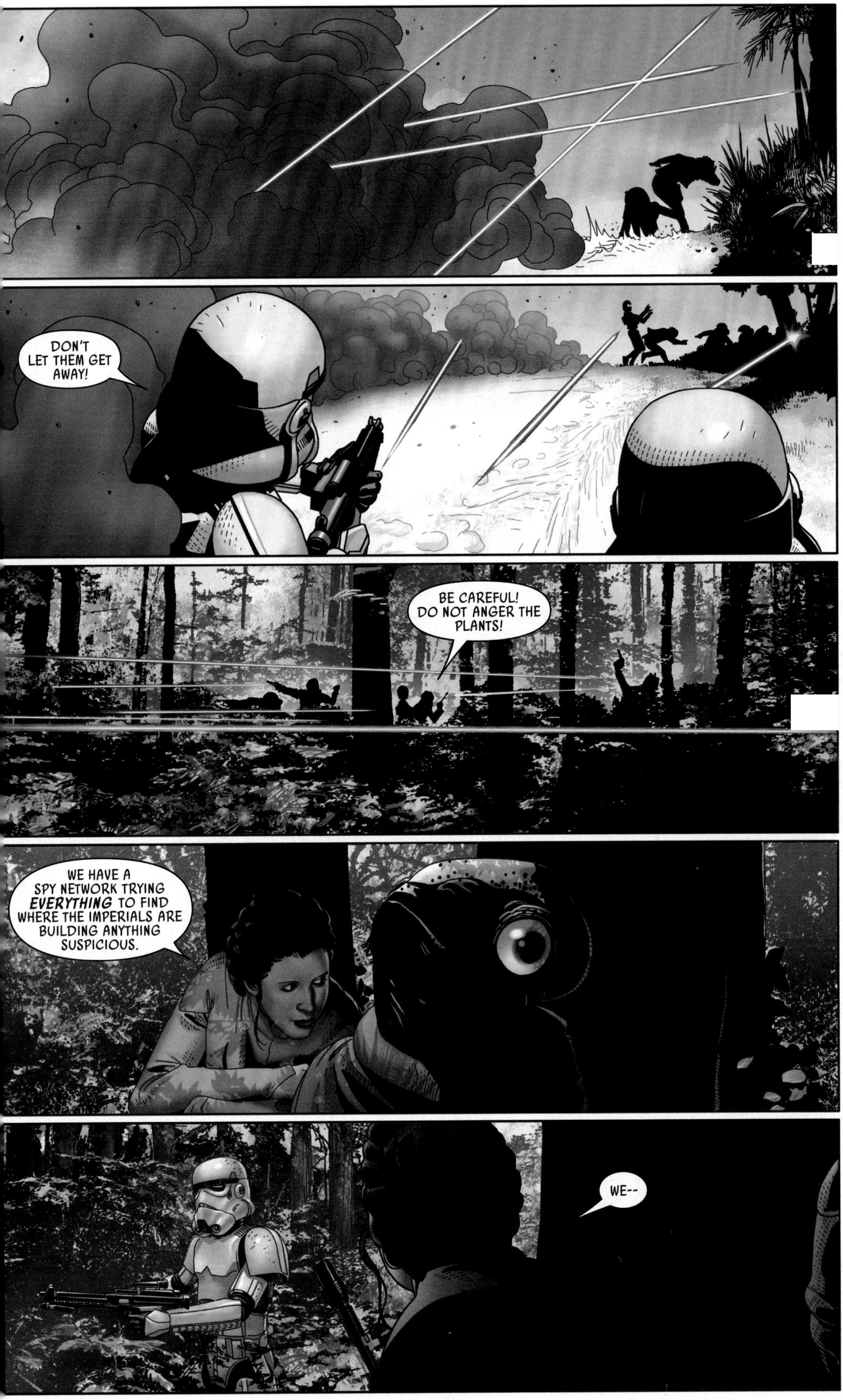
DON'T LET THEM GET AWAY!
BE CAREFUL! DO NOT ANGER THE PLANTS!
WE HAVE A SPY NETWORK TRYING *EVERYTHING* TO FIND WHERE THE IMPERIALS ARE BUILDING ANYTHING SUSPICIOUS.
WE--

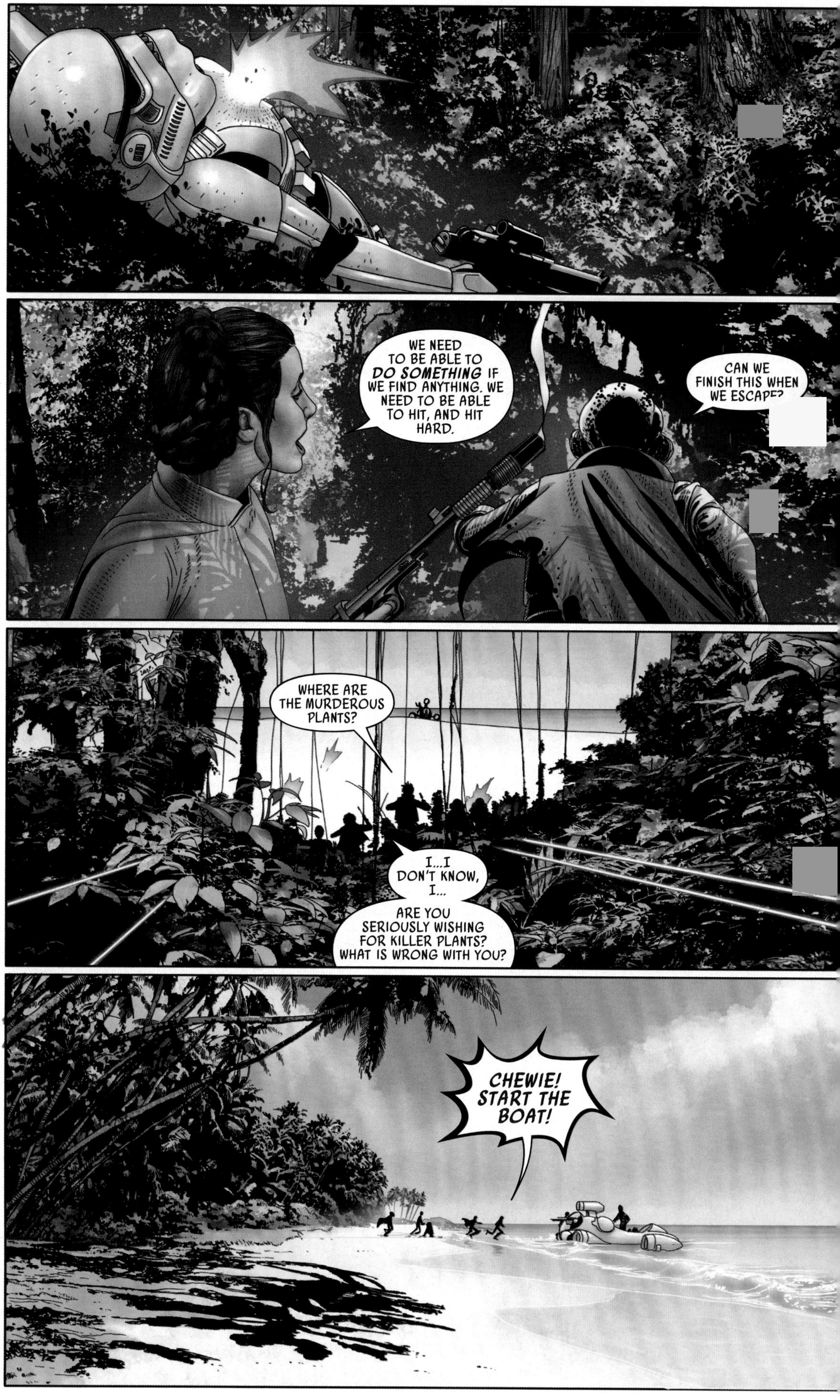

WE NEED TO BE ABLE TO DO SOMETHING IF WE FIND ANYTHING. WE NEED TO BE ABLE TO HIT, AND HIT HARD.
CAN WE FINISH THIS WHEN WE ESCAPE?
WHERE ARE THE MURDEROUS PLANTS?
I...I DON'T KNOW, I...
ARE YOU SERIOUSLY WISHING FOR KILLER PLANTS? WHAT IS WRONG WITH YOU?
CHEWIE! START THE BOAT!

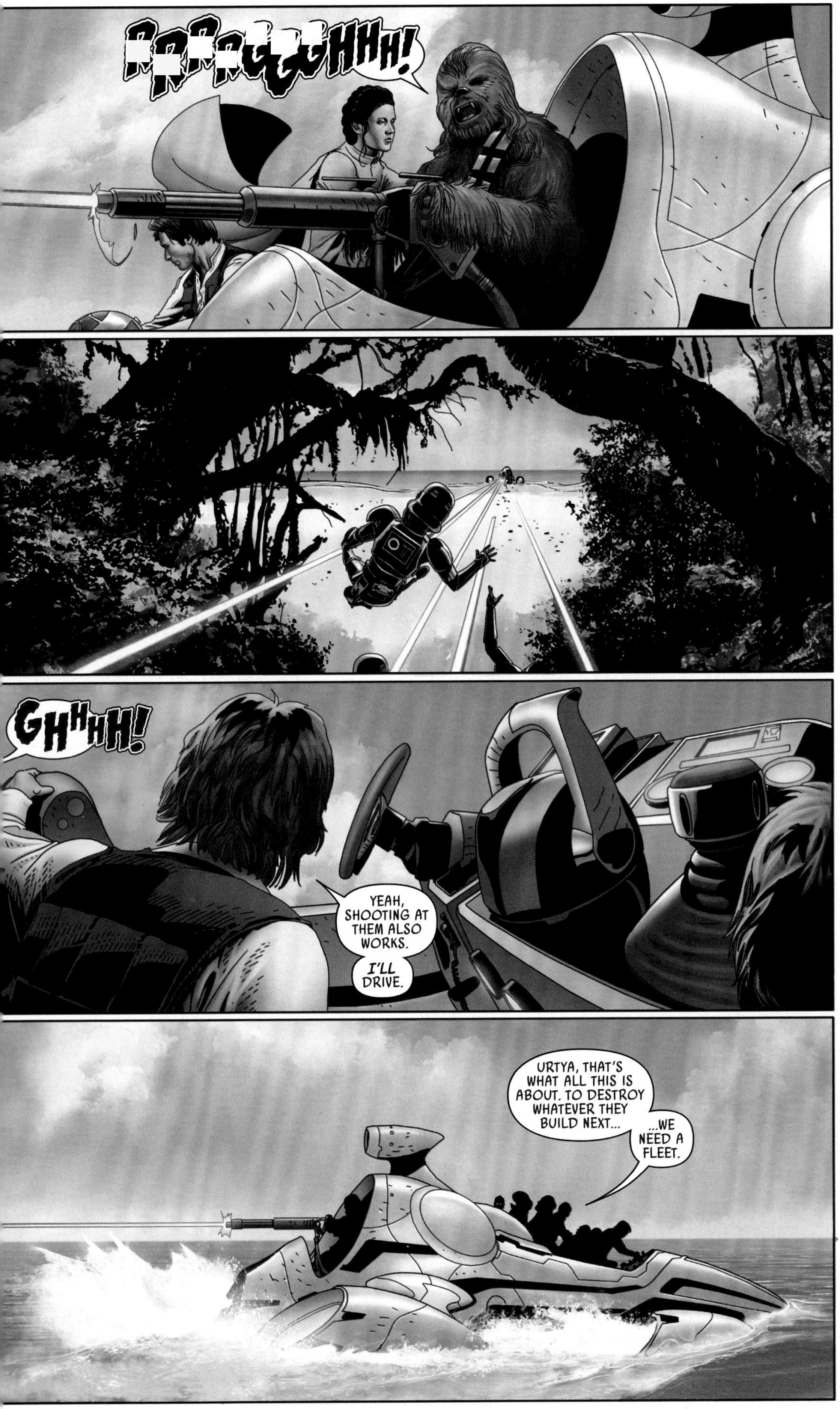
GHHHH!
YEAH, SHOOTING AT THEM ALSO WORKS.
I'LL DRIVE.
URTYA, THAT'S WHAT ALL THIS IS ABOUT. TO DESTROY WHATEVER THEY BUILD NEXT...
...WE NEED A FLEET.

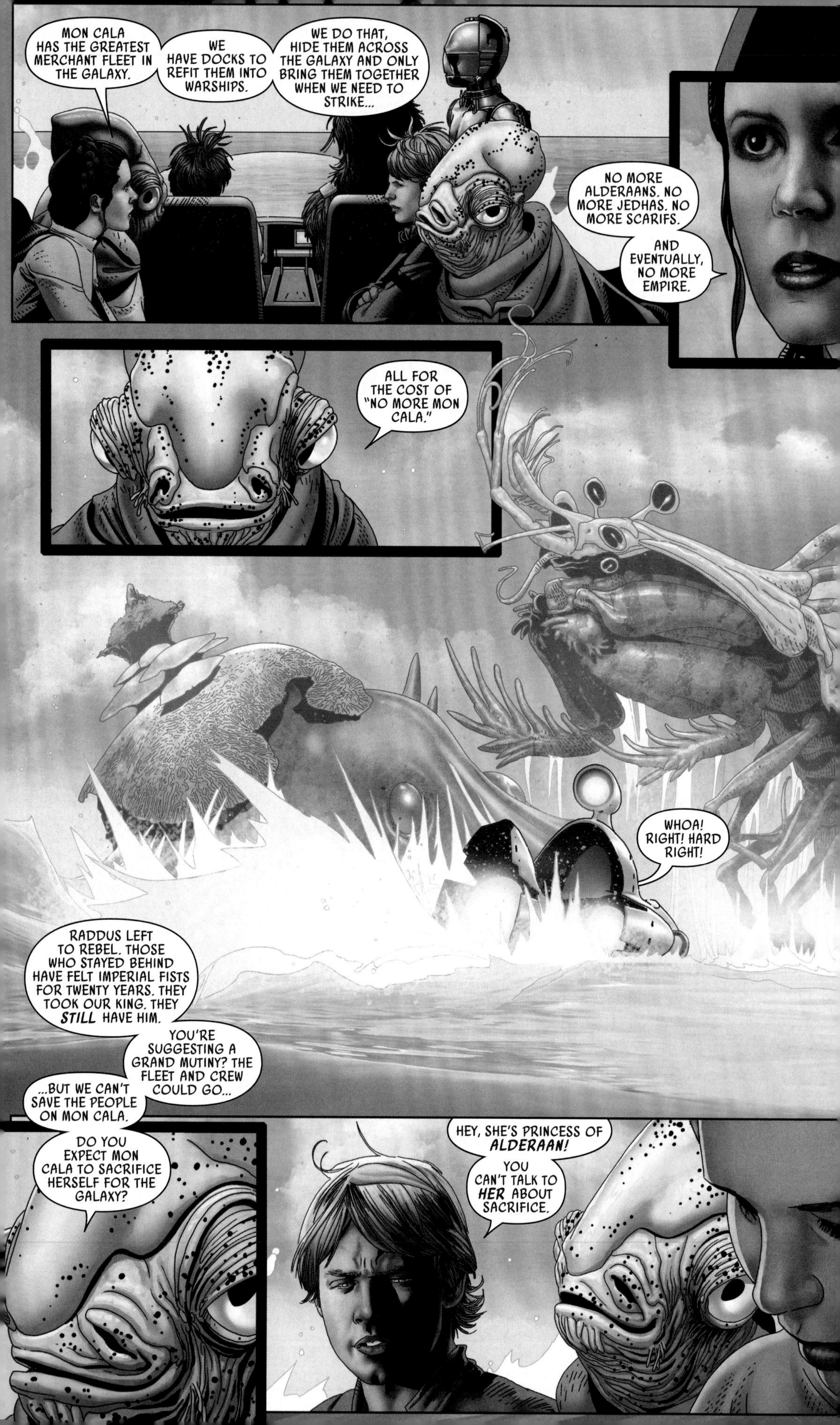
MON CALA HAS THE GREATEST MERCHANT FLEET IN THE GALAXY.
WE HAVE DOCKS TO REFIT THEM INTO WARSHIPS.
WE DO THAT, HIDE THEM ACROSS THE GALAXY AND ONLY BRING THEM TOGETHER WHEN WE NEED TO STRIKE...
NO MORE ALDERAANS. NO MORE JEDHAS. NO MORE SCARIFS.
AND EVENTUALLY, NO MORE EMPIRE.
ALL FOR THE COST OF "NO MORE MON CALA."
WHOA! RIGHT! HARD RIGHT!
RADDUS LEFT TO REBEL. THOSE WHO STAYED BEHIND HAVE FELT IMPERIAL FISTS FOR TWENTY YEARS. THEY TOOK OUR KING. THEY *STILL* HAVE HIM.
YOU'RE SUGGESTING A GRAND MUTINY? THE FLEET AND CREW COULD GO...
...BUT WE CAN'T SAVE THE PEOPLE ON MON CALA.
DO YOU EXPECT MON CALA TO SACRIFICE HERSELF FOR THE GALAXY?
HEY, SHE'S PRINCESS OF *ALDERAAN!*
YOU CAN'T TALK TO *HER* ABOUT SACRIFICE.

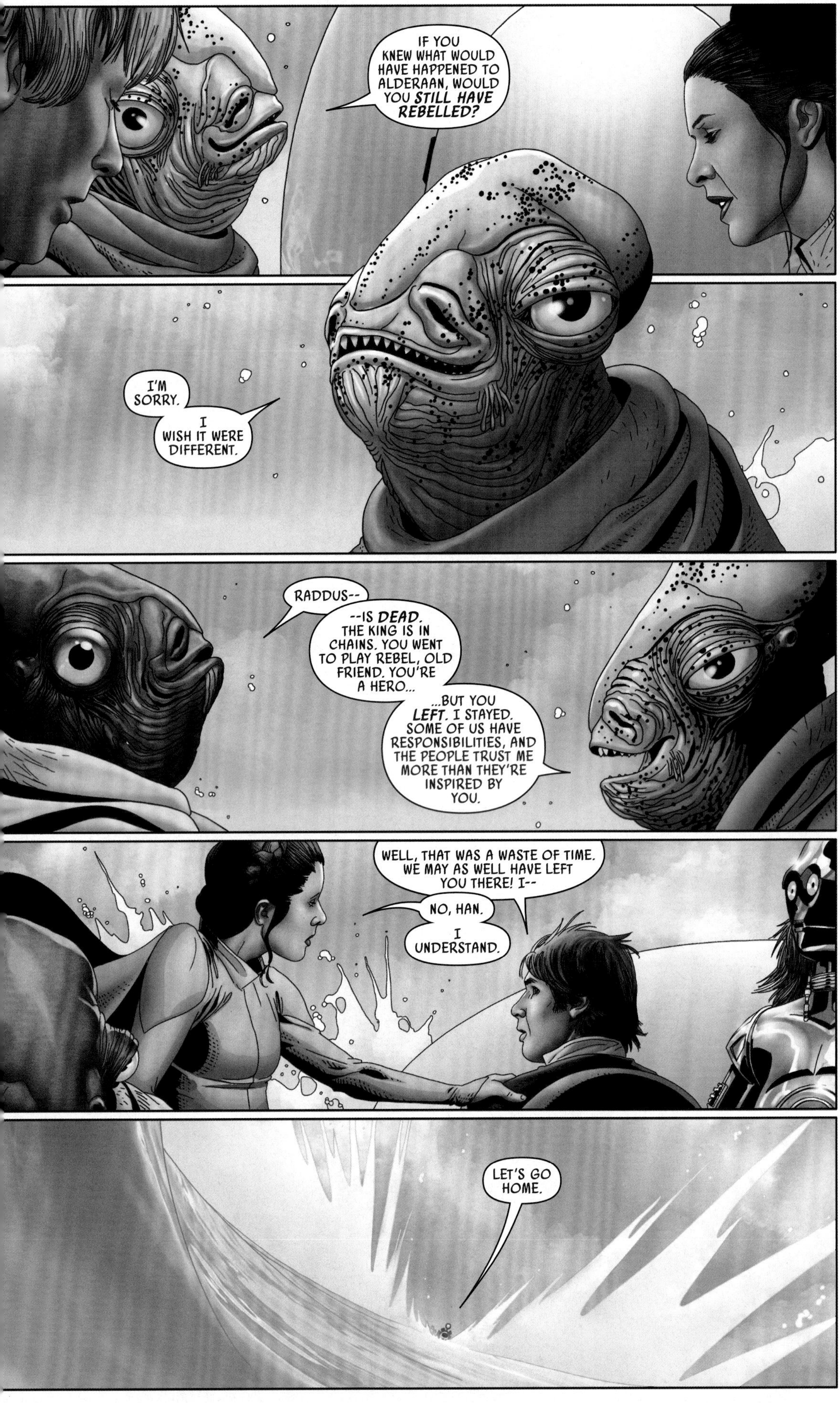
IF YOU KNEW WHAT WOULD HAVE HAPPENED TO ALDERAAN, WOULD YOU *STILL HAVE REBELLED?*
I'M SORRY.
I WISH IT WERE DIFFERENT.
RADDUS--
--IS *DEAD.* THE KING IS IN CHAINS. YOU WENT TO PLAY REBEL, OLD FRIEND. YOU'RE A HERO...
...BUT YOU *LEFT.* I STAYED. SOME OF US HAVE RESPONSIBILITIES, AND THE PEOPLE TRUST ME MORE THAN THEY'RE INSPIRED BY YOU.
WELL, THAT WAS A WASTE OF TIME. WE MAY AS WELL HAVE LEFT YOU THERE! I--
NO, HAN.
I UNDERSTAND.
LET'S GO HOME.

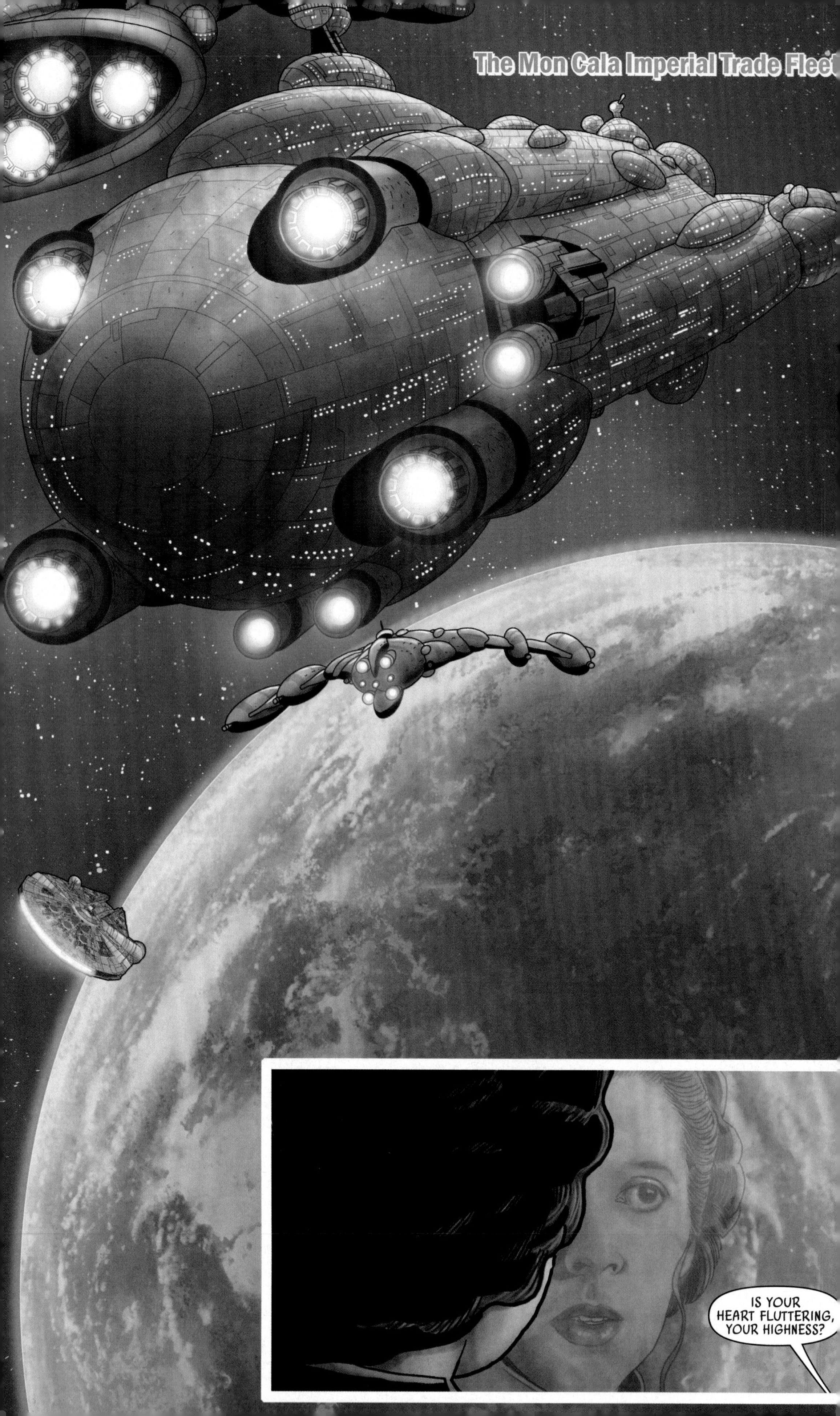
The Mon Cala Imperial Trade Fleet
IS YOUR HEART FLUTTERING, YOUR HIGHNESS?

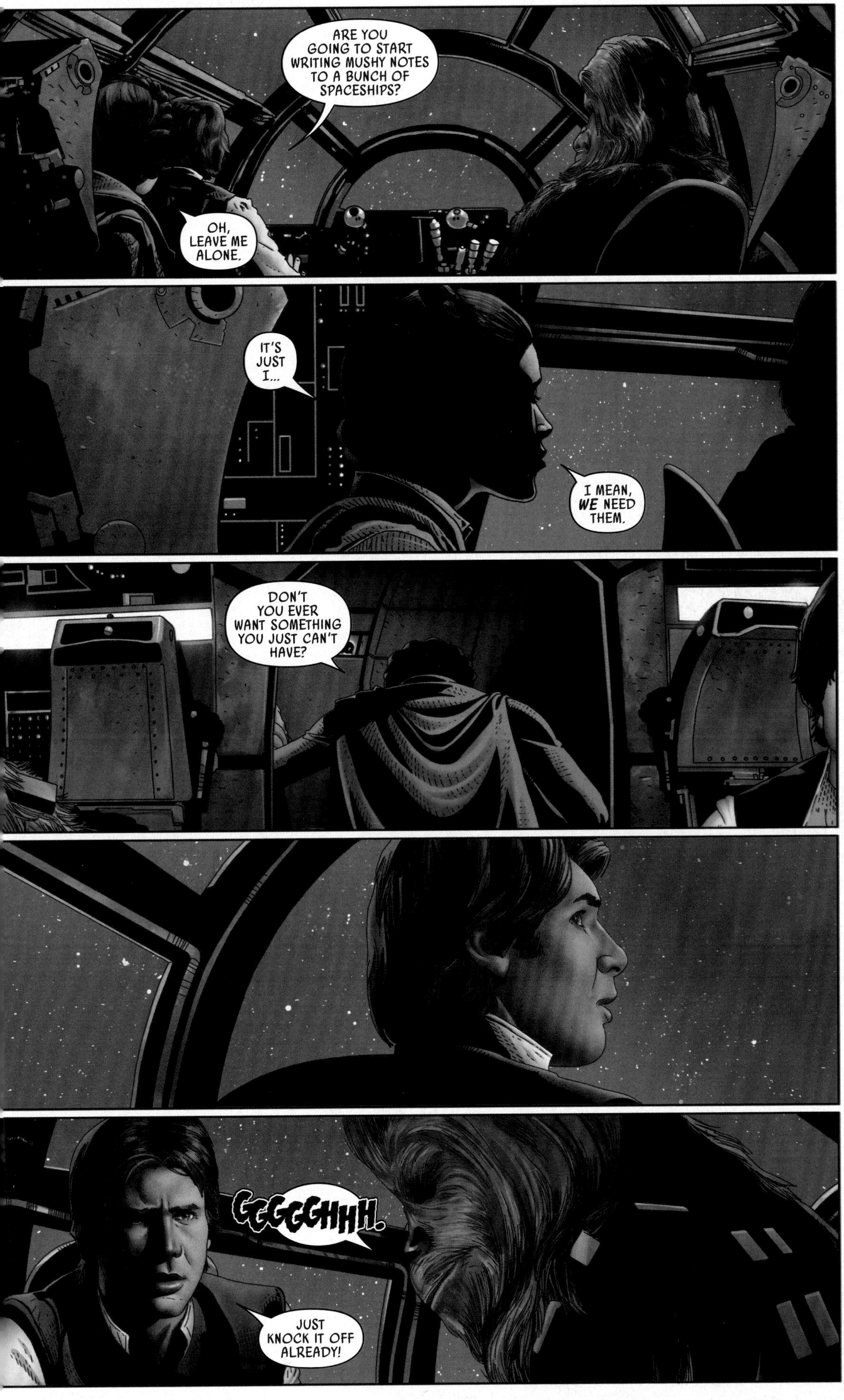
ARE YOU GOING TO START WRITING MUSHY NOTES TO A BUNCH OF SPACESHIPS?
OH, LEAVE ME ALONE.
IT'S JUST I...
I MEAN, *WE* NEED THEM.
DON'T YOU EVER WANT SOMETHING YOU JUST CAN'T HAVE?
GGGGGHHH.
JUST KNOCK IT OFF ALREADY!

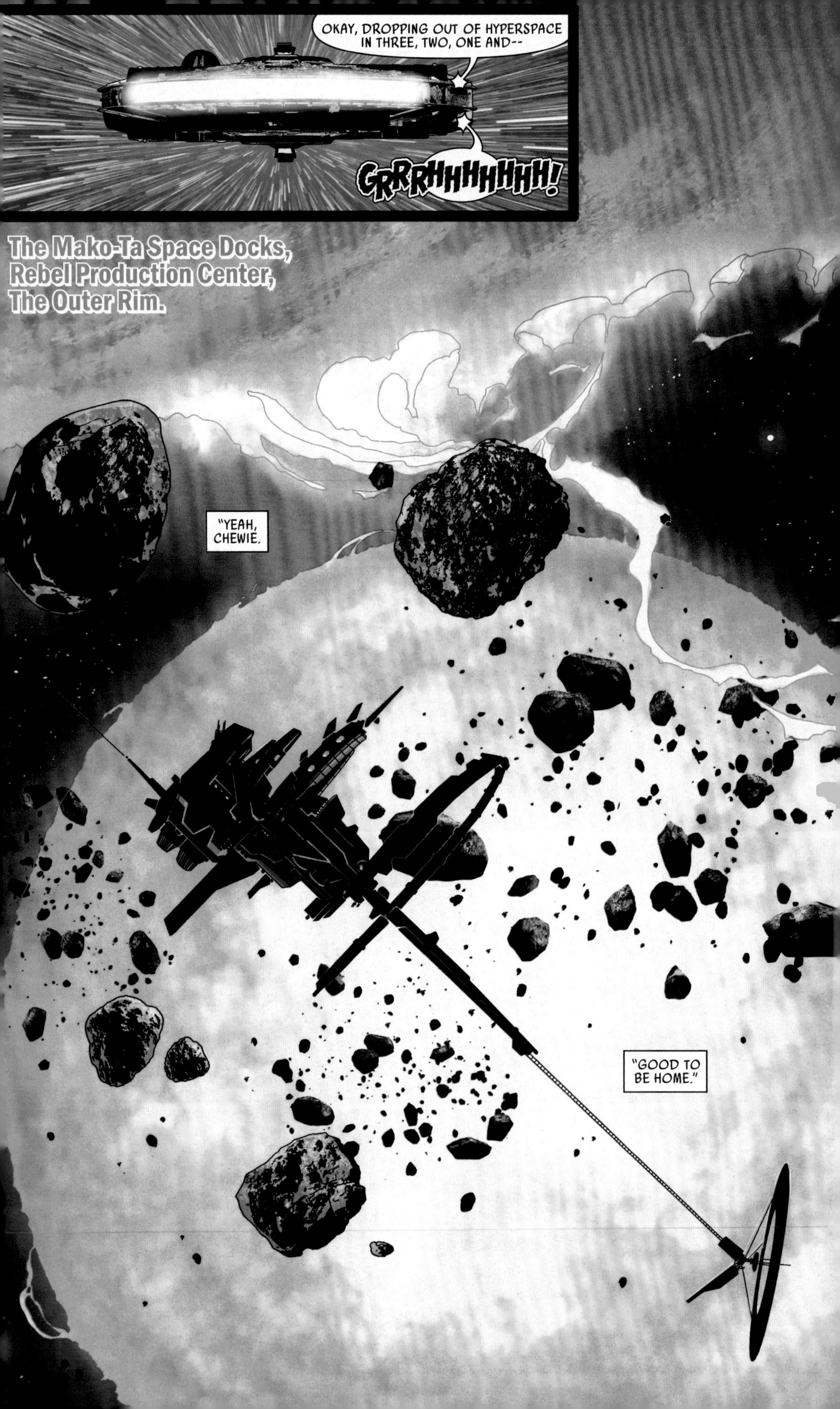
OKAY, DROPPING OUT OF HYPERSPACE IN THREE, TWO, ONE AND--
GRRRHHHHHHH!
The Mako-Ta Space Docks, Rebel Production Center, The Outer Rim.
"YEAH, CHEWIE.
"GOOD TO BE HOME."

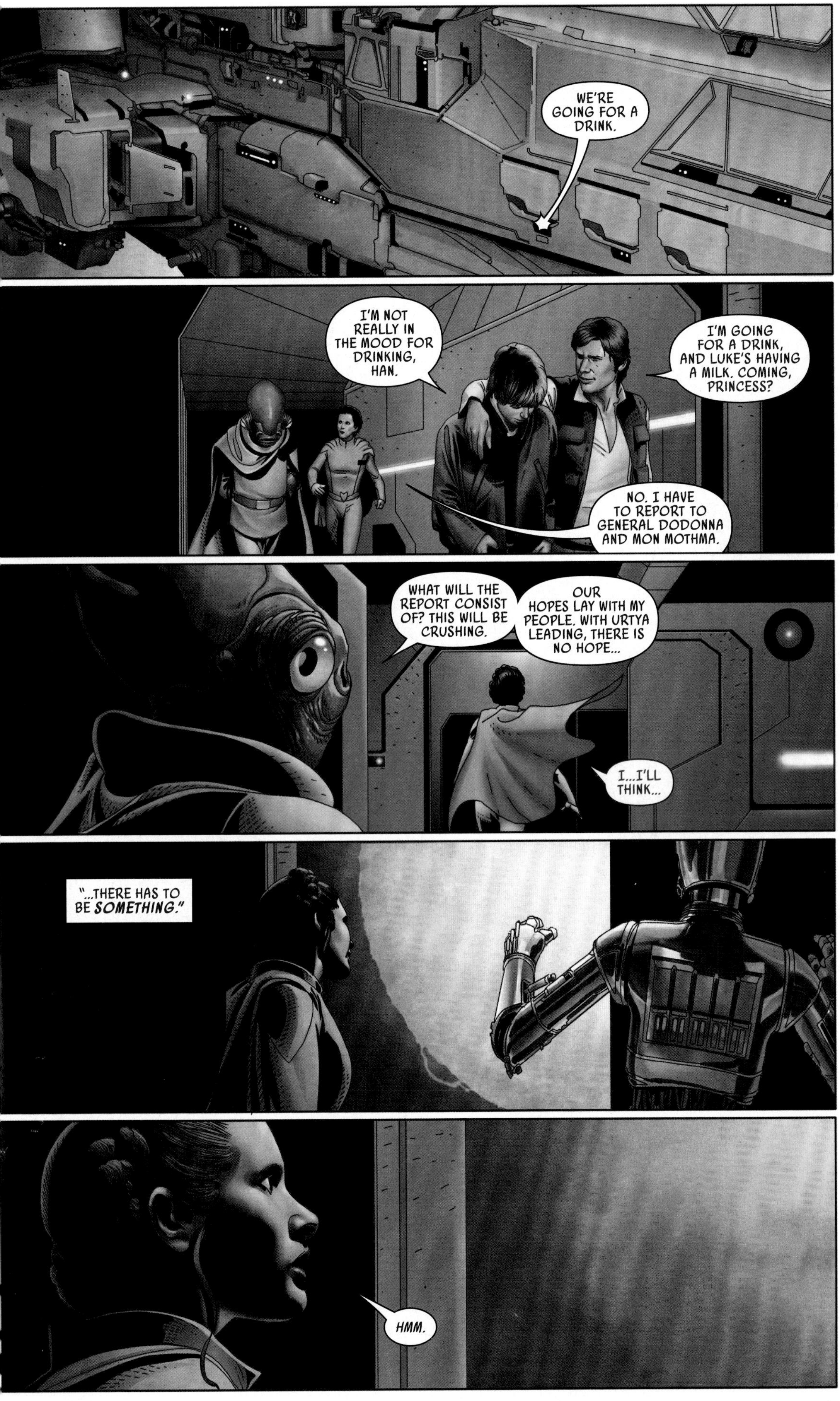
WE'RE GOING FOR A DRINK.
I'M NOT REALLY IN THE MOOD FOR DRINKING, HAN.
I'M GOING FOR A DRINK, AND LUKE'S HAVING A MILK. COMING, PRINCESS?
NO. I HAVE TO REPORT TO GENERAL DODONNA AND MON MOTHMA.
WHAT WILL THE REPORT CONSIST OF? THIS WILL BE CRUSHING.
OUR HOPES LAY WITH MY PEOPLE. WITH URTYA LEADING, THERE IS NO HOPE...
I...I'LL THINK...
"...THERE HAS TO BE *SOMETHING.*"
HMM.

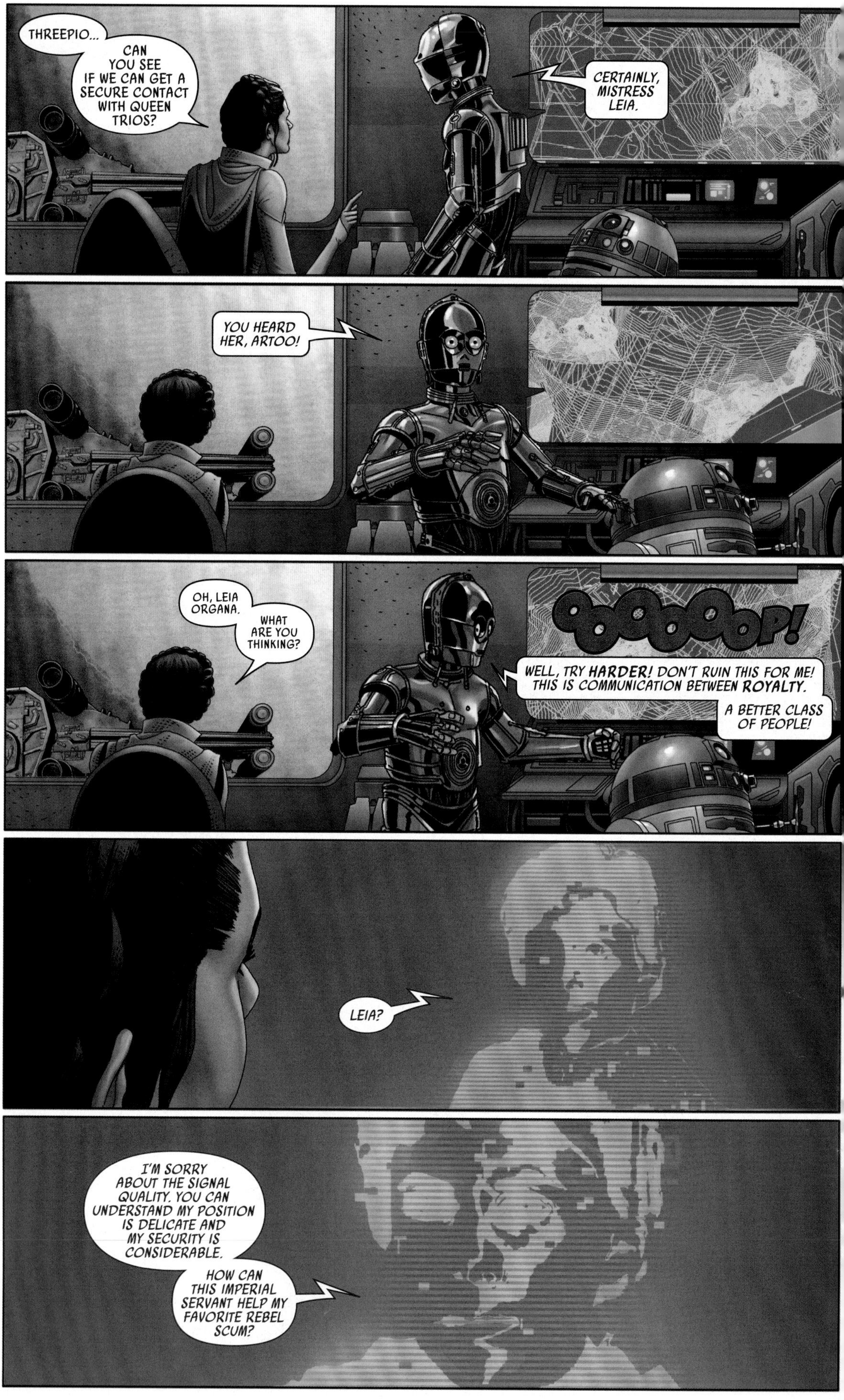
THREEPIO...
CAN YOU SEE IF WE CAN GET A SECURE CONTACT WITH QUEEN TRIOS?
CERTAINLY, MISTRESS LEIA.
YOU HEARD HER, ARTOO!
OH, LEIA ORGANA.
WHAT ARE YOU THINKING?
OOOOOOOP!
WELL, TRY HARDER! DON'T RUIN THIS FOR ME! THIS IS COMMUNICATION BETWEEN ROYALTY.
A BETTER CLASS OF PEOPLE!
LEIA?
I'M SORRY ABOUT THE SIGNAL QUALITY. YOU CAN UNDERSTAND MY POSITION IS DELICATE AND MY SECURITY IS CONSIDERABLE.
HOW CAN THIS IMPERIAL SERVANT HELP MY FAVORITE REBEL SCUM?

WHAT ACCESS COULD YOU GET TO THE ULTRA-HIGH-SECURITY IMPERIAL PRISON SYSTEM?
I... OH, LEIA. REALLY?
YOU AREN'T CONSIDERING SOME MANNER OF BREAKOUT? ISN'T THAT BENEATH A PRINCESS?
NOT IF YOU'RE SAVING A KING.

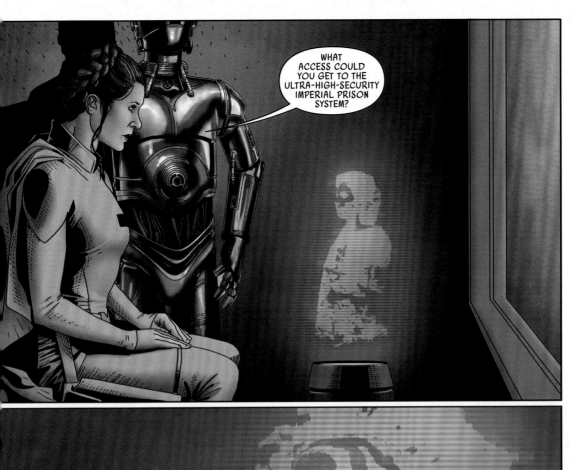

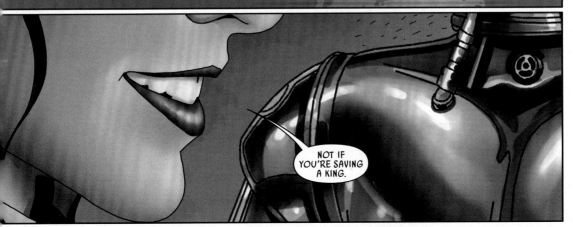

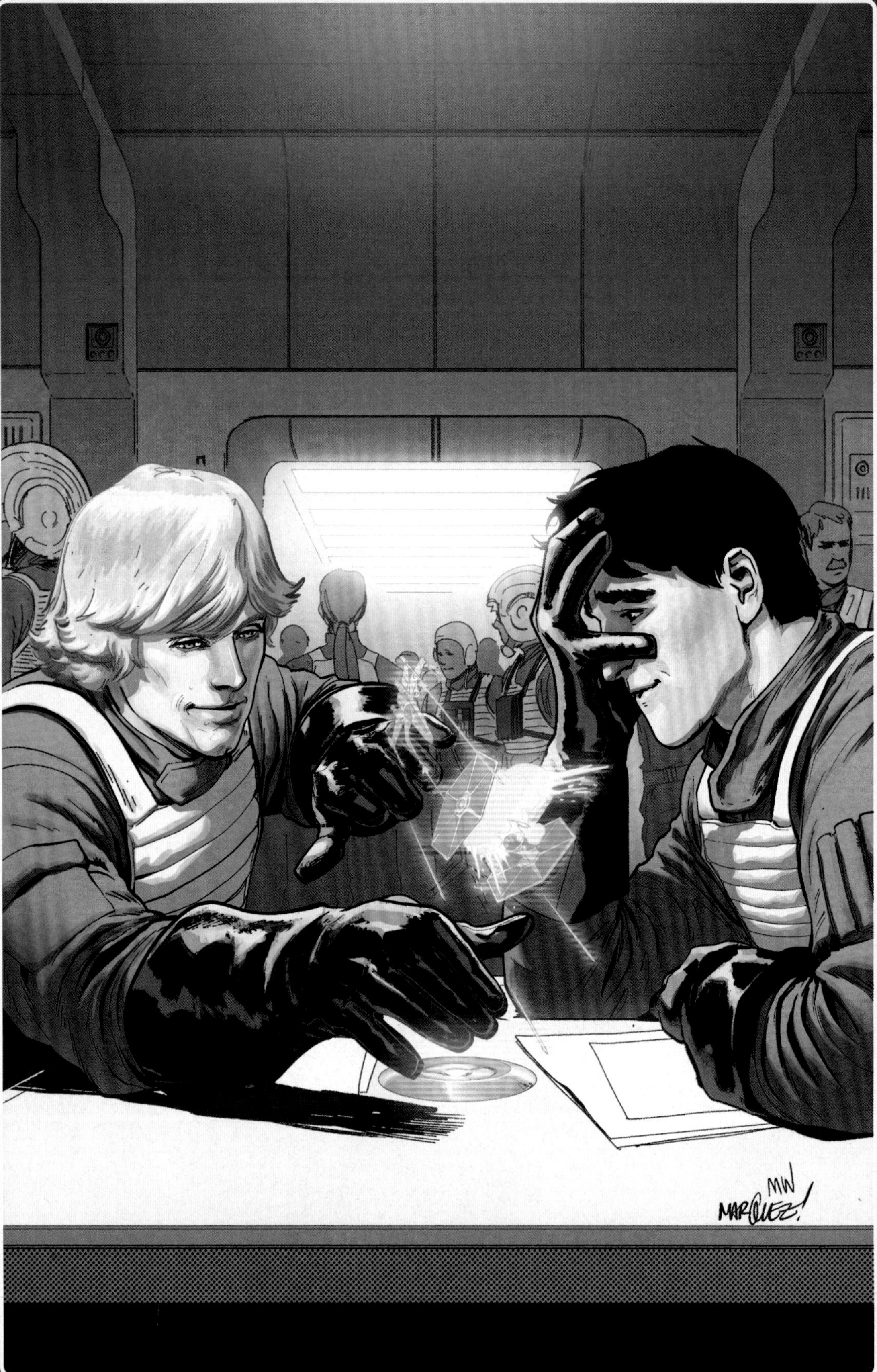
MW
MARQUEZ!

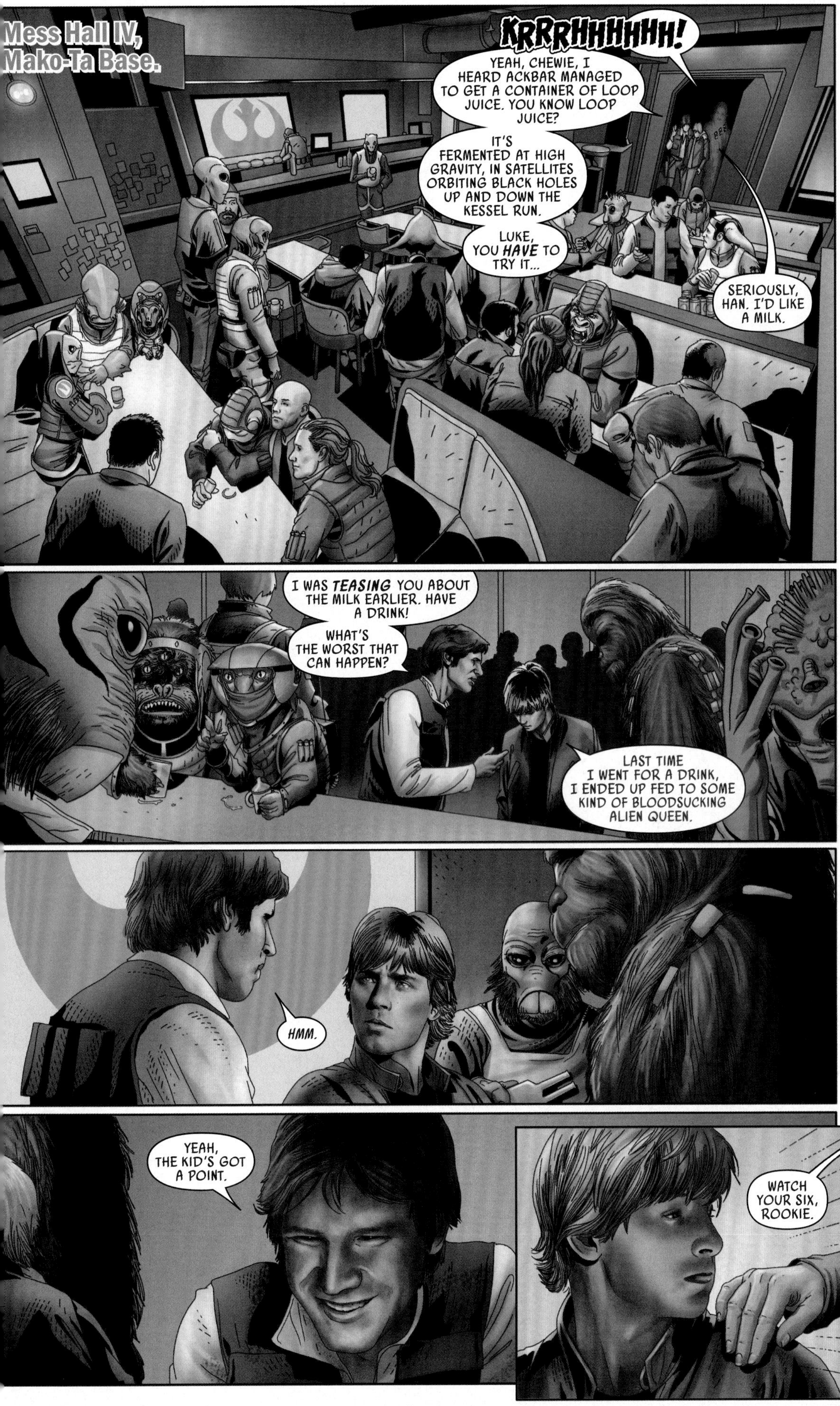
Mess Hall IV,
Mako-Ta Base.
KRRRHHHHHH!
YEAH, CHEWIE, I HEARD ACKBAR MANAGED TO GET A CONTAINER OF LOOP JUICE. YOU KNOW LOOP JUICE?
IT'S FERMENTED AT HIGH GRAVITY, IN SATELLITES ORBITING BLACK HOLES UP AND DOWN THE KESSEL RUN.
LUKE, YOU HAVE TO TRY IT...
SERIOUSLY, HAN. I'D LIKE A MILK.
I WAS TEASING YOU ABOUT THE MILK EARLIER. HAVE A DRINK!
WHAT'S THE WORST THAT CAN HAPPEN?
LAST TIME I WENT FOR A DRINK, I ENDED UP FED TO SOME KIND OF BLOODSUCKING ALIEN QUEEN.
HMM.
YEAH, THE KID'S GOT A POINT.
WATCH YOUR SIX, ROOKIE.

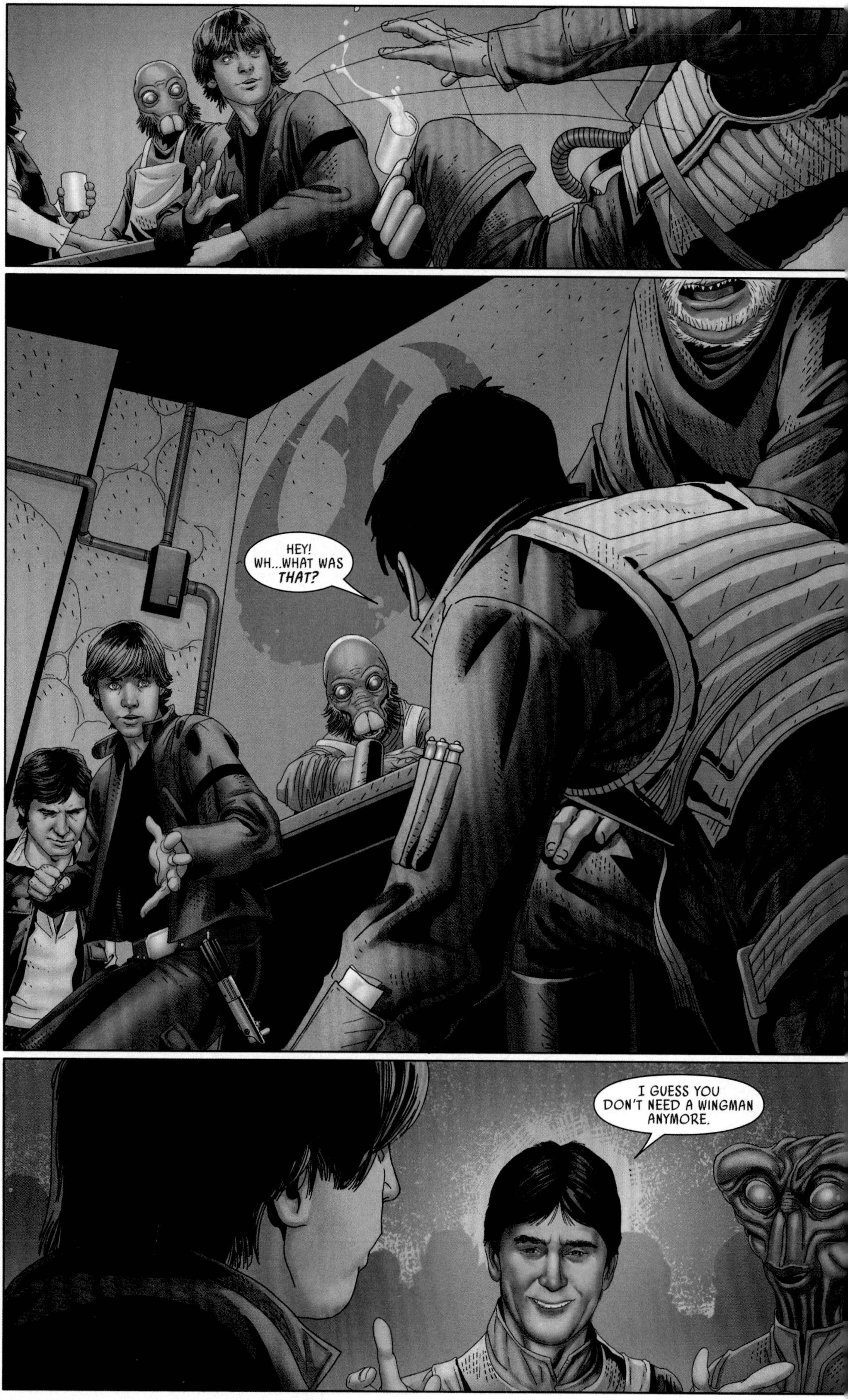
HEY! WH...WHAT WAS THAT?
I GUESS YOU DON'T NEED A WINGMAN ANYMORE.

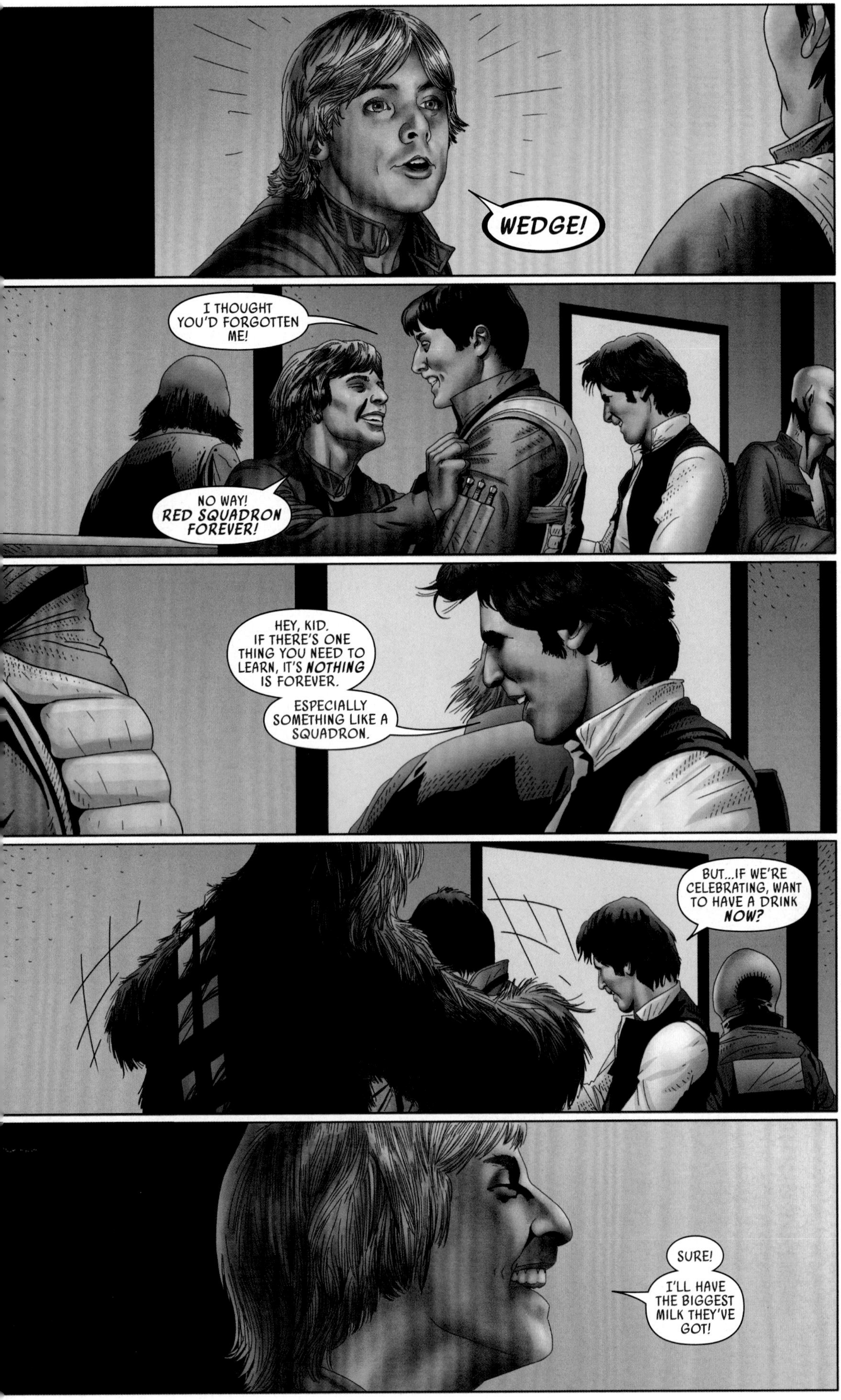
WEDGE!
I THOUGHT YOU'D FORGOTTEN ME!
NO WAY! RED SQUADRON FOREVER!
HEY, KID. IF THERE'S ONE THING YOU NEED TO LEARN, IT'S NOTHING IS FOREVER.
ESPECIALLY SOMETHING LIKE A SQUADRON.
BUT...IF WE'RE CELEBRATING, WANT TO HAVE A DRINK NOW?
SURE!
I'LL HAVE THE BIGGEST MILK THEY'VE GOT!

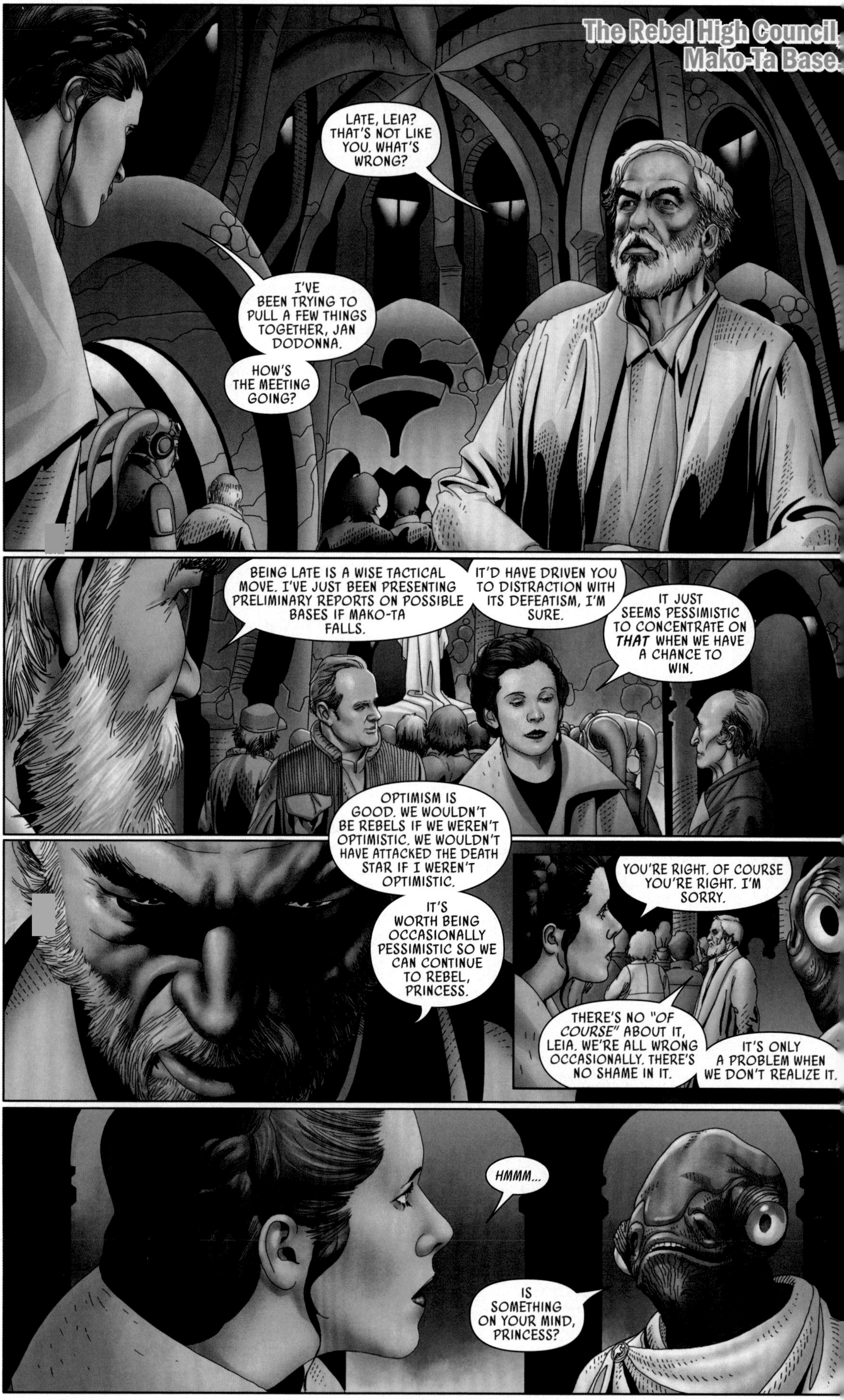
The Rebel High Council, Mako-Ta Base.
LATE, LEIA? THAT'S NOT LIKE YOU. WHAT'S WRONG?
I'VE BEEN TRYING TO PULL A FEW THINGS TOGETHER, JAN DODONNA.
HOW'S THE MEETING GOING?
BEING LATE IS A WISE TACTICAL MOVE. I'VE JUST BEEN PRESENTING PRELIMINARY REPORTS ON POSSIBLE BASES IF MAKO-TA FALLS.
IT'D HAVE DRIVEN YOU TO DISTRACTION WITH ITS DEFEATISM, I'M SURE.
IT JUST SEEMS PESSIMISTIC TO CONCENTRATE ON THAT WHEN WE HAVE A CHANCE TO WIN.
OPTIMISM IS GOOD. WE WOULDN'T BE REBELS IF WE WEREN'T OPTIMISTIC. WE WOULDN'T HAVE ATTACKED THE DEATH STAR IF I WEREN'T OPTIMISTIC.
IT'S WORTH BEING OCCASIONALLY PESSIMISTIC SO WE CAN CONTINUE TO REBEL, PRINCESS.
YOU'RE RIGHT. OF COURSE YOU'RE RIGHT. I'M SORRY.
THERE'S NO "OF COURSE" ABOUT IT, LEIA. WE'RE ALL WRONG OCCASIONALLY. THERE'S NO SHAME IN IT.
IT'S ONLY A PROBLEM WHEN WE DON'T REALIZE IT.
HMMM...
IS SOMETHING ON YOUR MIND, PRINCESS?

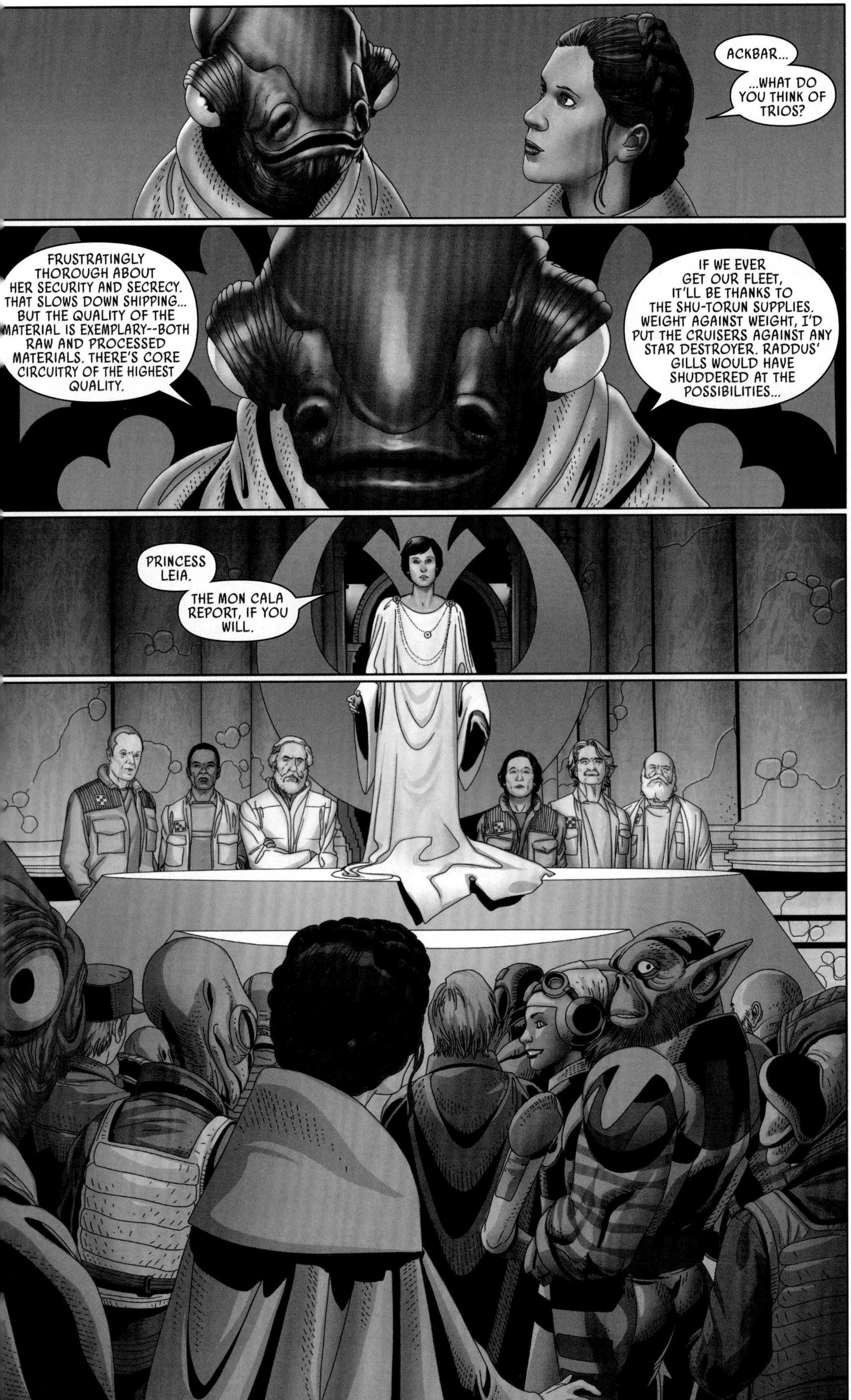

ACKBAR...
...WHAT DO YOU THINK OF TRIOS?
FRUSTRATINGLY THOROUGH ABOUT HER SECURITY AND SECRECY. THAT SLOWS DOWN SHIPPING... BUT THE QUALITY OF THE MATERIAL IS EXEMPLARY--BOTH RAW AND PROCESSED MATERIALS. THERE'S CORE CIRCUITRY OF THE HIGHEST QUALITY.
IF WE EVER GET OUR FLEET, IT'LL BE THANKS TO THE SHU-TORUN SUPPLIES. WEIGHT AGAINST WEIGHT, I'D PUT THE CRUISERS AGAINST ANY STAR DESTROYER. RADDUS' GILLS WOULD HAVE SHUDDERED AT THE POSSIBILITIES...
PRINCESS LEIA.
THE MON CALA REPORT, IF YOU WILL.

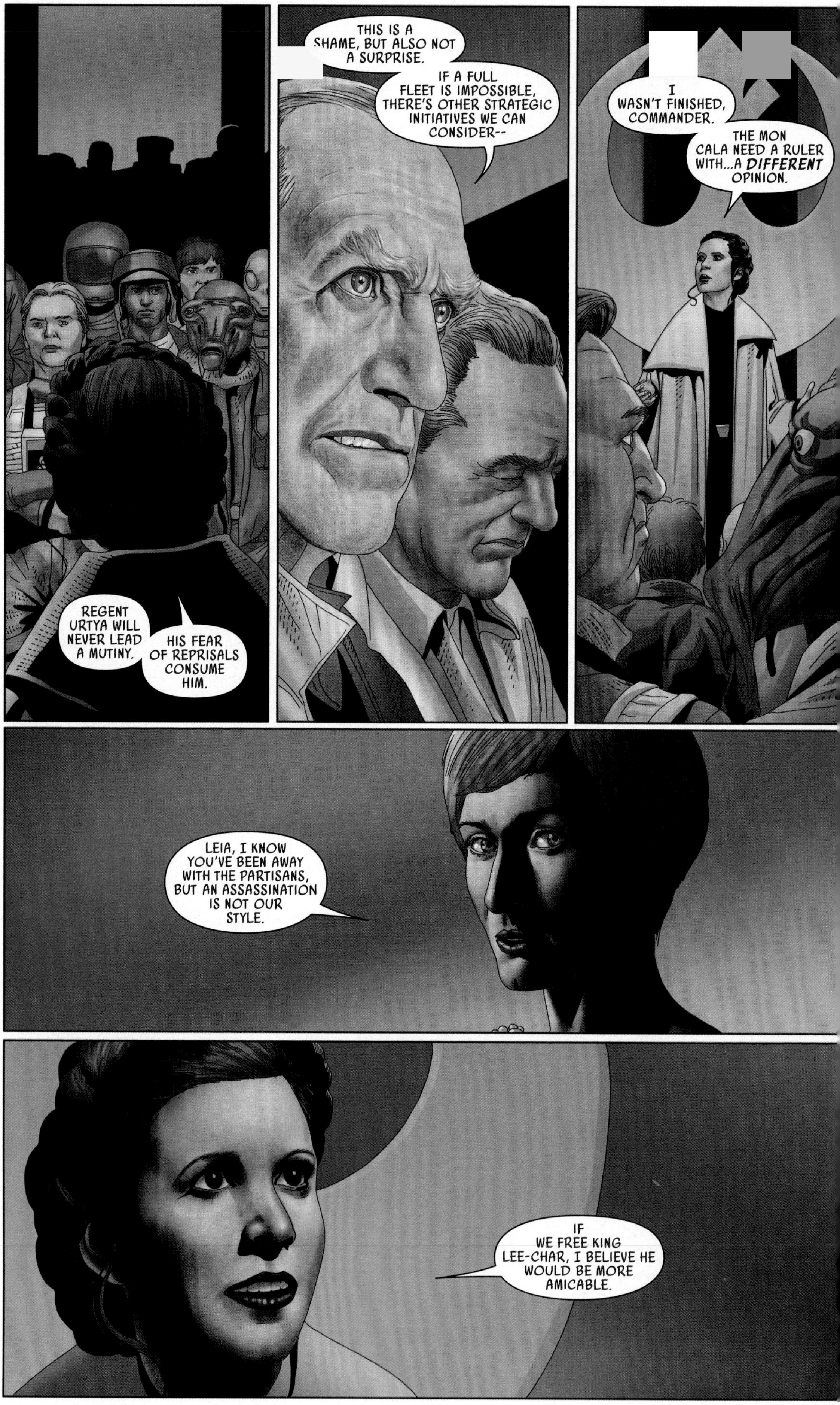
THIS IS A SHAME, BUT ALSO NOT A SURPRISE.
IF A FULL FLEET IS IMPOSSIBLE, THERE'S OTHER STRATEGIC INITIATIVES WE CAN CONSIDER--
REGENT URTYA WILL NEVER LEAD A MUTINY.
HIS FEAR OF REPRISALS CONSUME HIM.
I WASN'T FINISHED, COMMANDER.
THE MON CALA NEED A RULER WITH...A *DIFFERENT* OPINION.
LEIA, I KNOW YOU'VE BEEN AWAY WITH THE PARTISANS, BUT AN ASSASSINATION IS NOT OUR STYLE.
IF WE FREE KING LEE-CHAR, I BELIEVE HE WOULD BE MORE AMICABLE.

THIS SOUNDS LIKE A WONDERFUL PLAN, PRINCESS.

EXTRACTING LEE-CHAR FROM HIS PRISON HAS BEEN A REBEL OBJECTIVE FOR THE LAST *TWENTY YEARS*. IT WAS IMPOSSIBLE THEN. IT'S IMPOSSIBLE NOW.

HE WILL BE IN AN ULTRA-SECURITY FACILITY.

THEY HIDE THOSE FROM *US* AS WELL AS WE HIDE FROM *THEM*. IF WE KNEW WHERE HE WAS, DON'T YOU THINK WE'D HAVE TRIED?

I KNOW WHERE HE IS.

OUR... CONTACT HAS PROVIDED THE REQUISITE INFORMATION.

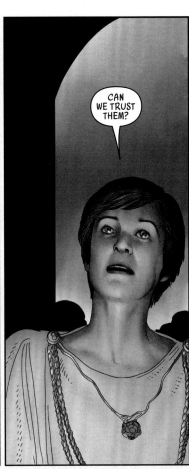

CAN WE TRUST THEM?

THEY TAKE THEIR SECRECY SERIOUSLY. THAT WE'RE NOT REFERRING TO THEM BY NAME EVEN IN A MEETING OF THE REBEL HIGH COMMAND SAYS AS MUCH.

THEY ARE *PETRIFIED* OF DISCOVERY.

DO *YOU* TRUST THEM, LEIA?

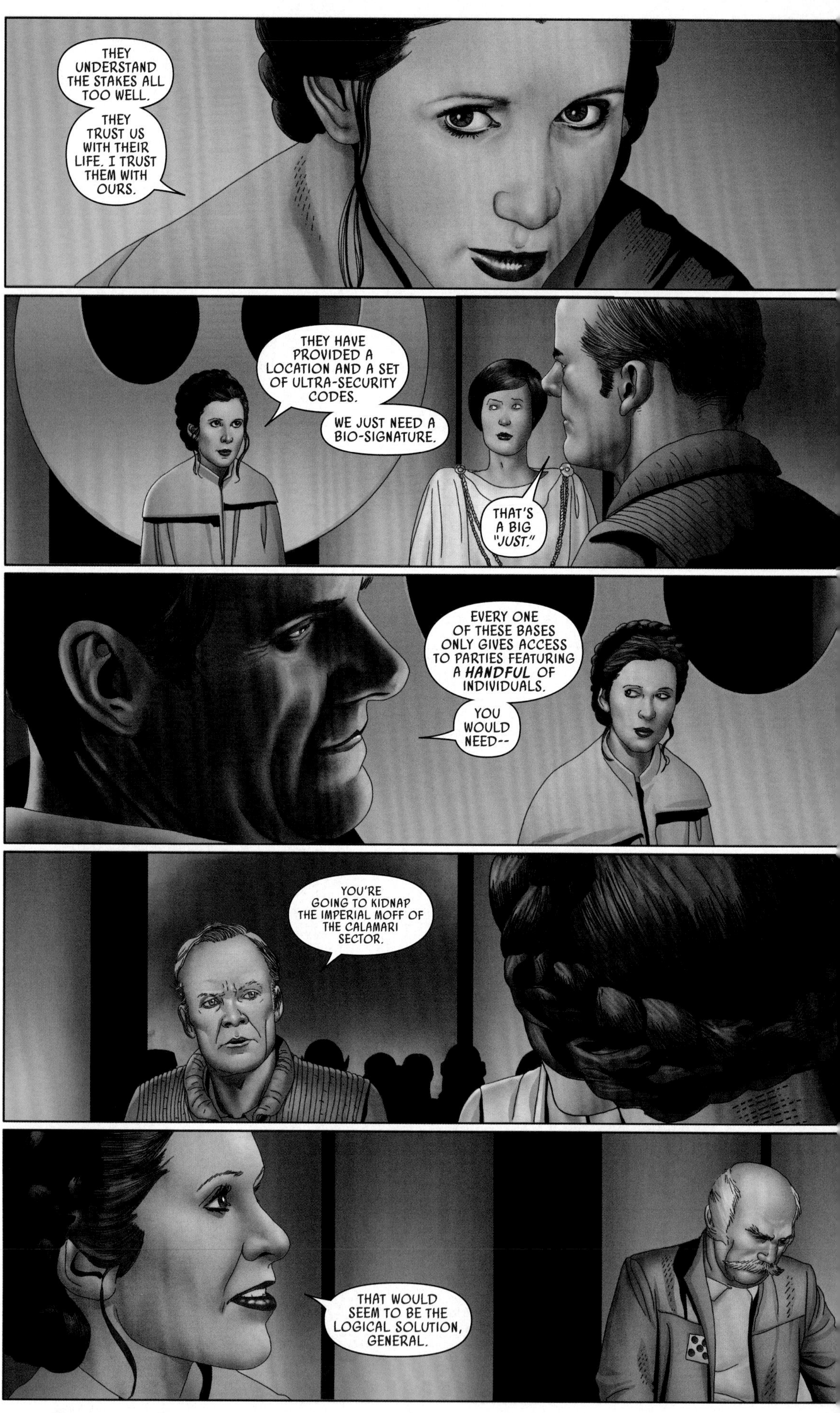
THEY UNDERSTAND THE STAKES ALL TOO WELL.
THEY TRUST US WITH THEIR LIFE. I TRUST THEM WITH OURS.
THEY HAVE PROVIDED A LOCATION AND A SET OF ULTRA-SECURITY CODES.
WE JUST NEED A BIO-SIGNATURE.
THAT'S A BIG "JUST."
EVERY ONE OF THESE BASES ONLY GIVES ACCESS TO PARTIES FEATURING A HANDFUL OF INDIVIDUALS.
YOU WOULD NEED--
YOU'RE GOING TO KIDNAP THE IMPERIAL MOFF OF THE CALAMARI SECTOR.
THAT WOULD SEEM TO BE THE LOGICAL SOLUTION, GENERAL.

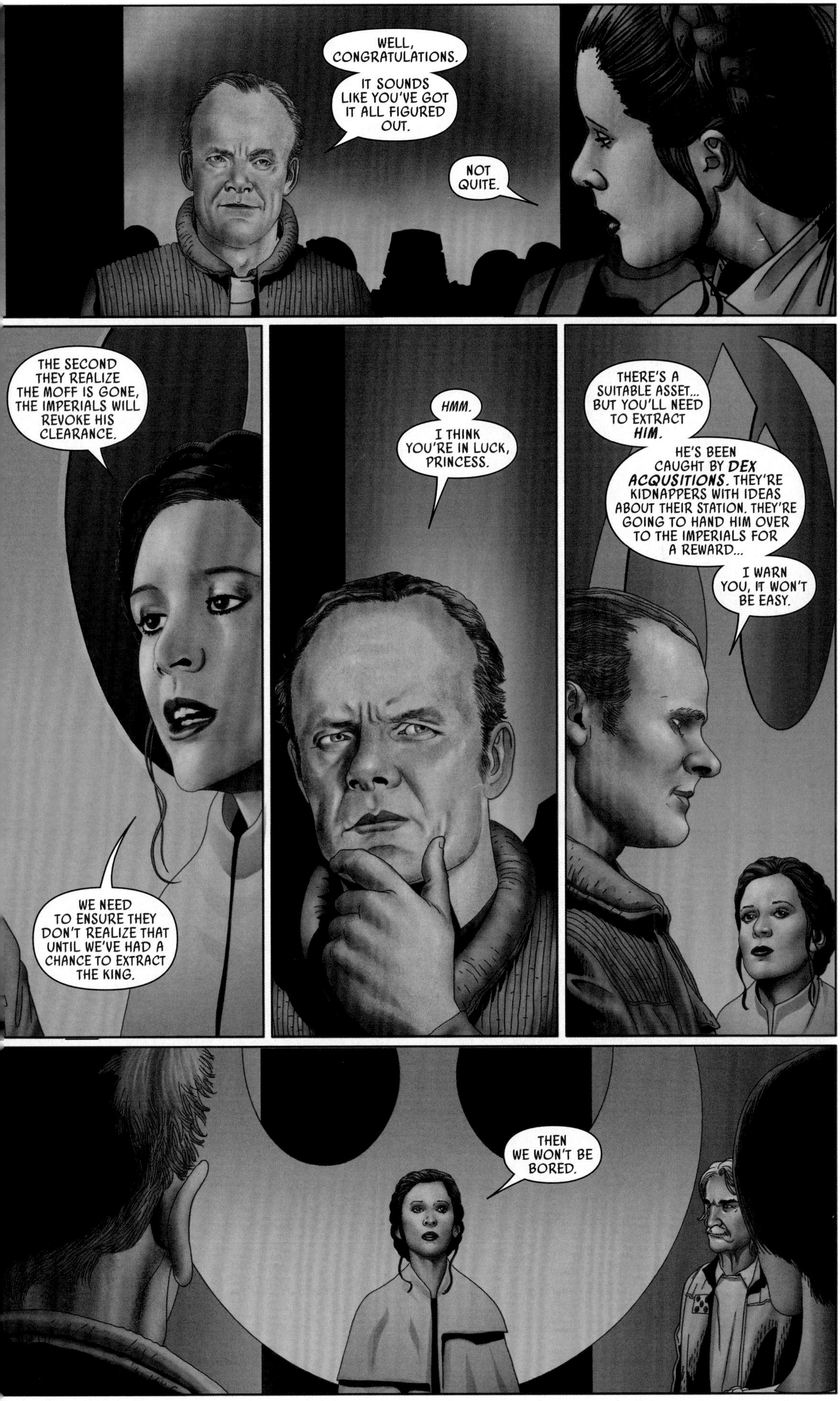
WELL, CONGRATULATIONS.
IT SOUNDS LIKE YOU'VE GOT IT ALL FIGURED OUT.
NOT QUITE.
THE SECOND THEY REALIZE THE MOFF IS GONE, THE IMPERIALS WILL REVOKE HIS CLEARANCE.
WE NEED TO ENSURE THEY DON'T REALIZE THAT UNTIL WE'VE HAD A CHANCE TO EXTRACT THE KING.
HMM.
I THINK YOU'RE IN LUCK, PRINCESS.
THERE'S A SUITABLE ASSET... BUT YOU'LL NEED TO EXTRACT HIM.
HE'S BEEN CAUGHT BY DEX ACQUSITIONS. THEY'RE KIDNAPPERS WITH IDEAS ABOUT THEIR STATION. THEY'RE GOING TO HAND HIM OVER TO THE IMPERIALS FOR A REWARD...
I WARN YOU, IT WON'T BE EASY.
THEN WE WON'T BE BORED.

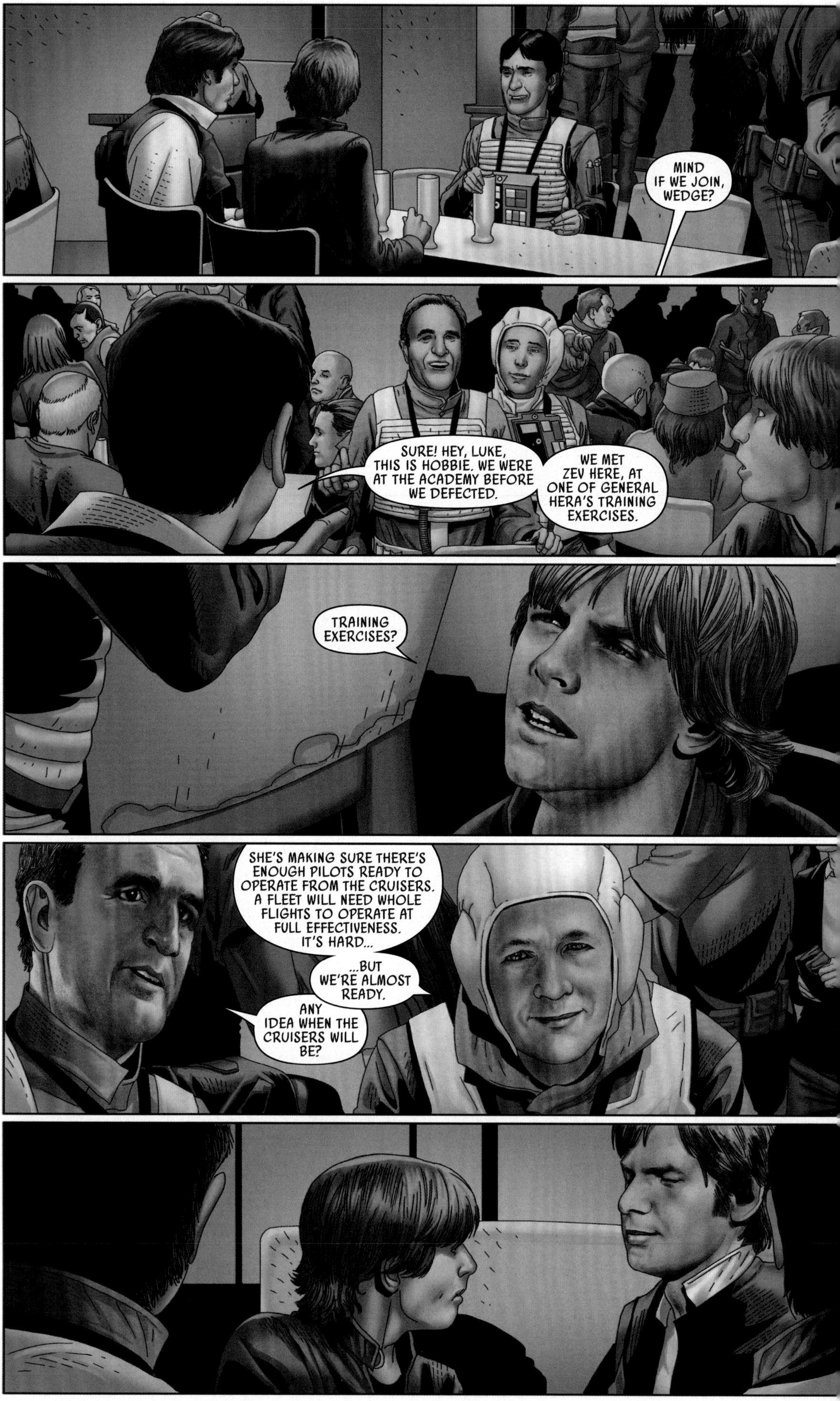
MIND IF WE JOIN, WEDGE?
SURE! HEY, LUKE, THIS IS HOBBIE. WE WERE AT THE ACADEMY BEFORE WE DEFECTED.
WE MET ZEV HERE, AT ONE OF GENERAL HERA'S TRAINING EXERCISES.
TRAINING EXERCISES?
SHE'S MAKING SURE THERE'S ENOUGH PILOTS READY TO OPERATE FROM THE CRUISERS. A FLEET WILL NEED WHOLE FLIGHTS TO OPERATE AT FULL EFFECTIVENESS. IT'S HARD...
...BUT WE'RE ALMOST READY.
ANY IDEA WHEN THE CRUISERS WILL BE?

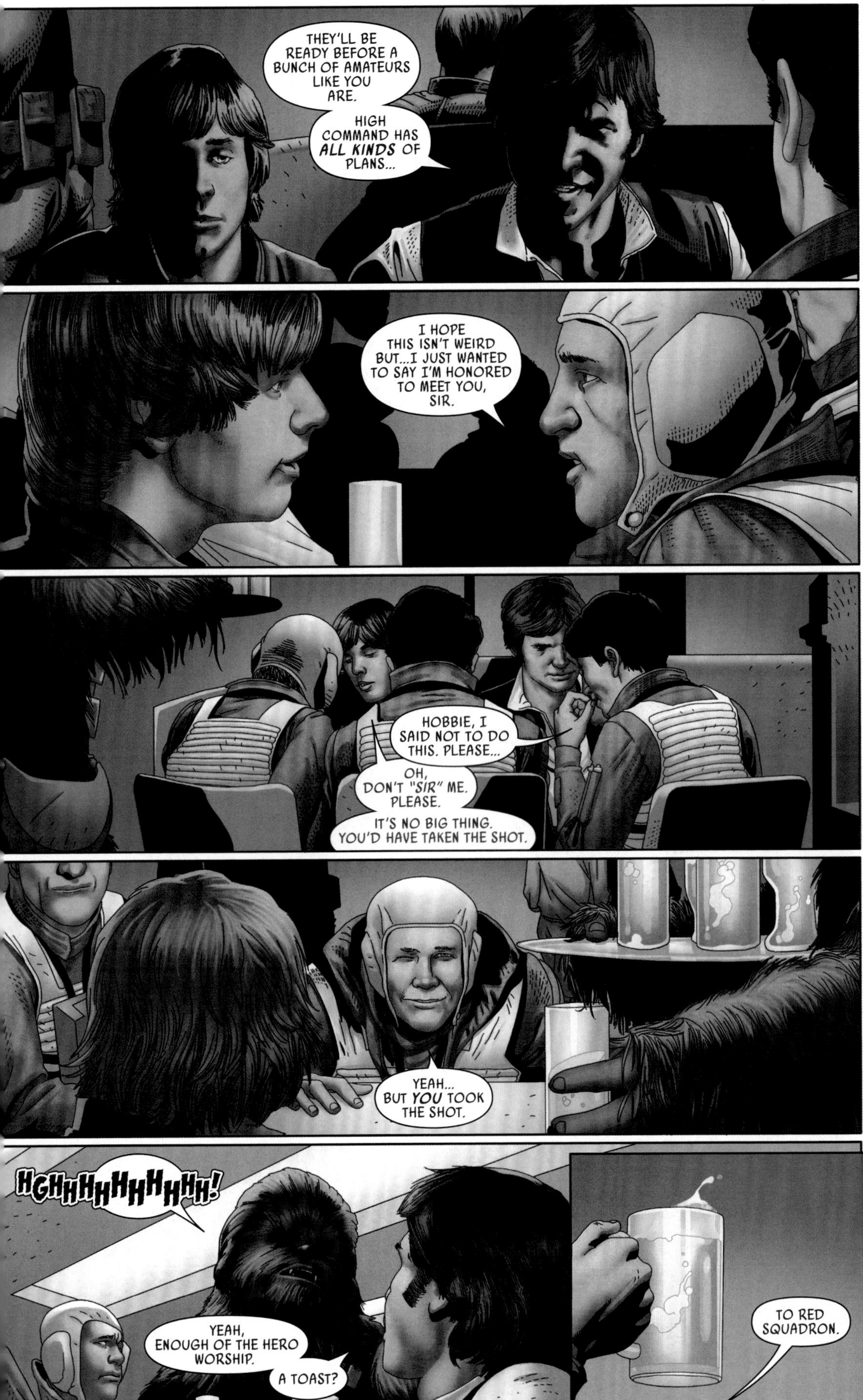
THEY'LL BE READY BEFORE A BUNCH OF AMATEURS LIKE YOU ARE.
HIGH COMMAND HAS ALL KINDS OF PLANS...
I HOPE THIS ISN'T WEIRD BUT...I JUST WANTED TO SAY I'M HONORED TO MEET YOU, SIR.
HOBBIE, I SAID NOT TO DO THIS. PLEASE...
OH, DON'T "SIR" ME. PLEASE.
IT'S NO BIG THING. YOU'D HAVE TAKEN THE SHOT.
YEAH... BUT YOU TOOK THE SHOT.
HGHHHHHHHHH!
YEAH, ENOUGH OF THE HERO WORSHIP.
A TOAST?
TO RED SQUADRON.

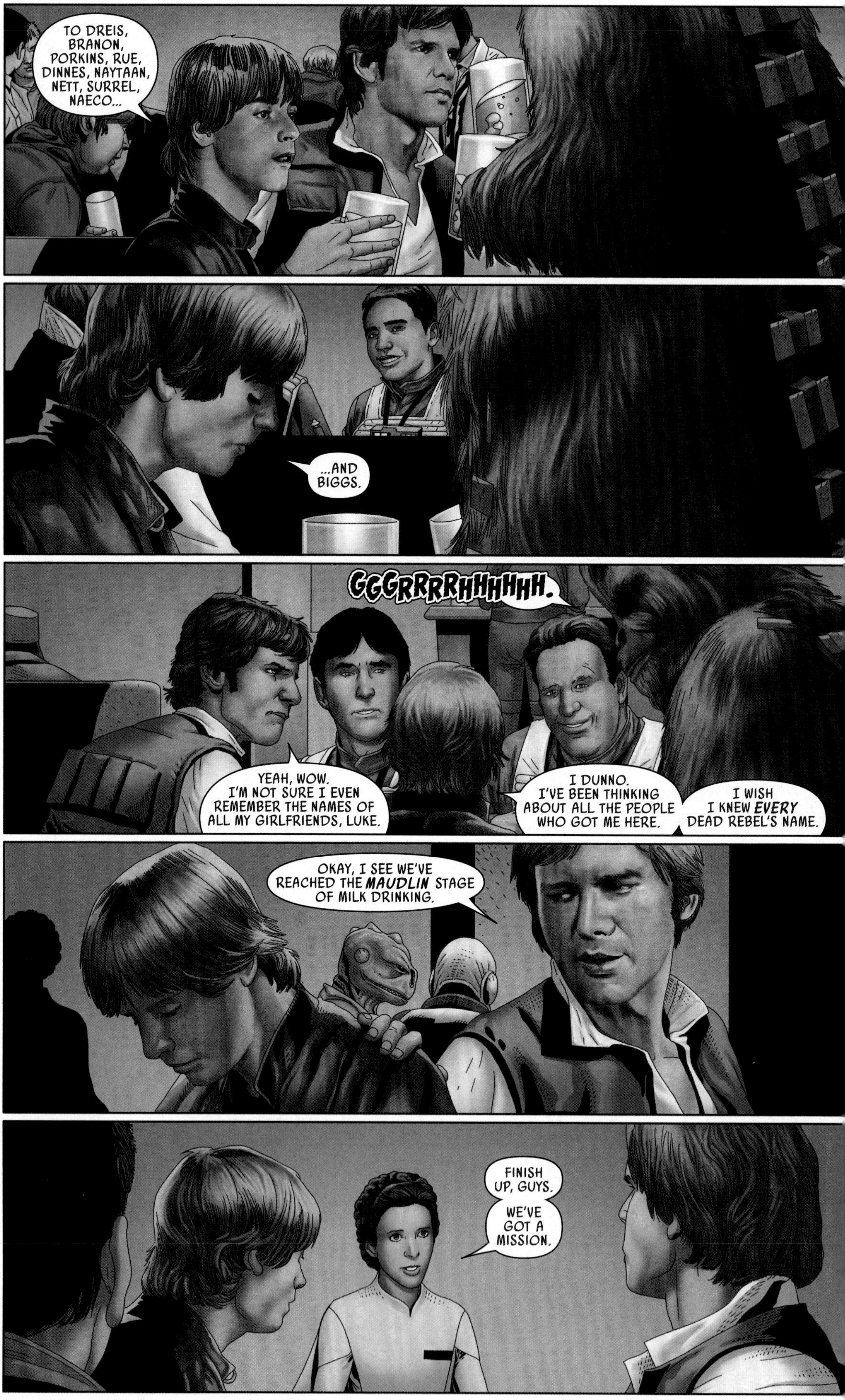
TO DREIS, BRANON, PORKINS, RUE, DINNES, NAYTAAN, NETT, SURREL, NAECO...
...AND BIGGS.
GGGRRRRHHHHHH.
YEAH, WOW. I'M NOT SURE I EVEN REMEMBER THE NAMES OF ALL MY GIRLFRIENDS, LUKE.
I DUNNO. I'VE BEEN THINKING ABOUT ALL THE PEOPLE WHO GOT ME HERE.
I WISH I KNEW EVERY DEAD REBEL'S NAME.
OKAY, I SEE WE'VE REACHED THE MAUDLIN STAGE OF MILK DRINKING.
FINISH UP, GUYS.
WE'VE GOT A MISSION.

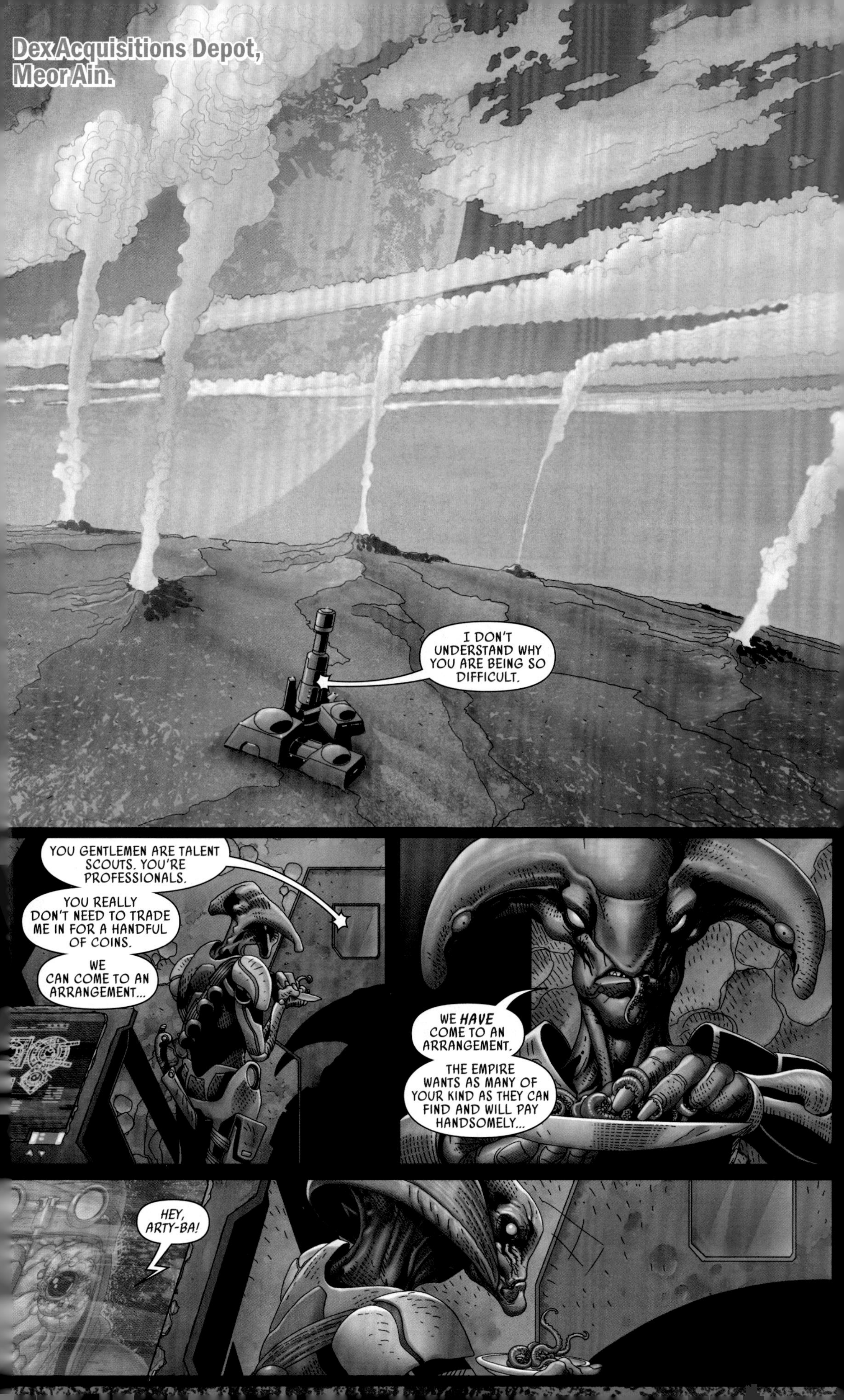
Dex Acquisitions Depot,
Meor Ain.
I DON'T UNDERSTAND WHY YOU ARE BEING SO DIFFICULT.
YOU GENTLEMEN ARE TALENT SCOUTS. YOU'RE PROFESSIONALS.
YOU REALLY DON'T NEED TO TRADE ME IN FOR A HANDFUL OF COINS.
WE CAN COME TO AN ARRANGEMENT...
WE *HAVE* COME TO AN ARRANGEMENT.
THE EMPIRE WANTS AS MANY OF YOUR KIND AS THEY CAN FIND AND WILL PAY HANDSOMELY...
HEY, ARTY-BA!

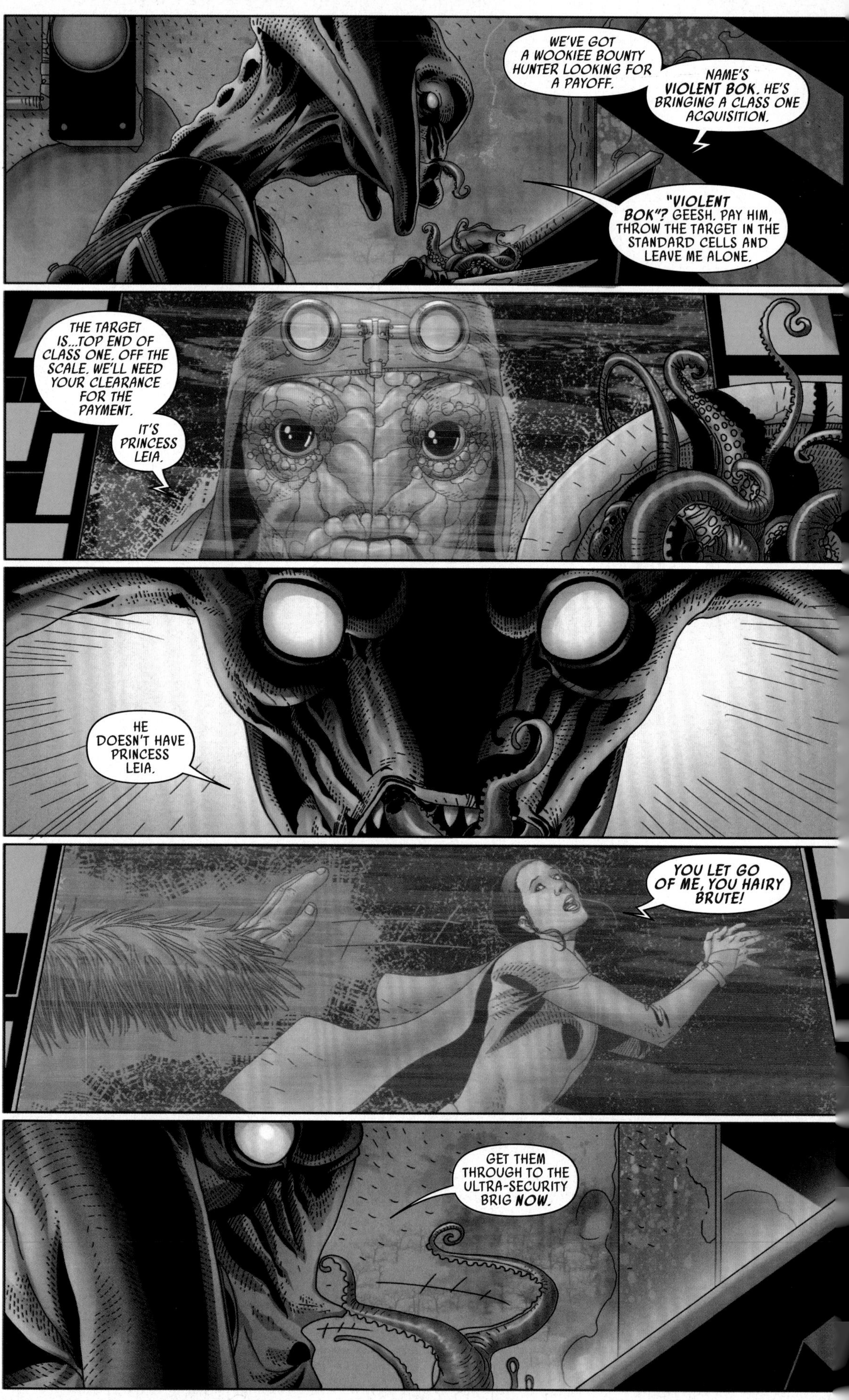

WE'VE GOT A WOOKIEE BOUNTY HUNTER LOOKING FOR A PAYOFF.
NAME'S VIOLENT BOK. HE'S BRINGING A CLASS ONE ACQUISITION.
"VIOLENT BOK"? GEESH. PAY HIM, THROW THE TARGET IN THE STANDARD CELLS AND LEAVE ME ALONE.
THE TARGET IS...TOP END OF CLASS ONE. OFF THE SCALE. WE'LL NEED YOUR CLEARANCE FOR THE PAYMENT.
IT'S PRINCESS LEIA.
HE DOESN'T HAVE PRINCESS LEIA.
YOU LET GO OF ME, YOU HAIRY BRUTE!
GET THEM THROUGH TO THE ULTRA-SECURITY BRIG NOW.

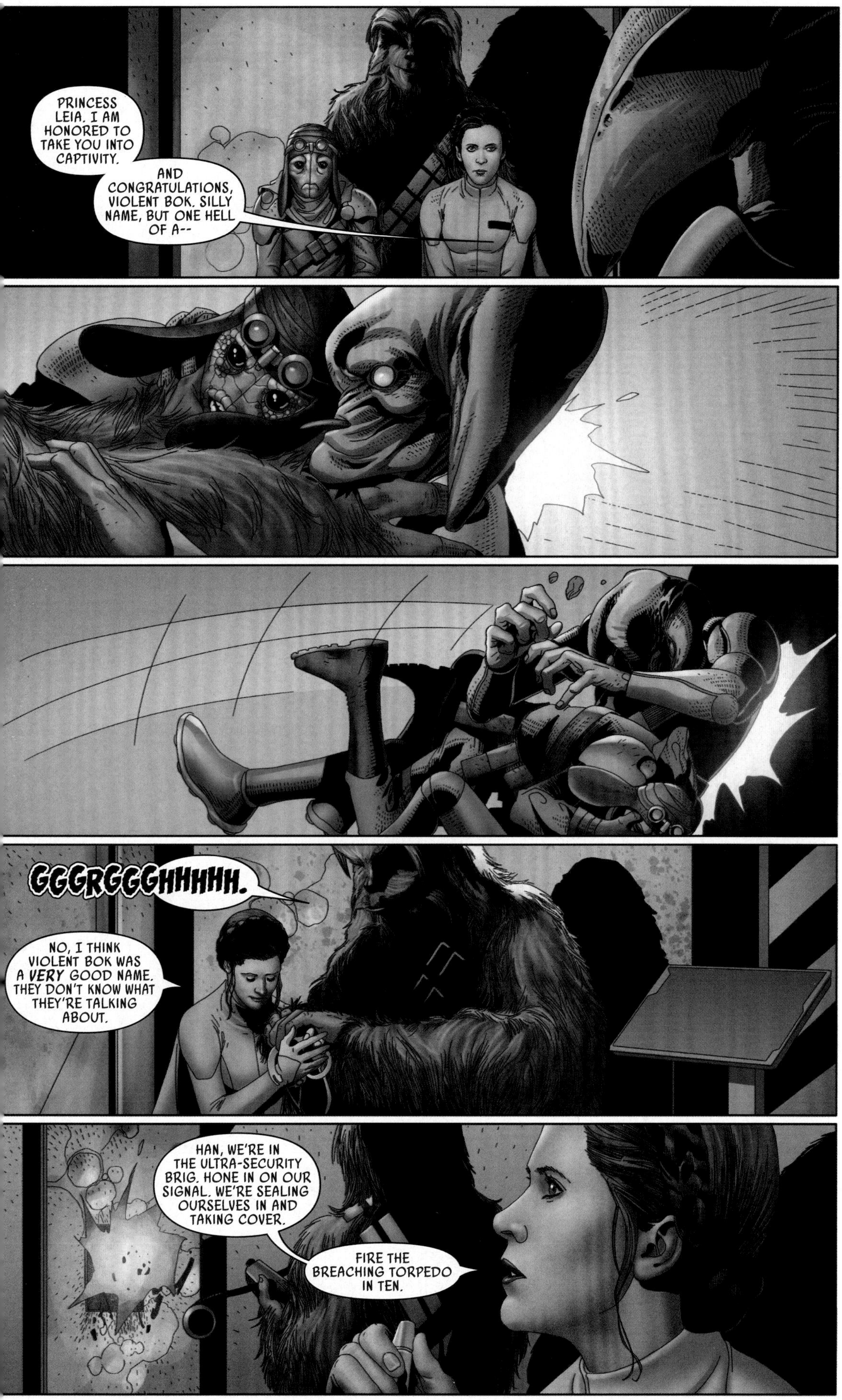
PRINCESS LEIA. I AM HONORED TO TAKE YOU INTO CAPTIVITY.
AND CONGRATULATIONS, VIOLENT BOK. SILLY NAME, BUT ONE HELL OF A--
GGGRGGGHHHHH.
NO, I THINK VIOLENT BOK WAS A *VERY* GOOD NAME. THEY DON'T KNOW WHAT THEY'RE TALKING ABOUT.
HAN, WE'RE IN THE ULTRA-SECURITY BRIG. HONE IN ON OUR SIGNAL. WE'RE SEALING OURSELVES IN AND TAKING COVER.
FIRE THE BREACHING TORPEDO IN TEN.

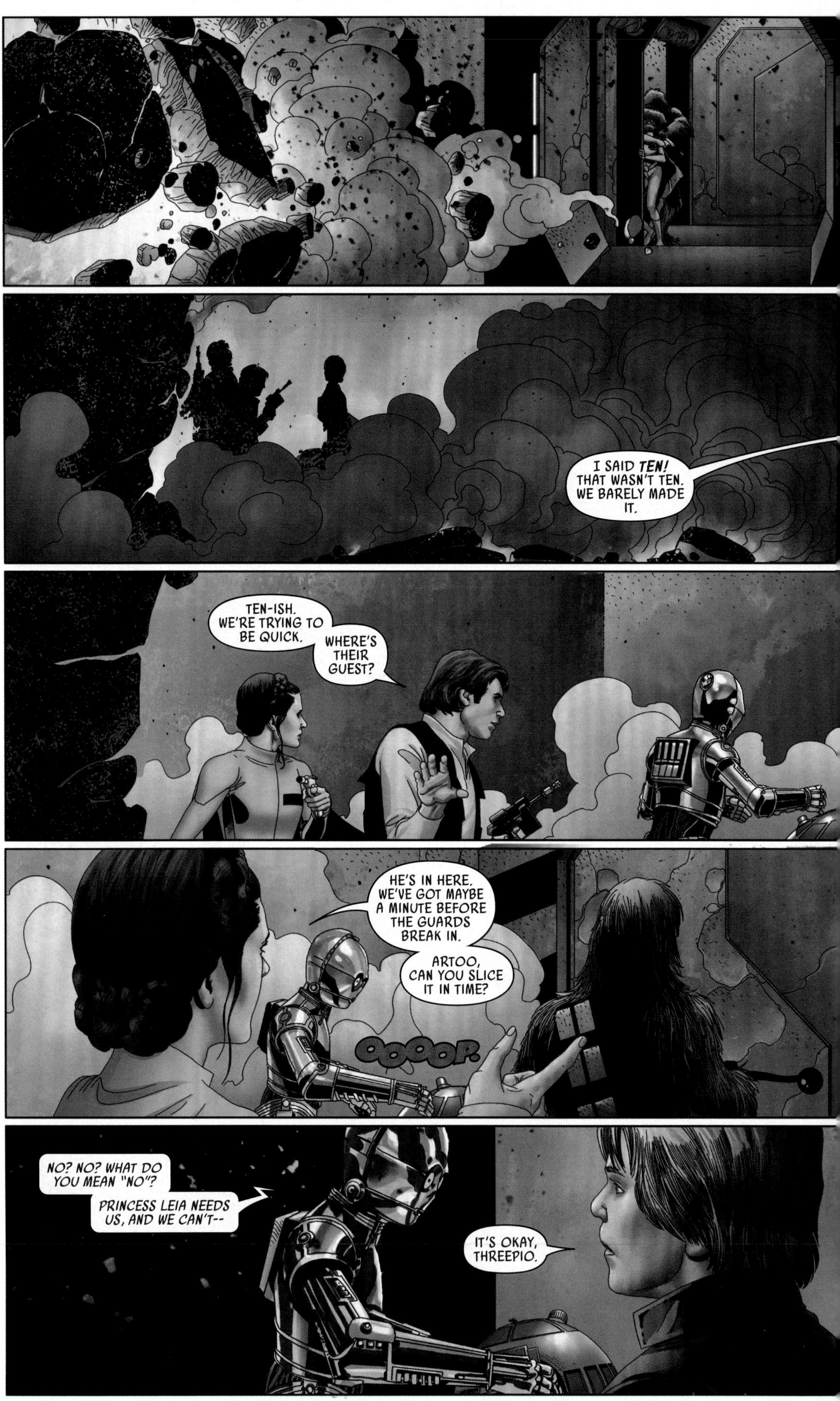
I SAID TEN! THAT WASN'T TEN. WE BARELY MADE IT.
TEN-ISH. WE'RE TRYING TO BE QUICK.
WHERE'S THEIR GUEST?
HE'S IN HERE. WE'VE GOT MAYBE A MINUTE BEFORE THE GUARDS BREAK IN.
ARTOO, CAN YOU SLICE IT IN TIME?
OOOOP.
NO? NO? WHAT DO YOU MEAN "NO"?
PRINCESS LEIA NEEDS US, AND WE CAN'T--
IT'S OKAY, THREEPIO.

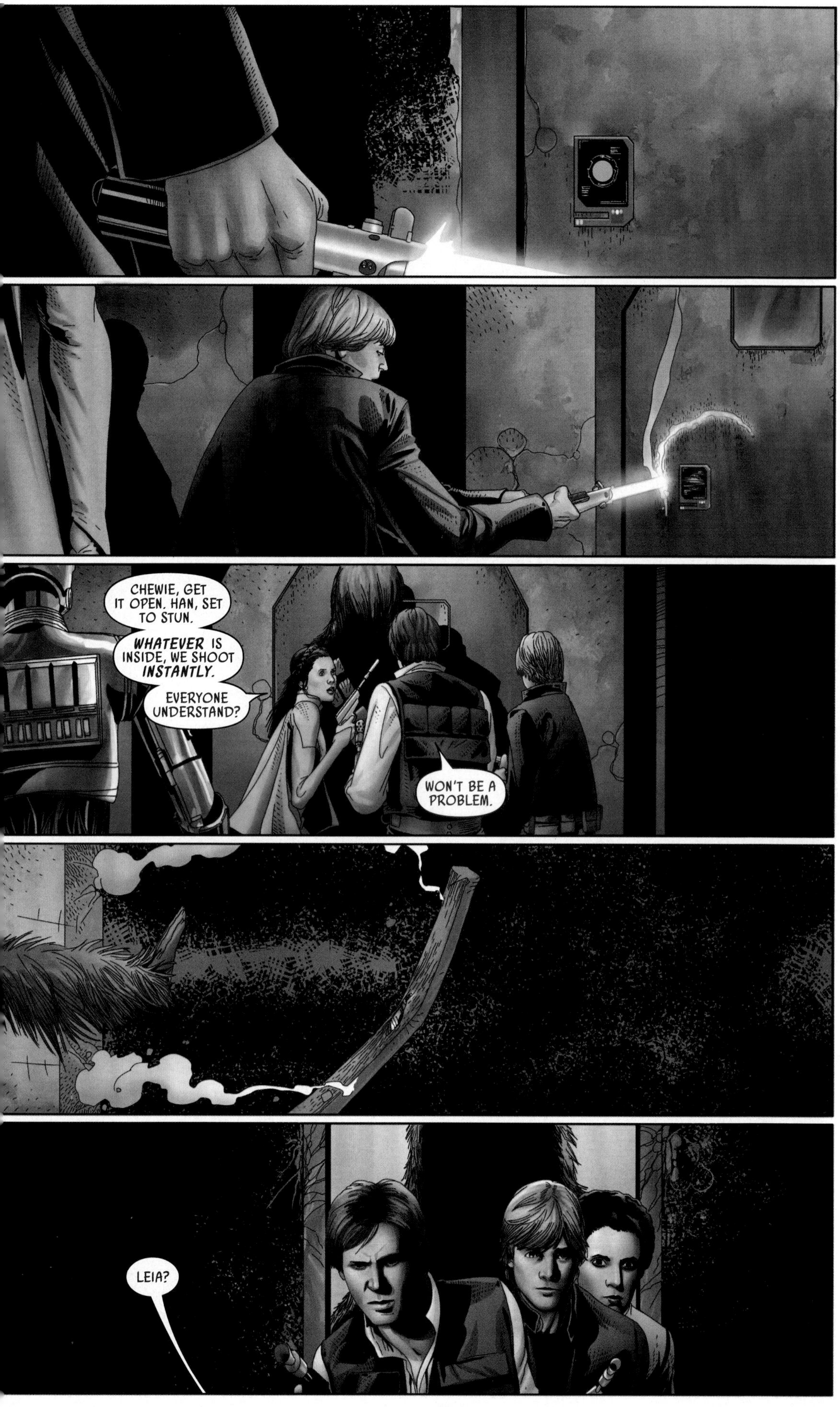
CHEWIE, GET IT OPEN. HAN, SET TO STUN.
WHATEVER IS INSIDE, WE SHOOT INSTANTLY.
EVERYONE UNDERSTAND?
WON'T BE A PROBLEM.
LEIA?

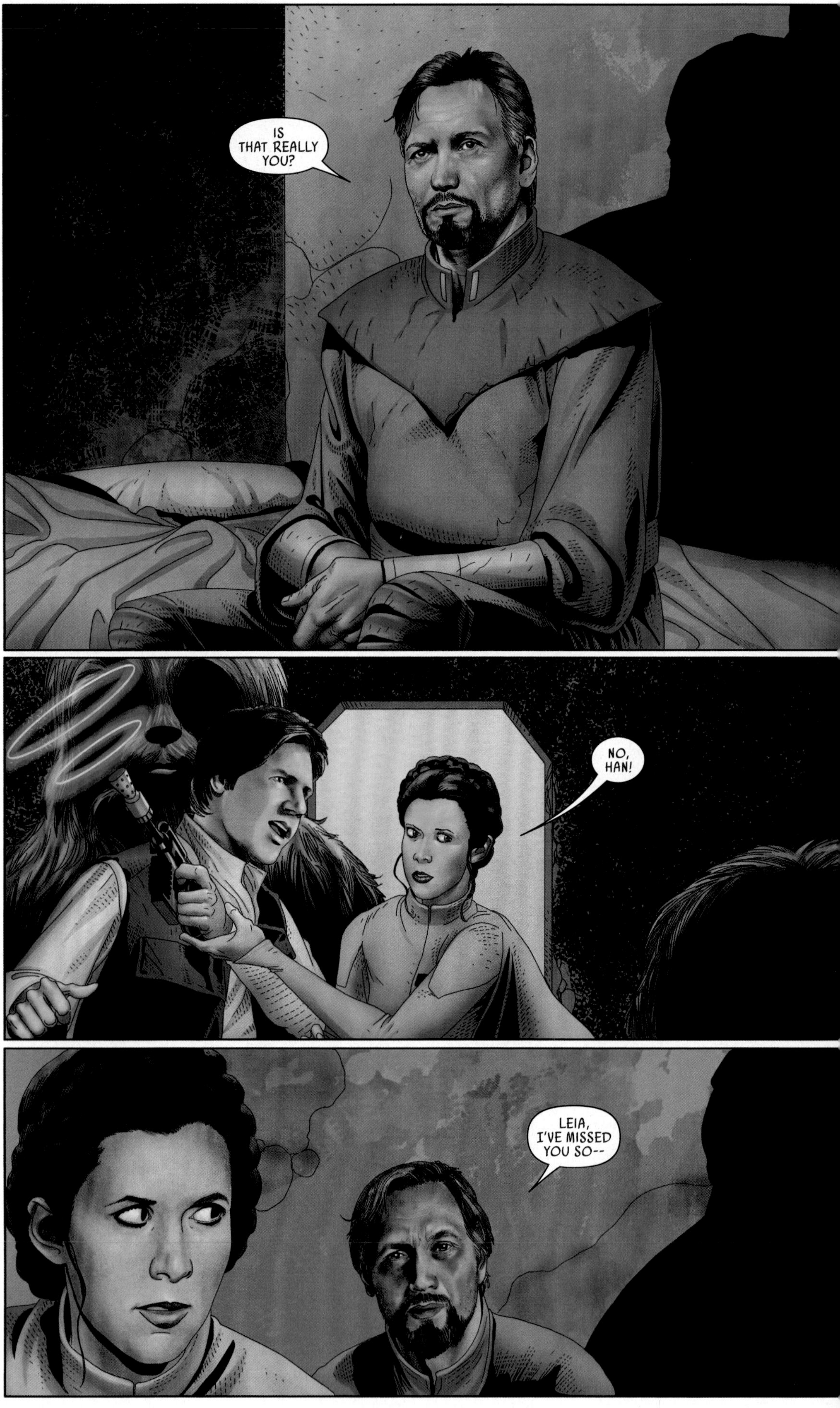
IS THAT REALLY YOU?
NO, HAN!
LEIA, I'VE MISSED YOU SO--

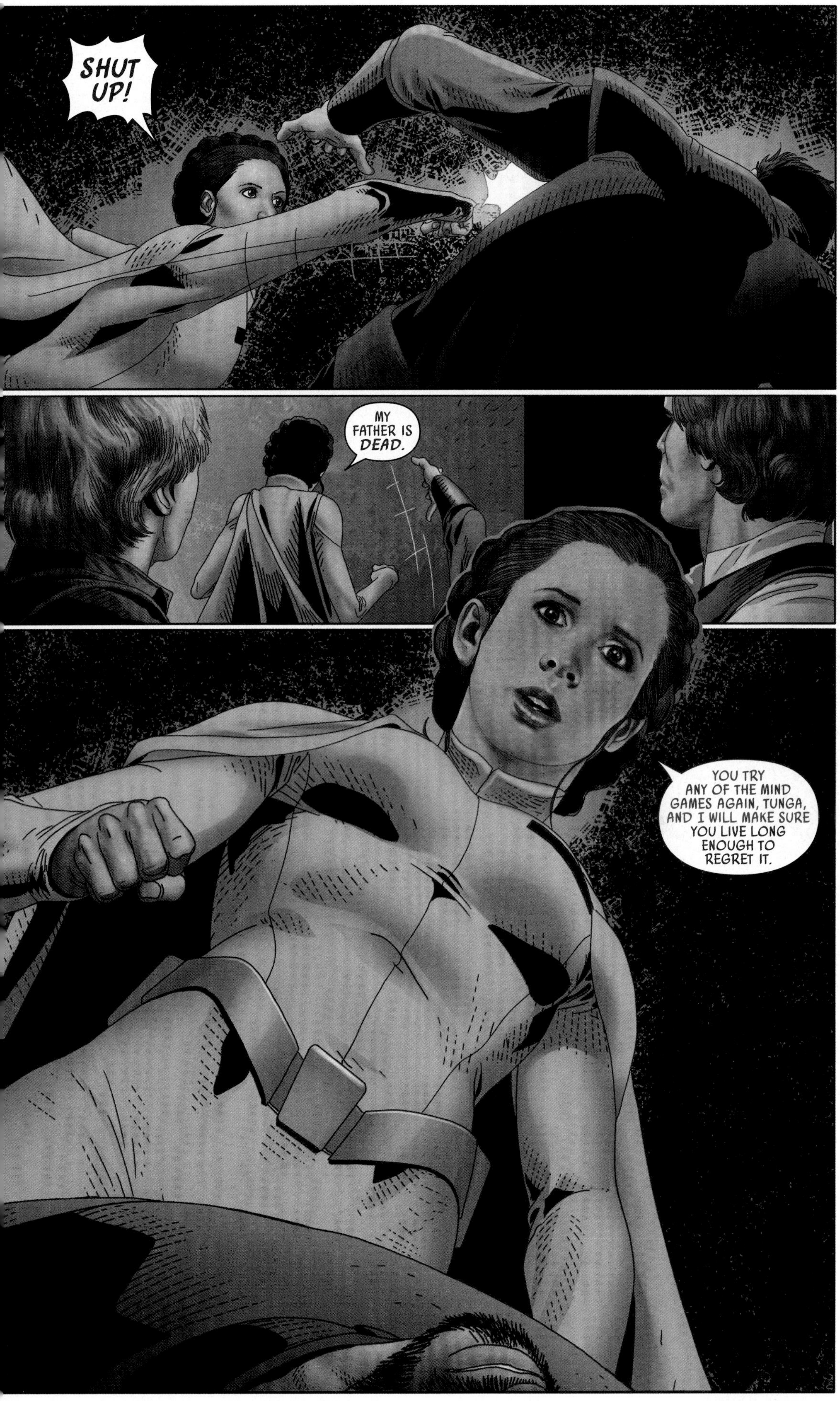
SHUT UP!
MY FATHER IS DEAD.
YOU TRY ANY OF THE MIND GAMES AGAIN, TUNGA, AND I WILL MAKE SURE YOU LIVE LONG ENOUGH TO REGRET IT.

YOU CAN'T BLAME A SHAPE-CHANGER FOR HAVING A LITTLE FUN.

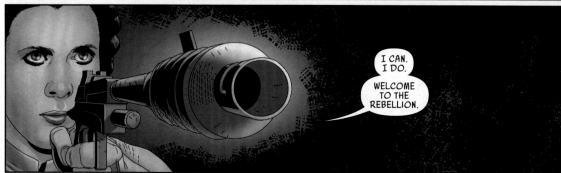

I CAN. I DO.

WELCOME TO THE REBELLION.

CHEWIE, PICK UP THE RECRUIT.

LET'S GET OUT OF HERE.

GGFGGGGGG.

YEAH, I'M IN THE MOOD FOR A STRONG MILK, TOO.

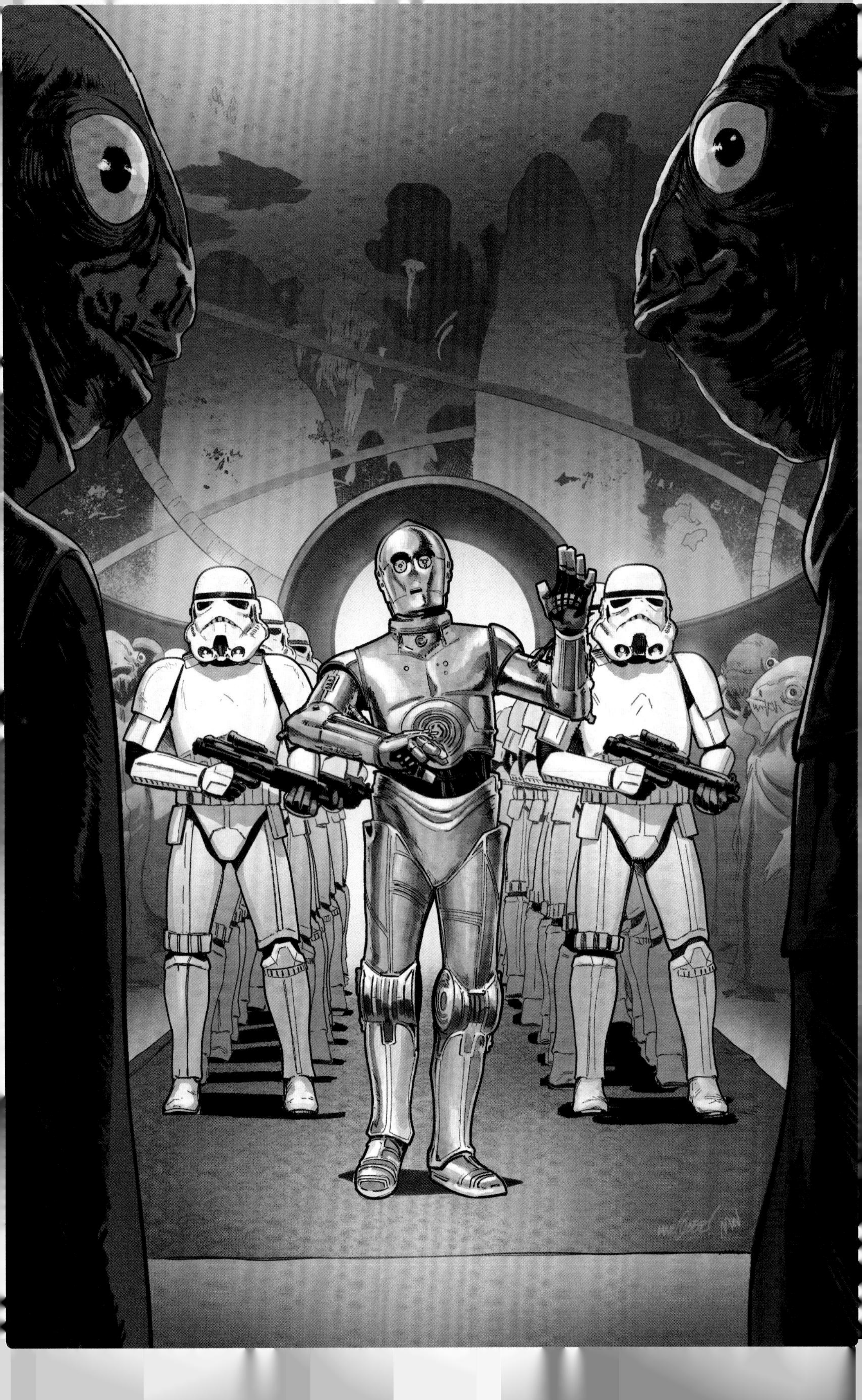

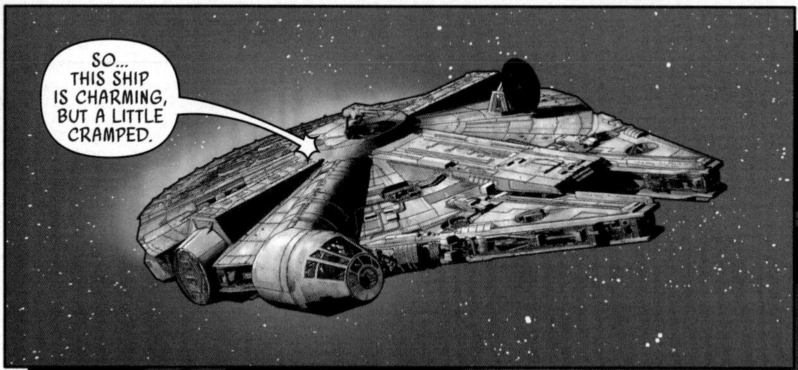
SO... THIS SHIP IS CHARMING, BUT A LITTLE CRAMPED.

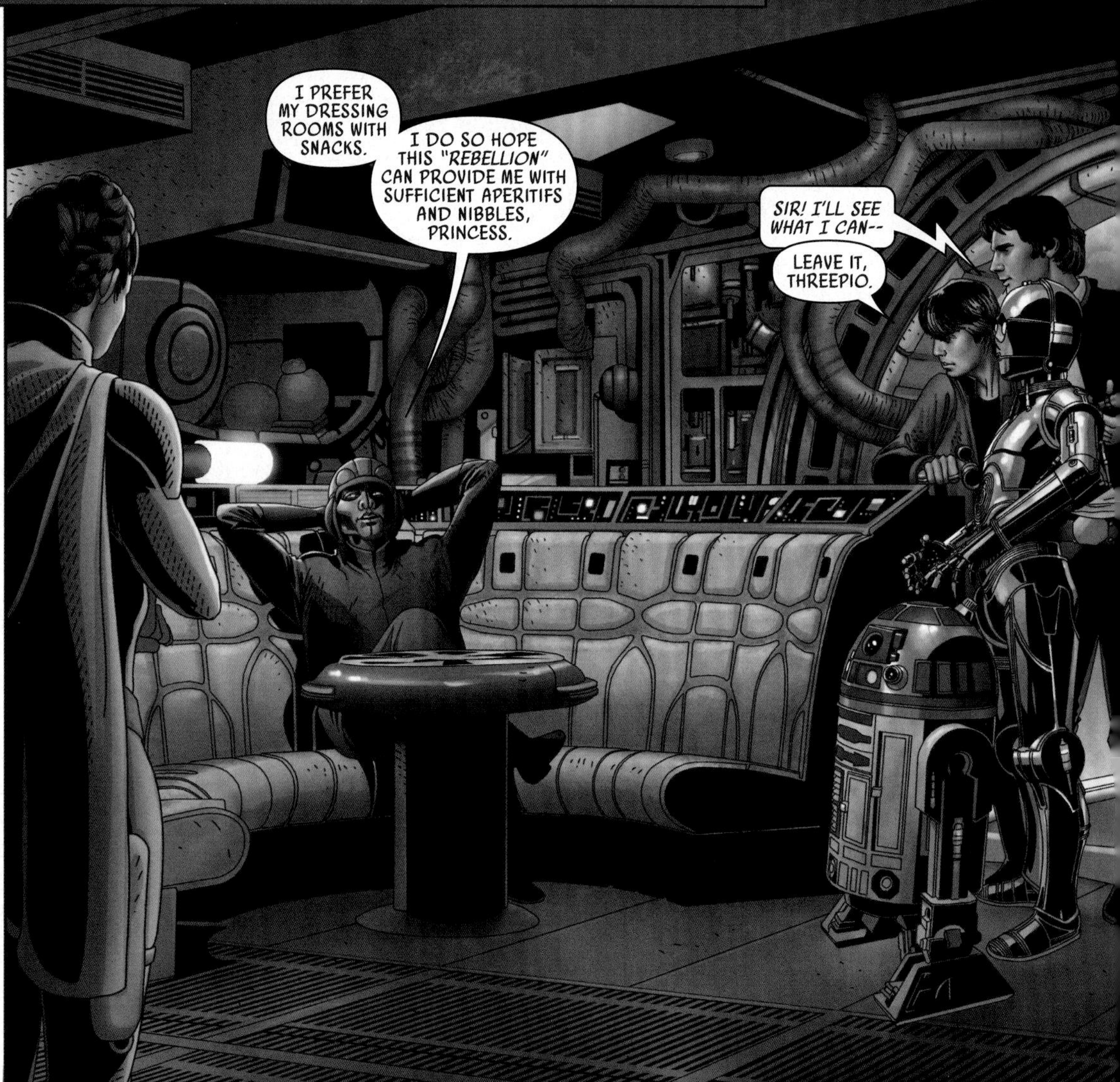
I PREFER MY DRESSING ROOMS WITH SNACKS.
I DO SO HOPE THIS "REBELLION" CAN PROVIDE ME WITH SUFFICIENT APERITIFS AND NIBBLES, PRINCESS.
SIR! I'LL SEE WHAT I CAN--
LEAVE IT, THREEPIO.

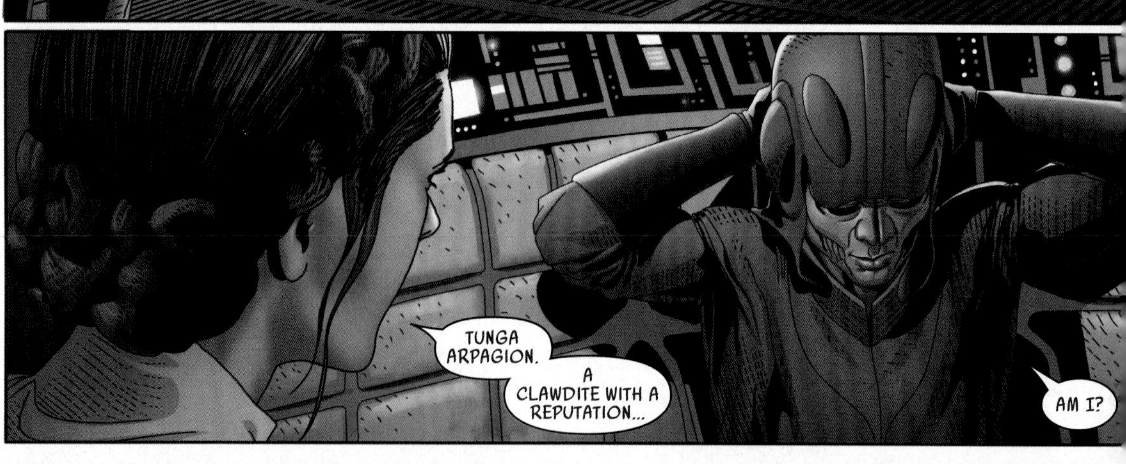
TUNGA ARPAGION.
A CLAWDITE WITH A REPUTATION...
AM I?

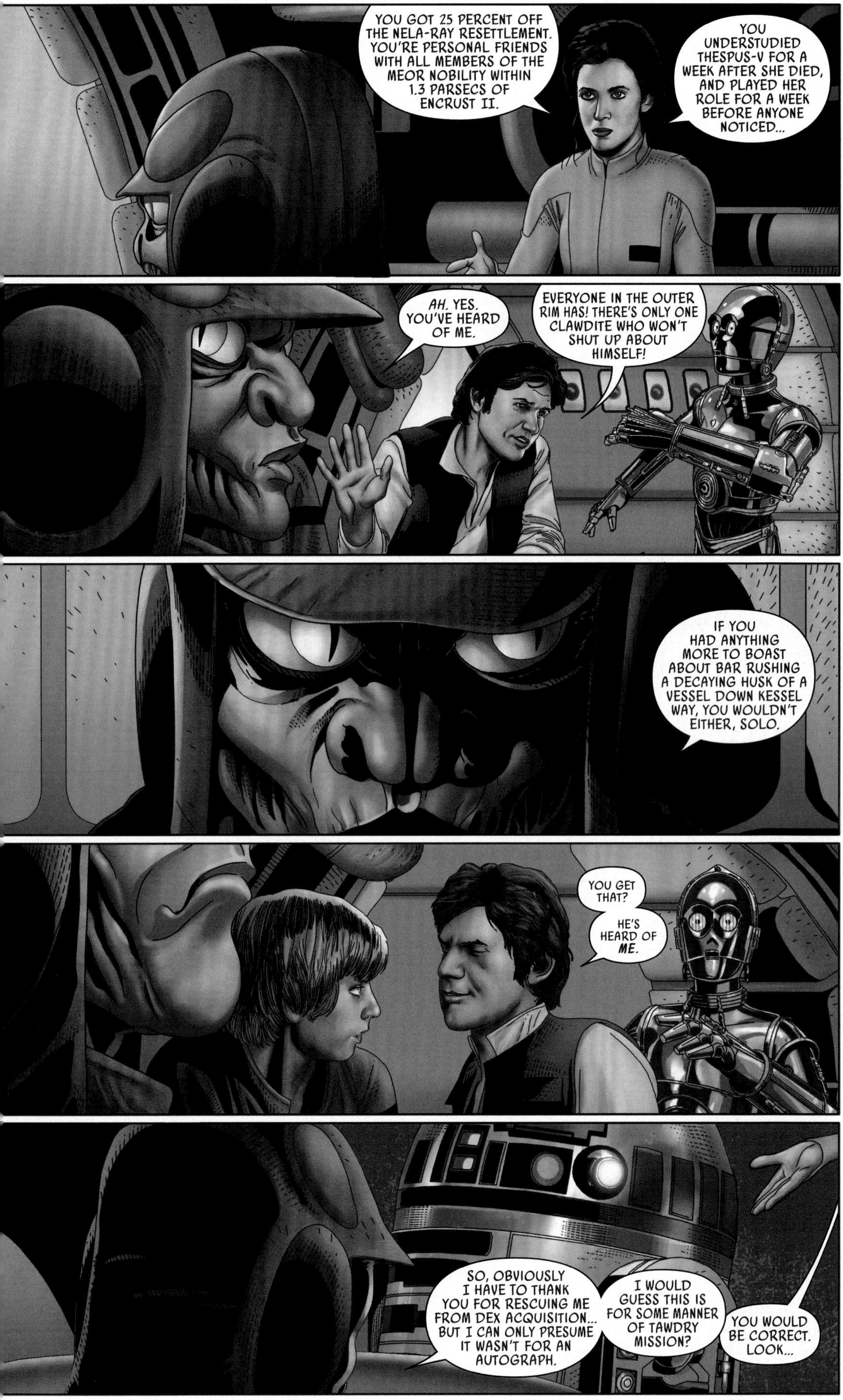
YOU GOT 25 PERCENT OFF THE NELA-RAY RESETTLEMENT. YOU'RE PERSONAL FRIENDS WITH ALL MEMBERS OF THE MEOR NOBILITY WITHIN 1.3 PARSECS OF ENCRUST II.
YOU UNDERSTUDIED THESPUS-V FOR A WEEK AFTER SHE DIED, AND PLAYED HER ROLE FOR A WEEK BEFORE ANYONE NOTICED...
AH. YES. YOU'VE HEARD OF ME.
EVERYONE IN THE OUTER RIM HAS! THERE'S ONLY ONE CLAWDITE WHO WON'T SHUT UP ABOUT HIMSELF!
IF YOU HAD ANYTHING MORE TO BOAST ABOUT BAR RUSHING A DECAYING HUSK OF A VESSEL DOWN KESSEL WAY, YOU WOULDN'T EITHER, SOLO.
YOU GET THAT?
HE'S HEARD OF ME.
SO, OBVIOUSLY I HAVE TO THANK YOU FOR RESCUING ME FROM DEX ACQUISITION... BUT I CAN ONLY PRESUME IT WASN'T FOR AN AUTOGRAPH.
I WOULD GUESS THIS IS FOR SOME MANNER OF TAWDRY MISSION?
YOU WOULD BE CORRECT. LOOK...

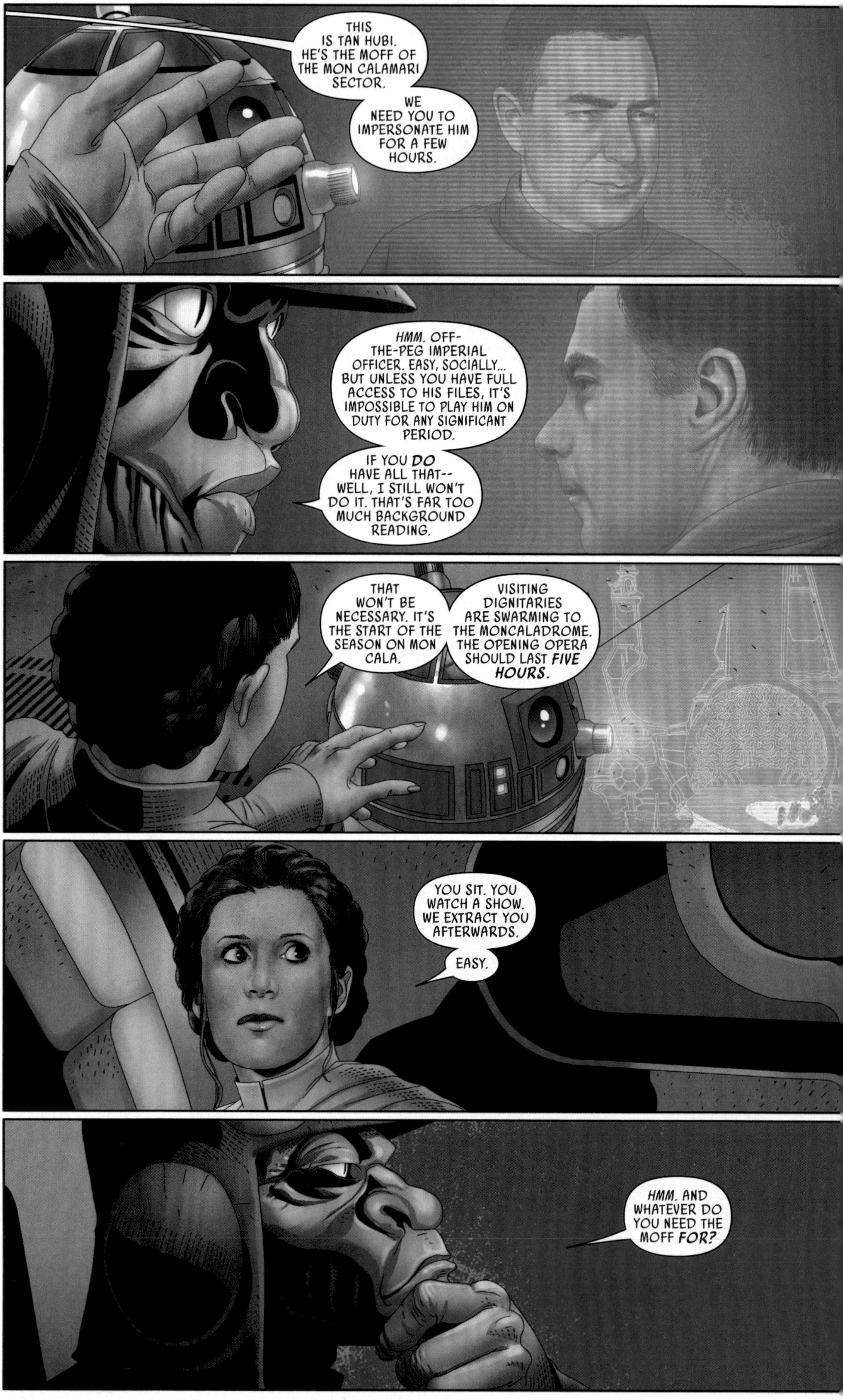
THIS IS TAN HUBI. HE'S THE MOFF OF THE MON CALAMARI SECTOR.
WE NEED YOU TO IMPERSONATE HIM FOR A FEW HOURS.
HMM. OFF-THE-PEG IMPERIAL OFFICER. EASY, SOCIALLY... BUT UNLESS YOU HAVE FULL ACCESS TO HIS FILES, IT'S IMPOSSIBLE TO PLAY HIM ON DUTY FOR ANY SIGNIFICANT PERIOD.
IF YOU ***DO*** HAVE ALL THAT--WELL, I STILL WON'T DO IT. THAT'S FAR TOO MUCH BACKGROUND READING.
THAT WON'T BE NECESSARY. IT'S THE START OF THE SEASON ON MON CALA.
VISITING DIGNITARIES ARE SWARMING TO THE MONCALADROME. THE OPENING OPERA SHOULD LAST ***FIVE HOURS.***
YOU SIT. YOU WATCH A SHOW. WE EXTRACT YOU AFTERWARDS.
EASY.
HMM. AND WHATEVER DO YOU NEED THE MOFF ***FOR?***

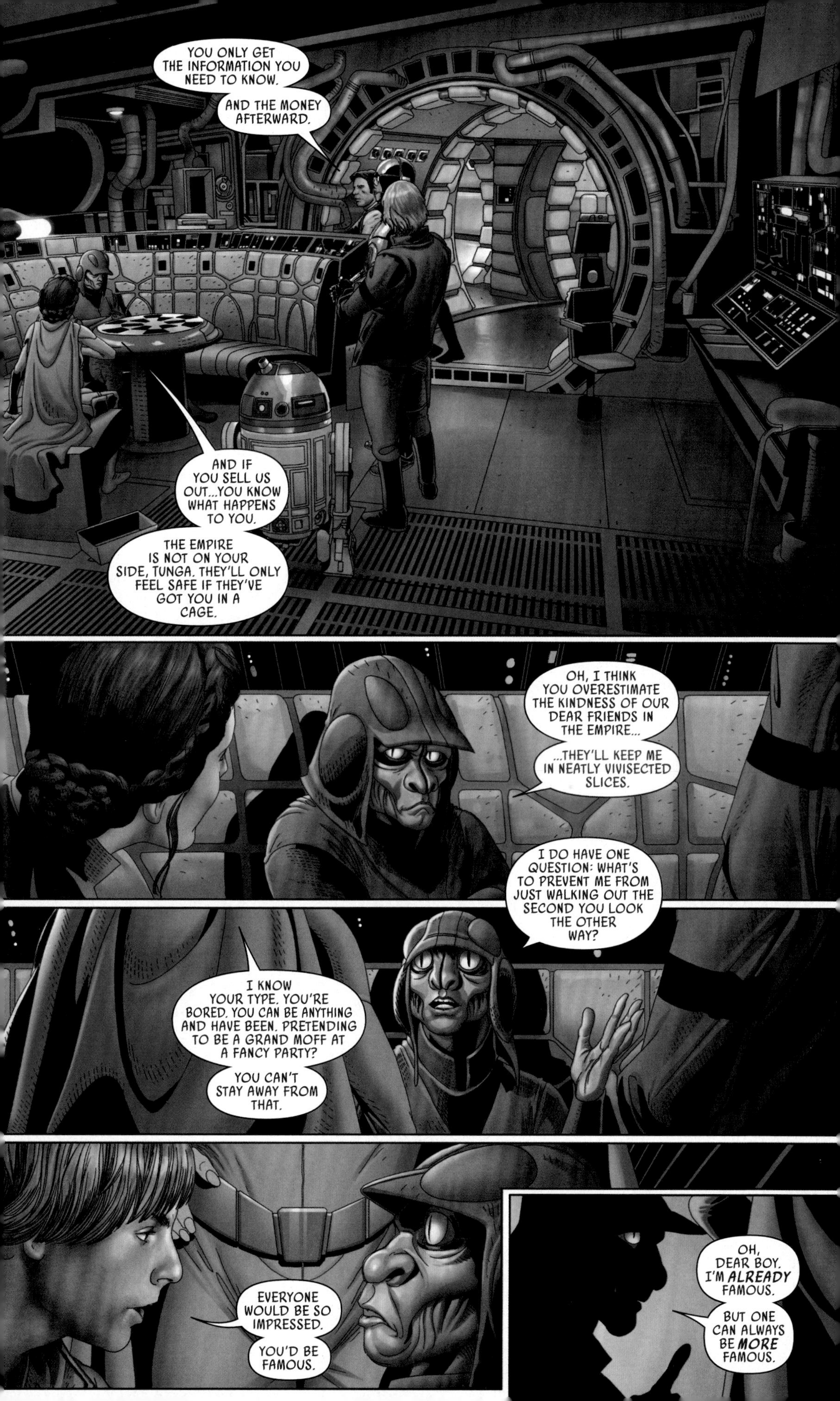
YOU ONLY GET THE INFORMATION YOU NEED TO KNOW.
AND THE MONEY AFTERWARD.
AND IF YOU SELL US OUT...YOU KNOW WHAT HAPPENS TO YOU.
THE EMPIRE IS NOT ON YOUR SIDE, TUNGA. THEY'LL ONLY FEEL SAFE IF THEY'VE GOT YOU IN A CAGE.
OH, I THINK YOU OVERESTIMATE THE KINDNESS OF OUR DEAR FRIENDS IN THE EMPIRE...
...THEY'LL KEEP ME IN NEATLY VIVISECTED SLICES.
I DO HAVE ONE QUESTION: WHAT'S TO PREVENT ME FROM JUST WALKING OUT THE SECOND YOU LOOK THE OTHER WAY?
I KNOW YOUR TYPE. YOU'RE BORED. YOU CAN BE ANYTHING AND HAVE BEEN. PRETENDING TO BE A GRAND MOFF AT A FANCY PARTY?
YOU CAN'T STAY AWAY FROM THAT.
EVERYONE WOULD BE SO IMPRESSED.
YOU'D BE FAMOUS.
OH, DEAR BOY. I'M *ALREADY* FAMOUS.
BUT ONE CAN ALWAYS BE *MORE* FAMOUS.

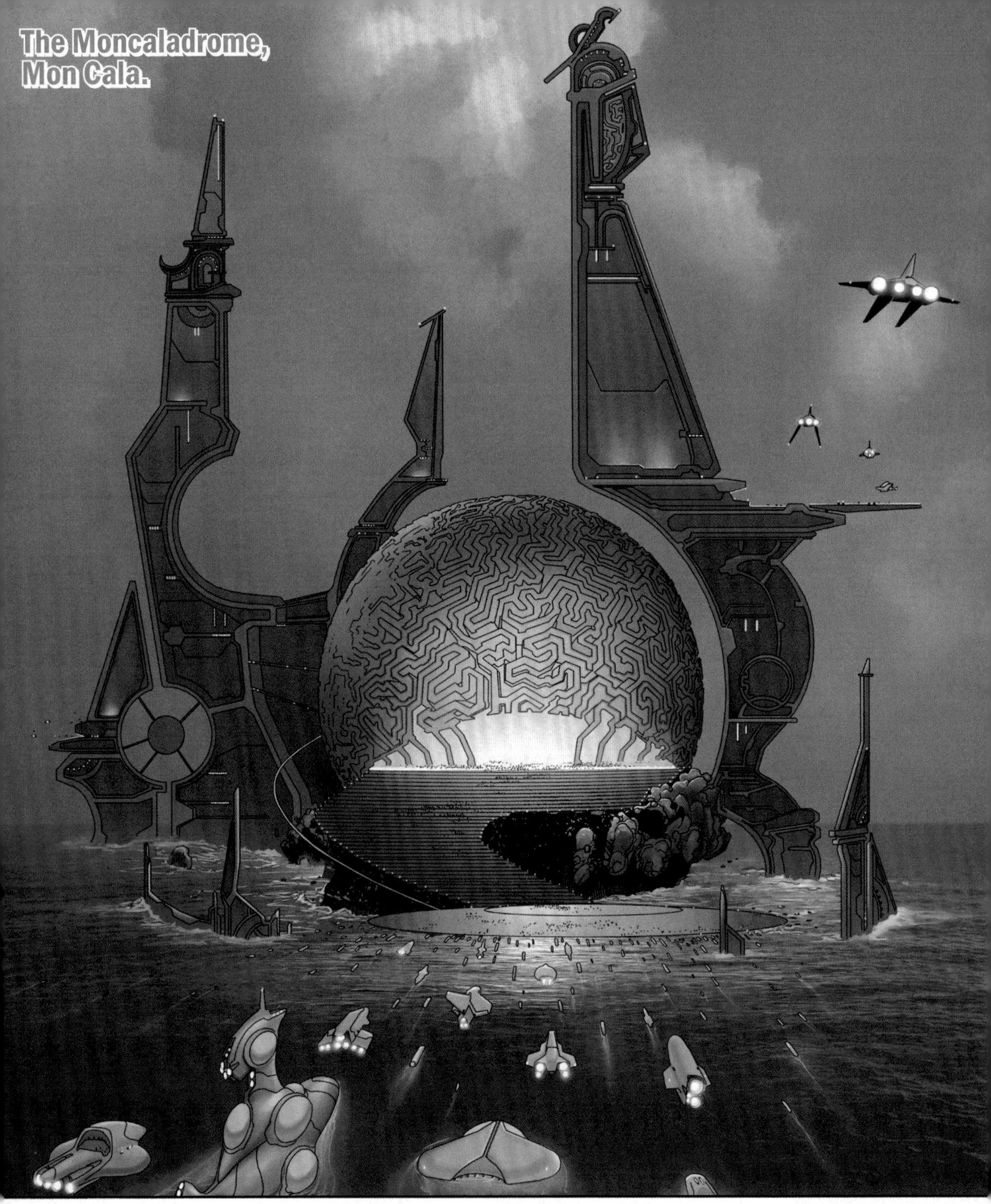
The Moncaladrome,
Mon Cala.

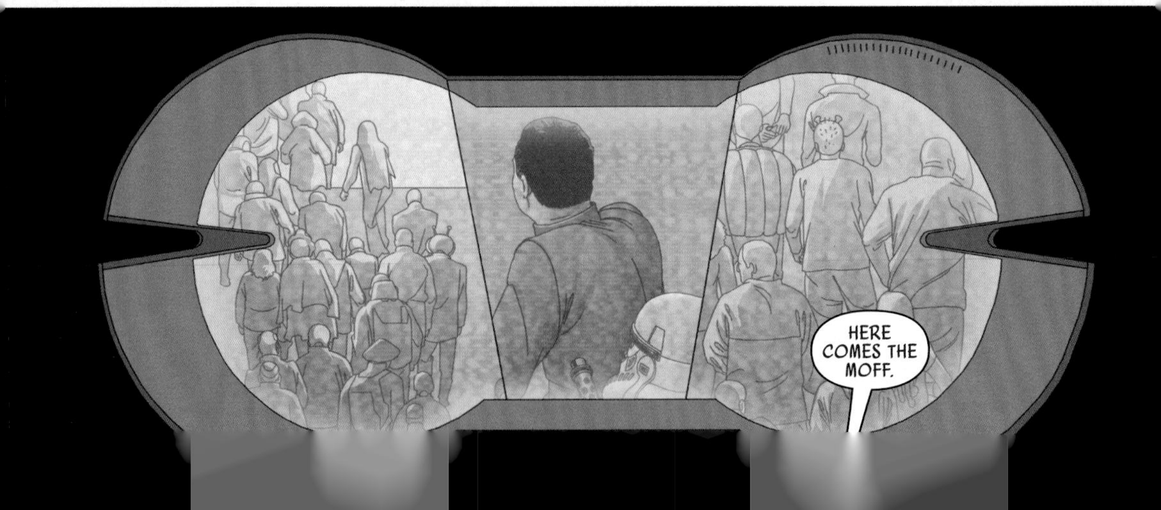
HERE COMES THE MOFF.

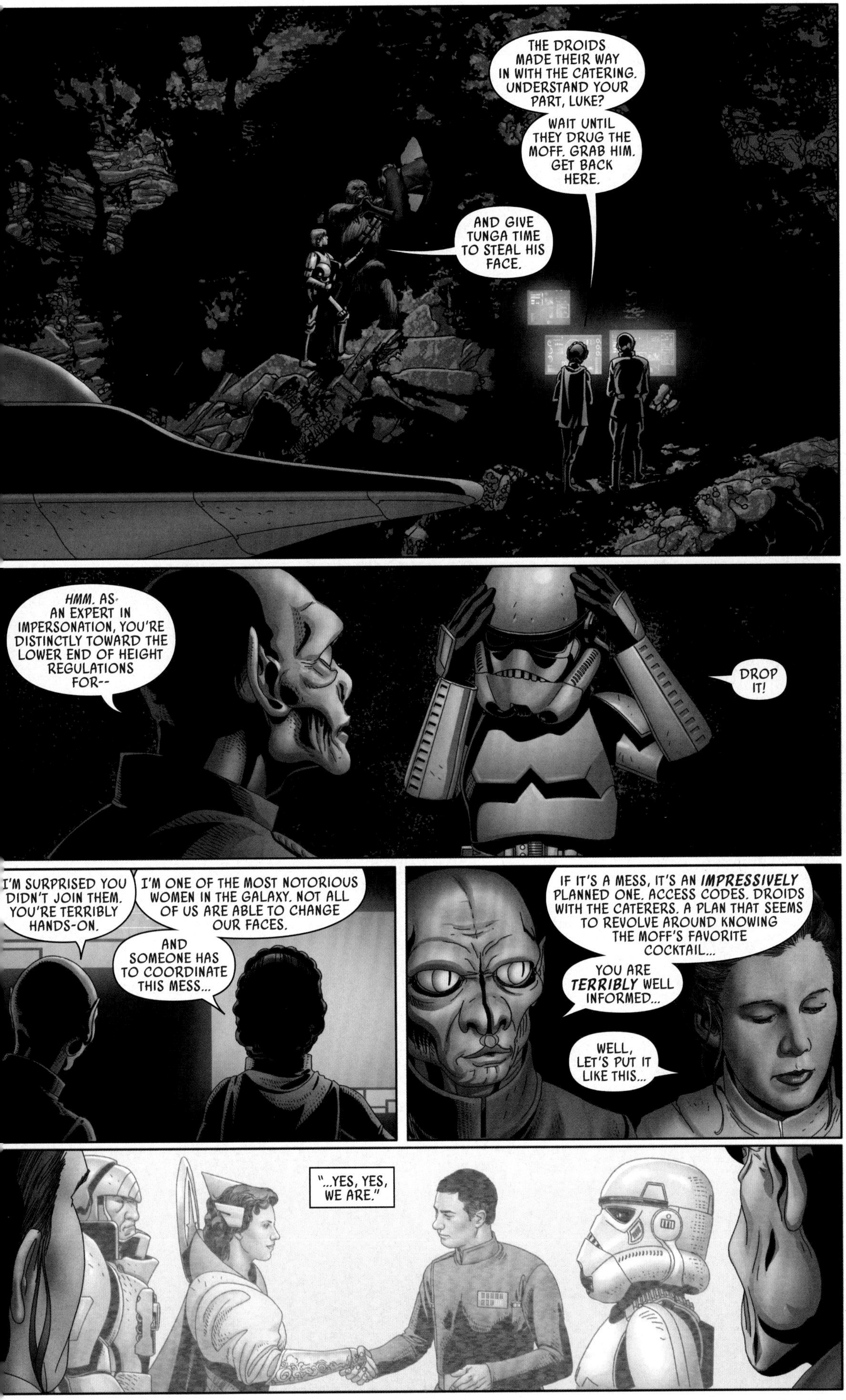

THE DROIDS MADE THEIR WAY IN WITH THE CATERING. UNDERSTAND YOUR PART, LUKE?
WAIT UNTIL THEY DRUG THE MOFF. GRAB HIM. GET BACK HERE.
AND GIVE TUNGA TIME TO STEAL HIS FACE.
HMM. AS AN EXPERT IN IMPERSONATION, YOU'RE DISTINCTLY TOWARD THE LOWER END OF HEIGHT REGULATIONS FOR--
DROP IT!
I'M SURPRISED YOU DIDN'T JOIN THEM. YOU'RE TERRIBLY HANDS-ON.
I'M ONE OF THE MOST NOTORIOUS WOMEN IN THE GALAXY. NOT ALL OF US ARE ABLE TO CHANGE OUR FACES.
AND SOMEONE HAS TO COORDINATE THIS MESS...
IF IT'S A MESS, IT'S AN *IMPRESSIVELY* PLANNED ONE. ACCESS CODES. DROIDS WITH THE CATERERS. A PLAN THAT SEEMS TO REVOLVE AROUND KNOWING THE MOFF'S FAVORITE COCKTAIL...
YOU ARE *TERRIBLY* WELL INFORMED...
WELL, LET'S PUT IT LIKE THIS...
"...YES, YES, WE ARE."

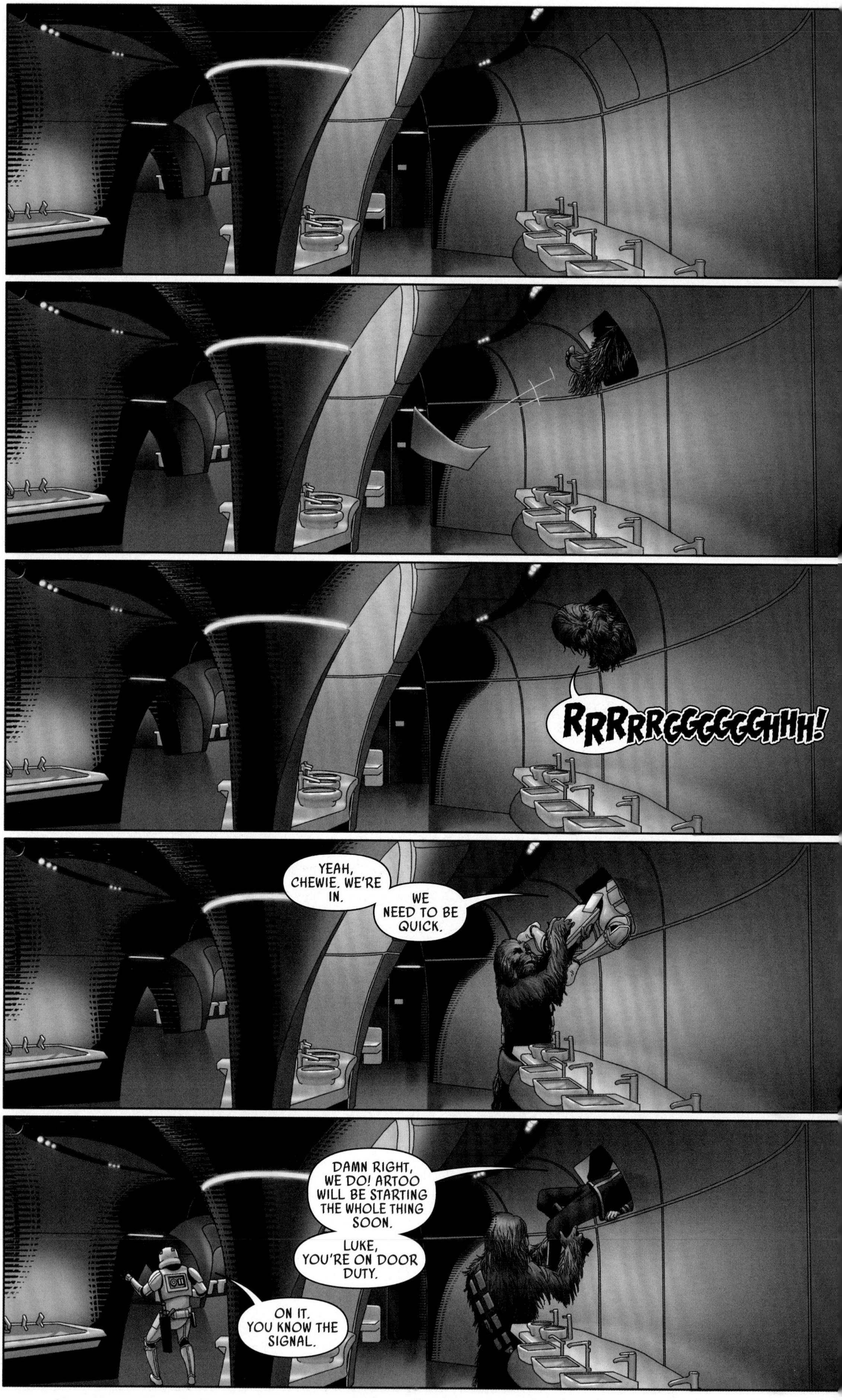

RRRRRGGGGGGHHH!
YEAH, CHEWIE. WE'RE IN.
WE NEED TO BE QUICK.
DAMN RIGHT, WE DO! ARTOO WILL BE STARTING THE WHOLE THING SOON.
LUKE, YOU'RE ON DOOR DUTY.
ON IT. YOU KNOW THE SIGNAL.

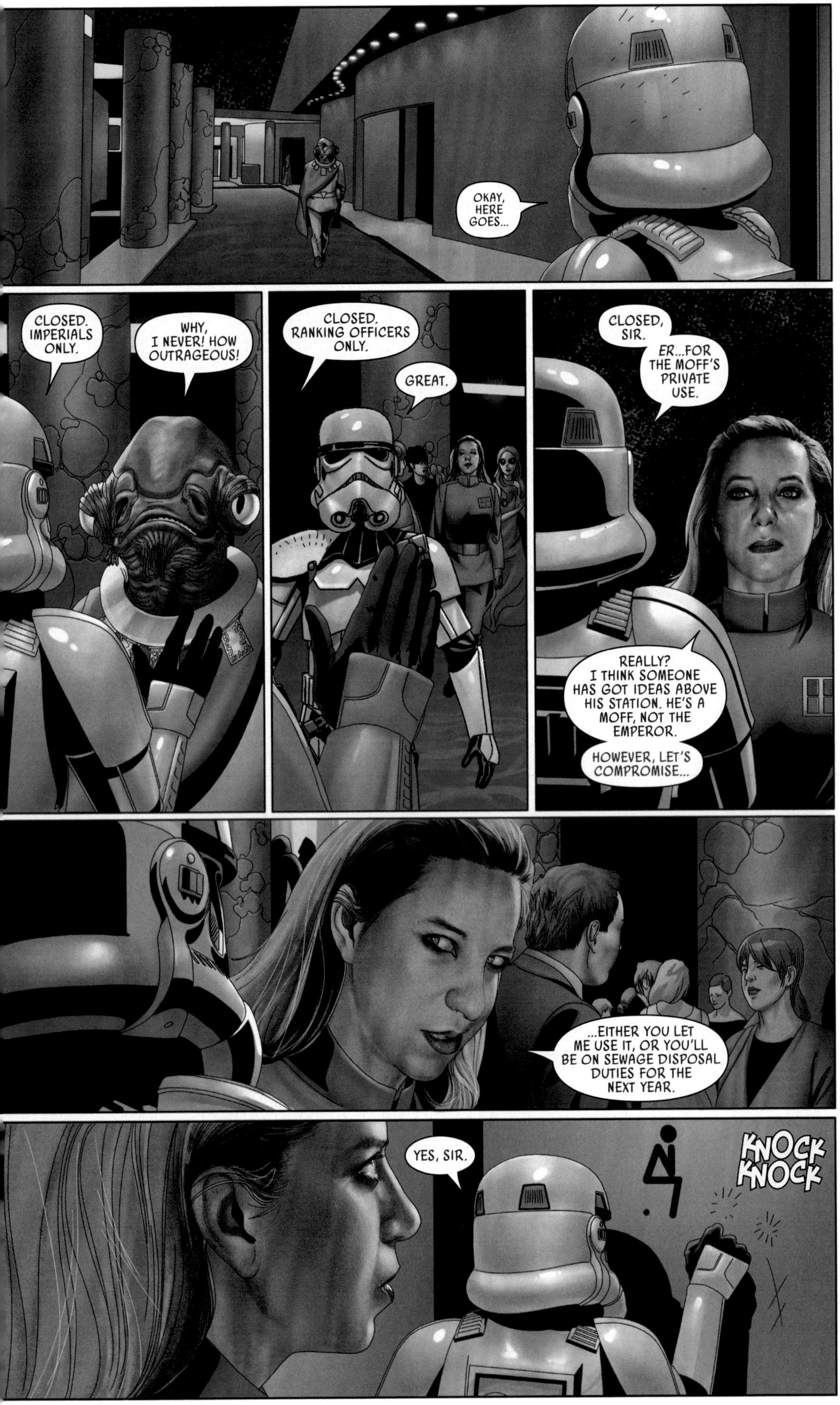
OKAY, HERE GOES...
CLOSED. IMPERIALS ONLY.
WHY, I NEVER! HOW OUTRAGEOUS!
CLOSED. RANKING OFFICERS ONLY.
GREAT.
CLOSED, SIR.
ER...FOR THE MOFF'S PRIVATE USE.
REALLY? I THINK SOMEONE HAS GOT IDEAS ABOVE HIS STATION. HE'S A MOFF, NOT THE EMPEROR.
HOWEVER, LET'S COMPROMISE...
...EITHER YOU LET ME USE IT, OR YOU'LL BE ON SEWAGE DISPOSAL DUTIES FOR THE NEXT YEAR.
YES, SIR.
KNOCK KNOCK

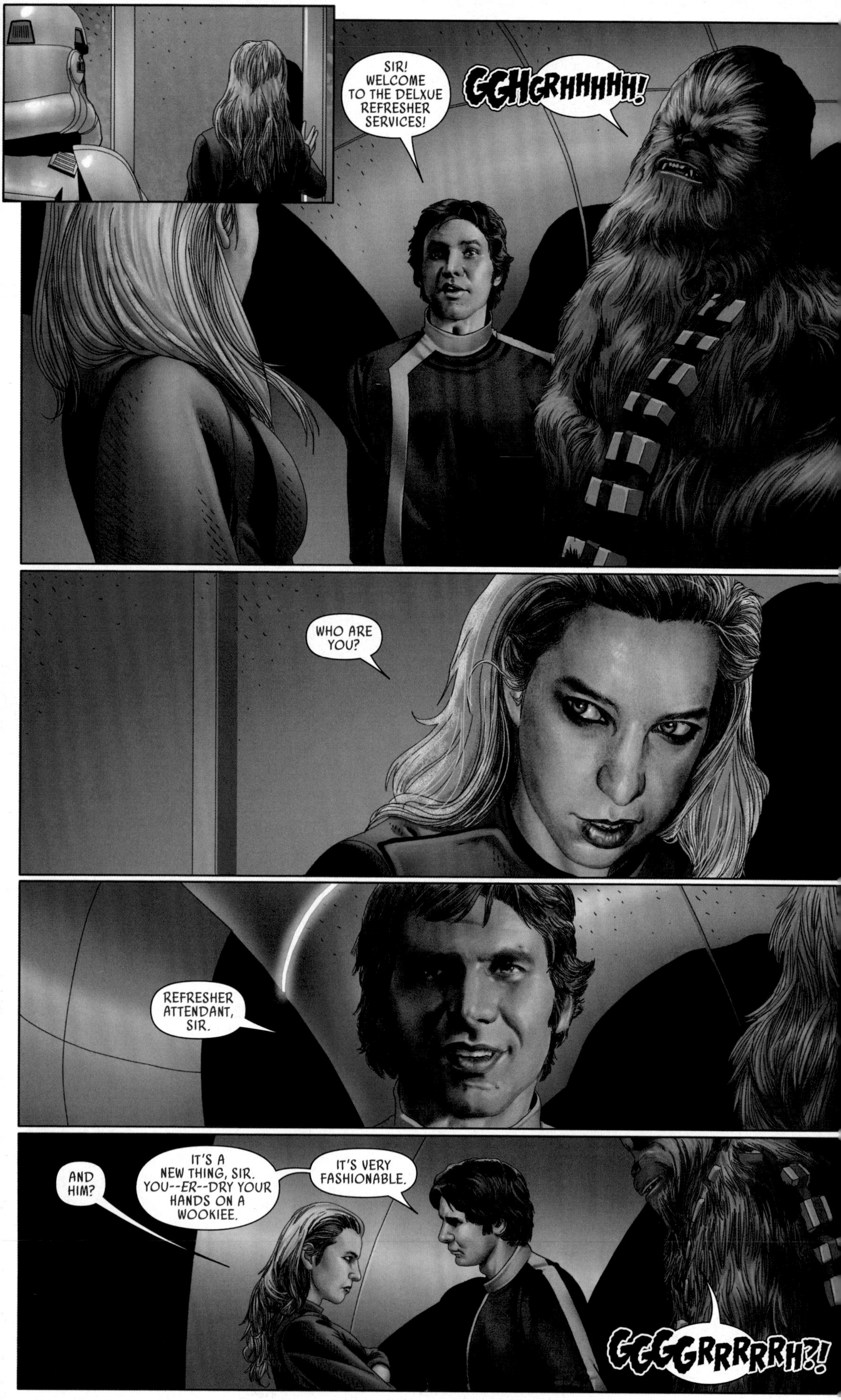
SIR! WELCOME TO THE DELXUE REFRESHER SERVICES!
GGHGRHHHHH!
WHO ARE YOU?
REFRESHER ATTENDANT, SIR.
AND HIM?
IT'S A NEW THING, SIR. YOU--ER--DRY YOUR HANDS ON A WOOKIEE.
IT'S VERY FASHIONABLE.
GGGGRRRRRH?!

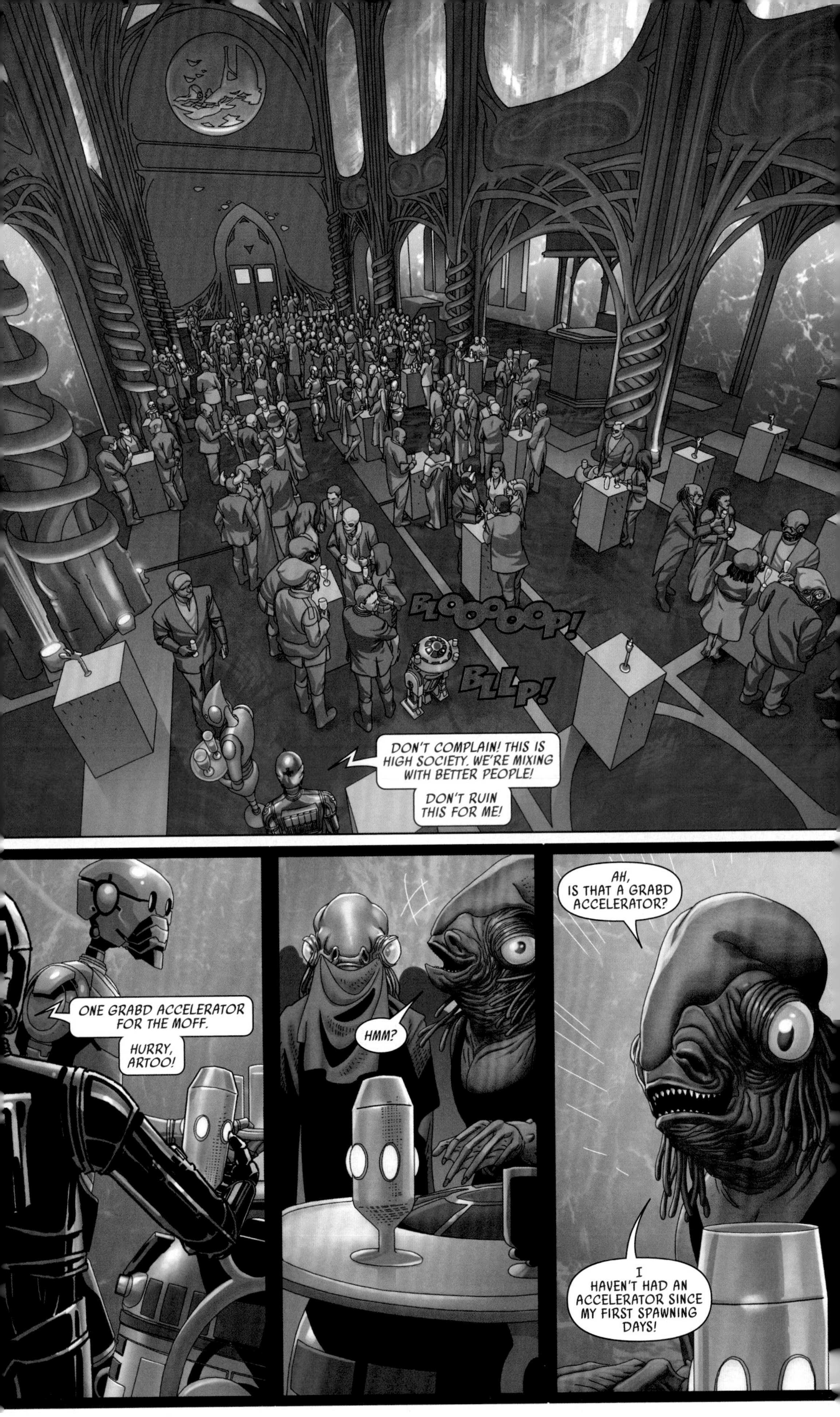
BLOOOOOOP!
BLLP!
DON'T COMPLAIN! THIS IS HIGH SOCIETY. WE'RE MIXING WITH BETTER PEOPLE!
DON'T RUIN THIS FOR ME!
ONE GRABD ACCELERATOR FOR THE MOFF.
HURRY, ARTOO!
HMM?
AH, IS THAT A GRABD ACCELERATOR?
I HAVEN'T HAD AN ACCELERATOR SINCE MY FIRST SPAWNING DAYS!

BLOOOOP!
BOO!

ZZZZZZP

HE... HE...

OH, I'M SORRY, MA'AM. HE'S MALFUNCTIONING.

I BELIEVE I SAW A BETTER DROID OVER THERE. A MUCH MORE RESPECTFUL SORT.

THEY'LL FIX YOU UP A NICE ACCELERATOR, I'M SURE.

HOW DREADFUL!

HE IS! HE REALLY IS.

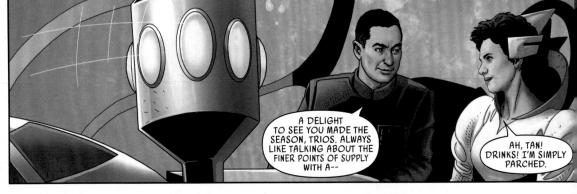

A DELIGHT TO SEE YOU MADE THE SEASON, TRIOS. ALWAYS LIKE TALKING ABOUT THE FINER POINTS OF SUPPLY WITH A--

AH, TAN! DRINKS! I'M SIMPLY PARCHED.

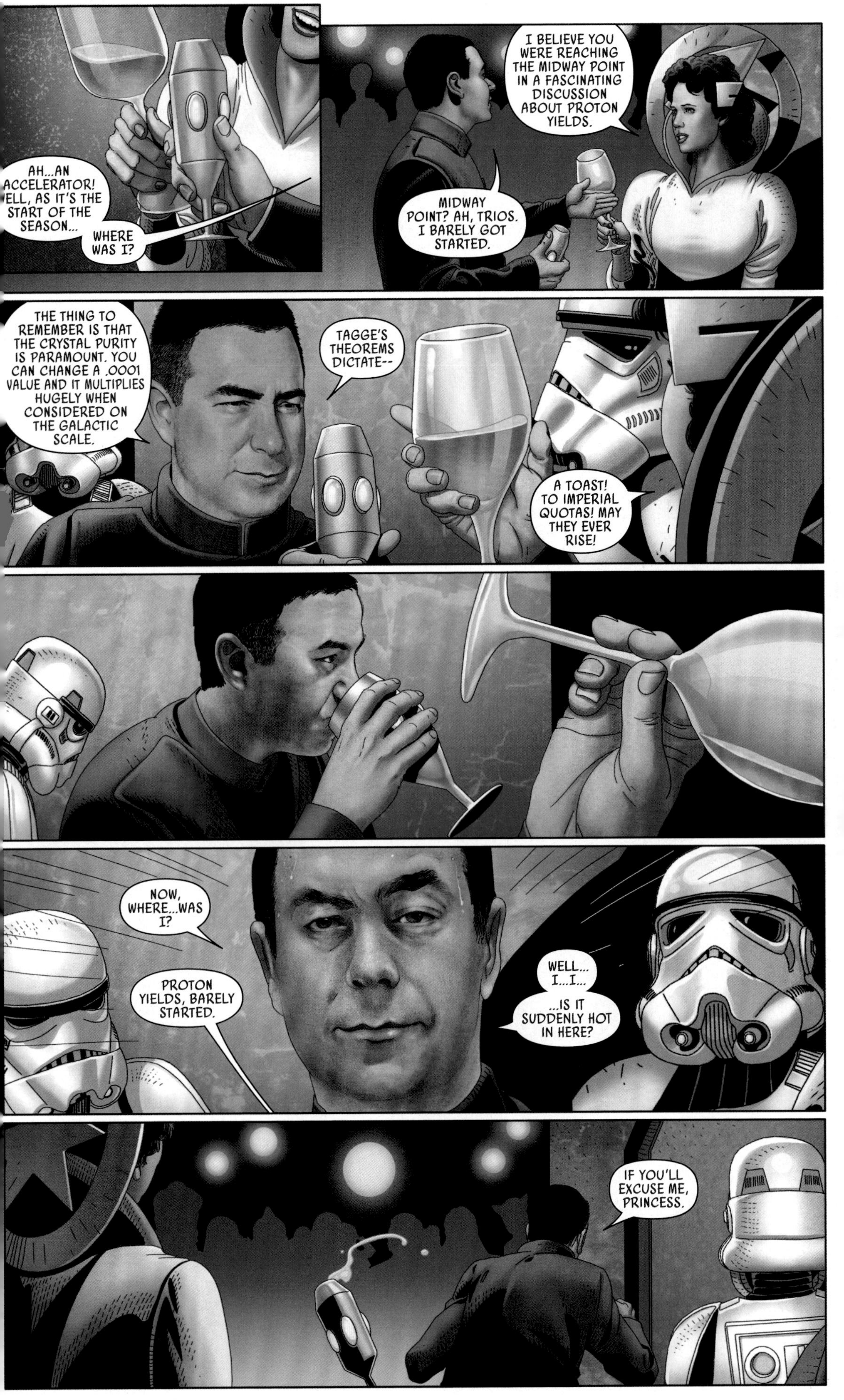

AH...AN ACCELERATOR! ELL, AS IT'S THE START OF THE SEASON...
WHERE WAS I?
I BELIEVE YOU WERE REACHING THE MIDWAY POINT IN A FASCINATING DISCUSSION ABOUT PROTON YIELDS.
MIDWAY POINT? AH, TRIOS. I BARELY GOT STARTED.
THE THING TO REMEMBER IS THAT THE CRYSTAL PURITY IS PARAMOUNT. YOU CAN CHANGE A .0001 VALUE AND IT MULTIPLIES HUGELY WHEN CONSIDERED ON THE GALACTIC SCALE.
TAGGE'S THEOREMS DICTATE--
A TOAST! TO IMPERIAL QUOTAS! MAY THEY EVER RISE!
NOW, WHERE...WAS I?
PROTON YIELDS, BARELY STARTED.
WELL... I...I...
...IS IT SUDDENLY HOT IN HERE?
IF YOU'LL EXCUSE ME, PRINCESS.

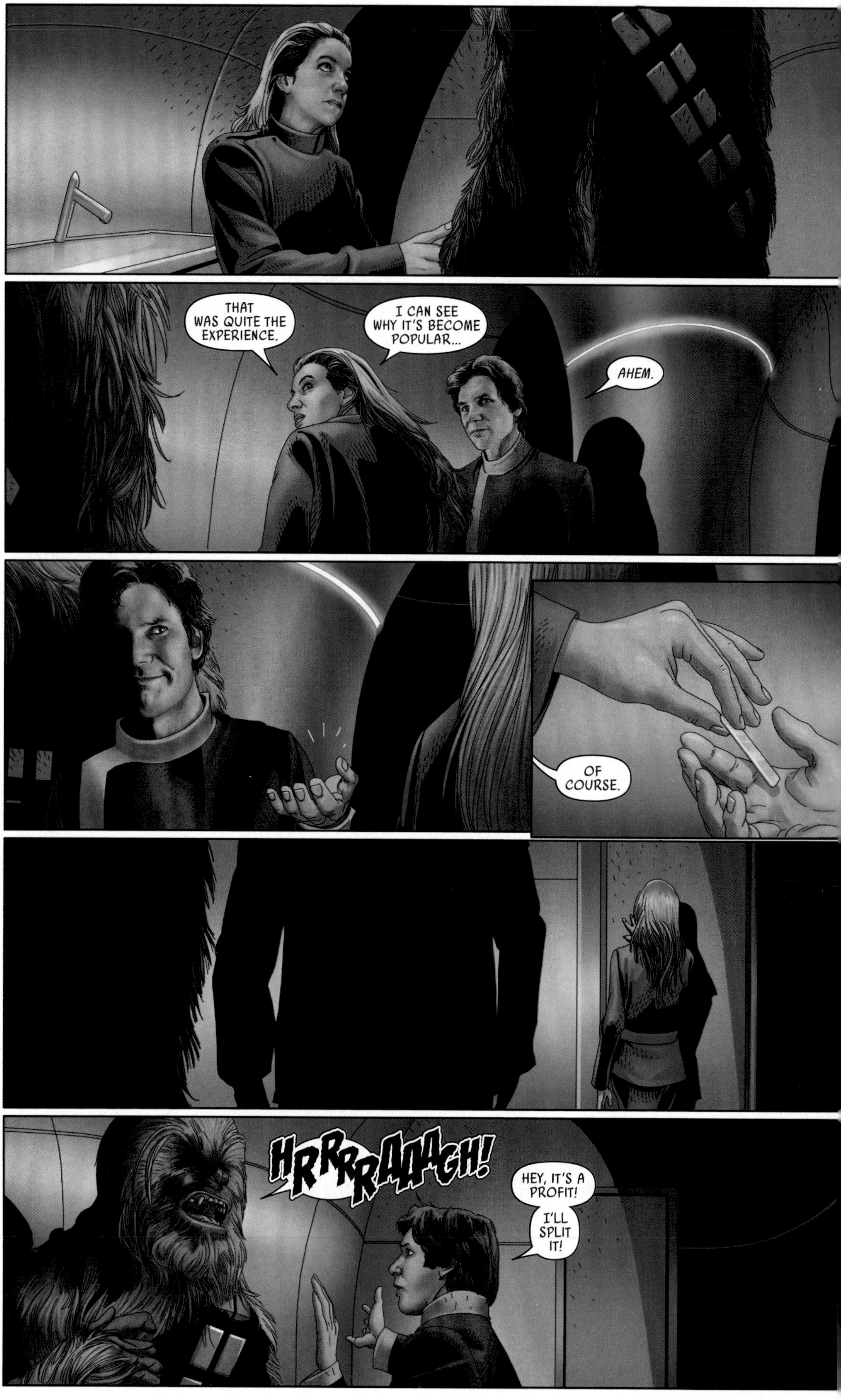
THAT WAS QUITE THE EXPERIENCE.
I CAN SEE WHY IT'S BECOME POPULAR...
AHEM.
OF COURSE.
HRRRRAAAGH!
HEY, IT'S A PROFIT!
I'LL SPLIT IT!

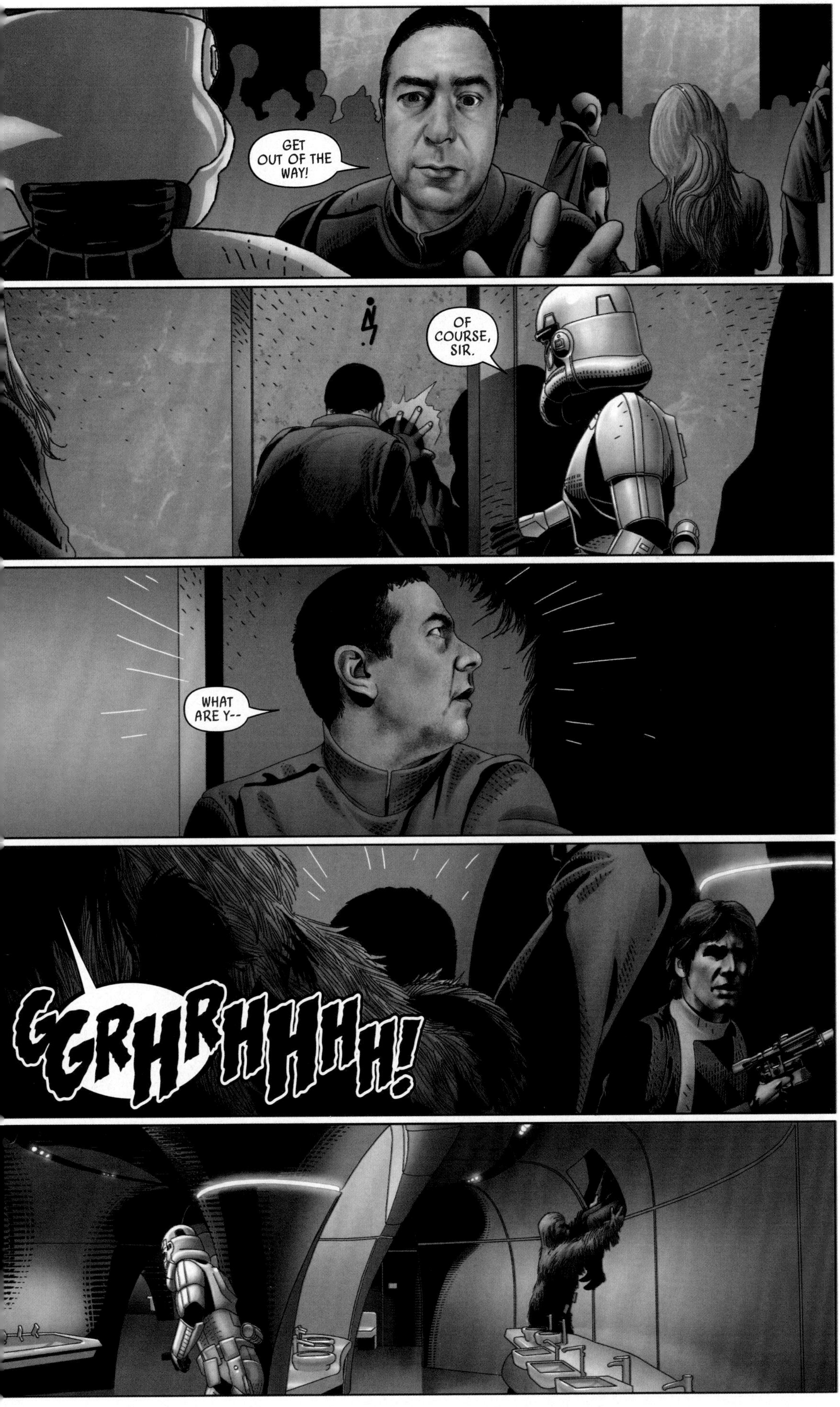
GET OUT OF THE WAY!
OF COURSE, SIR.
WHAT ARE Y--
GGRHRHHHH!

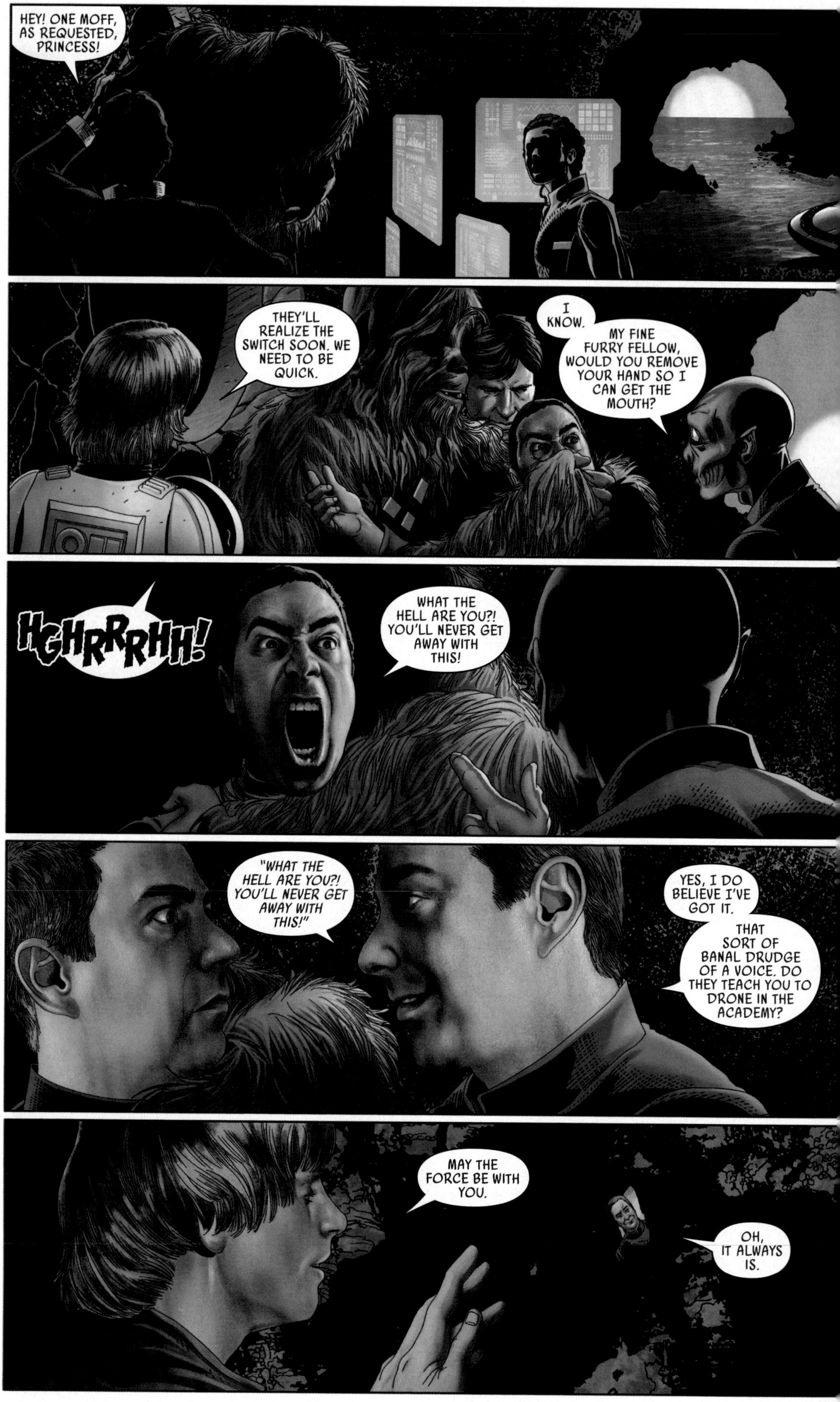
HEY! ONE MOFF, AS REQUESTED, PRINCESS!
THEY'LL REALIZE THE SWITCH SOON. WE NEED TO BE QUICK.
I KNOW.
MY FINE FURRY FELLOW, WOULD YOU REMOVE YOUR HAND SO I CAN GET THE MOUTH?
HGHRRRHH!
WHAT THE HELL ARE YOU?! YOU'LL NEVER GET AWAY WITH THIS!
"WHAT THE HELL ARE YOU?! YOU'LL NEVER GET AWAY WITH THIS!"
YES, I DO BELIEVE I'VE GOT IT.
THAT SORT OF BANAL DRUDGE OF A VOICE. DO THEY TEACH YOU TO DRONE IN THE ACADEMY?
MAY THE FORCE BE WITH YOU.
OH, IT ALWAYS IS.

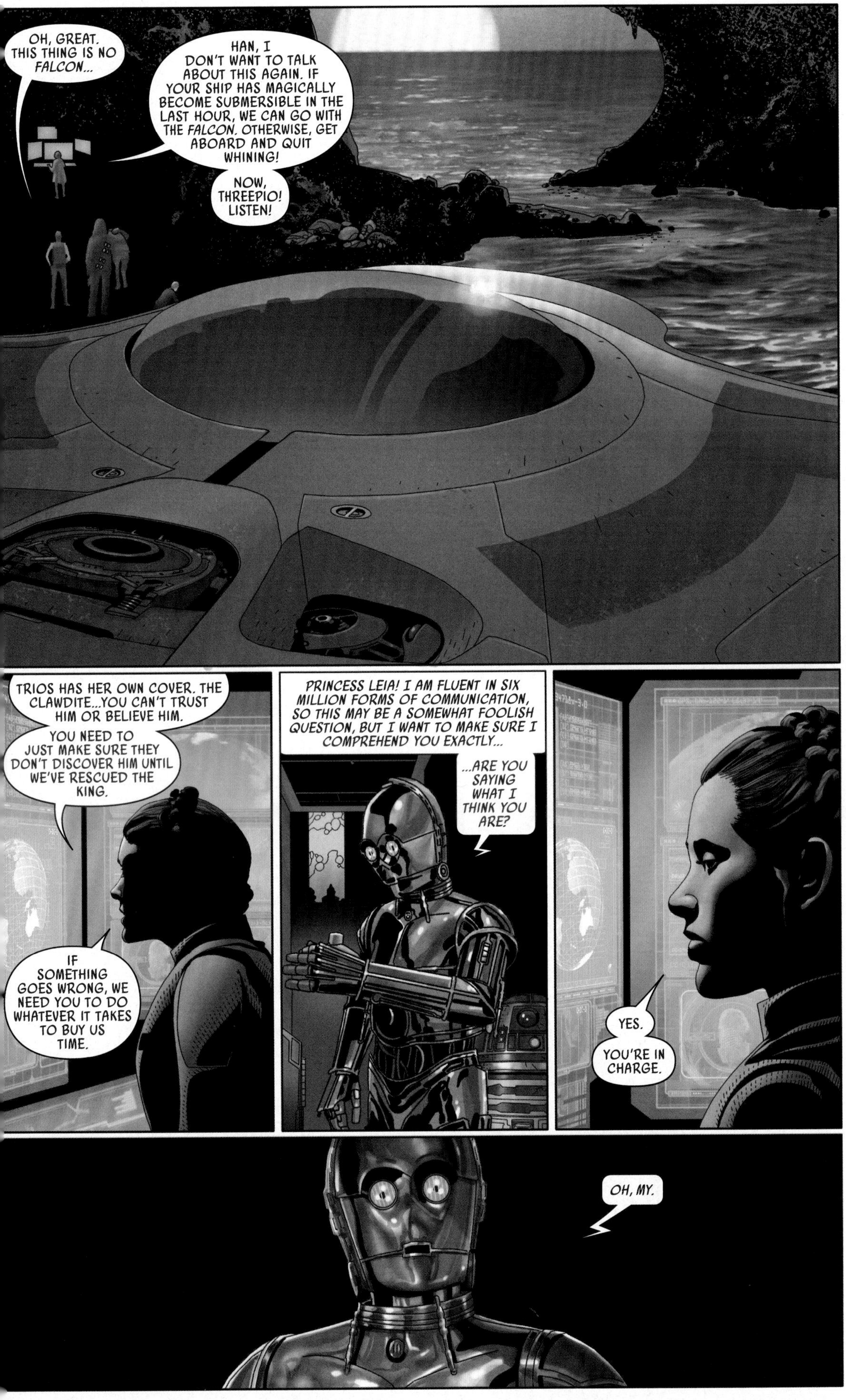

OH, GREAT. THIS THING IS NO FALCON...
HAN, I DON'T WANT TO TALK ABOUT THIS AGAIN. IF YOUR SHIP HAS MAGICALLY BECOME SUBMERSIBLE IN THE LAST HOUR, WE CAN GO WITH THE FALCON. OTHERWISE, GET ABOARD AND QUIT WHINING!
NOW, THREEPIO! LISTEN!
TRIOS HAS HER OWN COVER. THE CLAWDITE...YOU CAN'T TRUST HIM OR BELIEVE HIM.
YOU NEED TO JUST MAKE SURE THEY DON'T DISCOVER HIM UNTIL WE'VE RESCUED THE KING.
IF SOMETHING GOES WRONG, WE NEED YOU TO DO WHATEVER IT TAKES TO BUY US TIME.
PRINCESS LEIA! I AM FLUENT IN SIX MILLION FORMS OF COMMUNICATION, SO THIS MAY BE A SOMEWHAT FOOLISH QUESTION, BUT I WANT TO MAKE SURE I COMPREHEND YOU EXACTLY...
...ARE YOU SAYING WHAT I THINK YOU ARE?
YES.
YOU'RE IN CHARGE.
OH, MY.

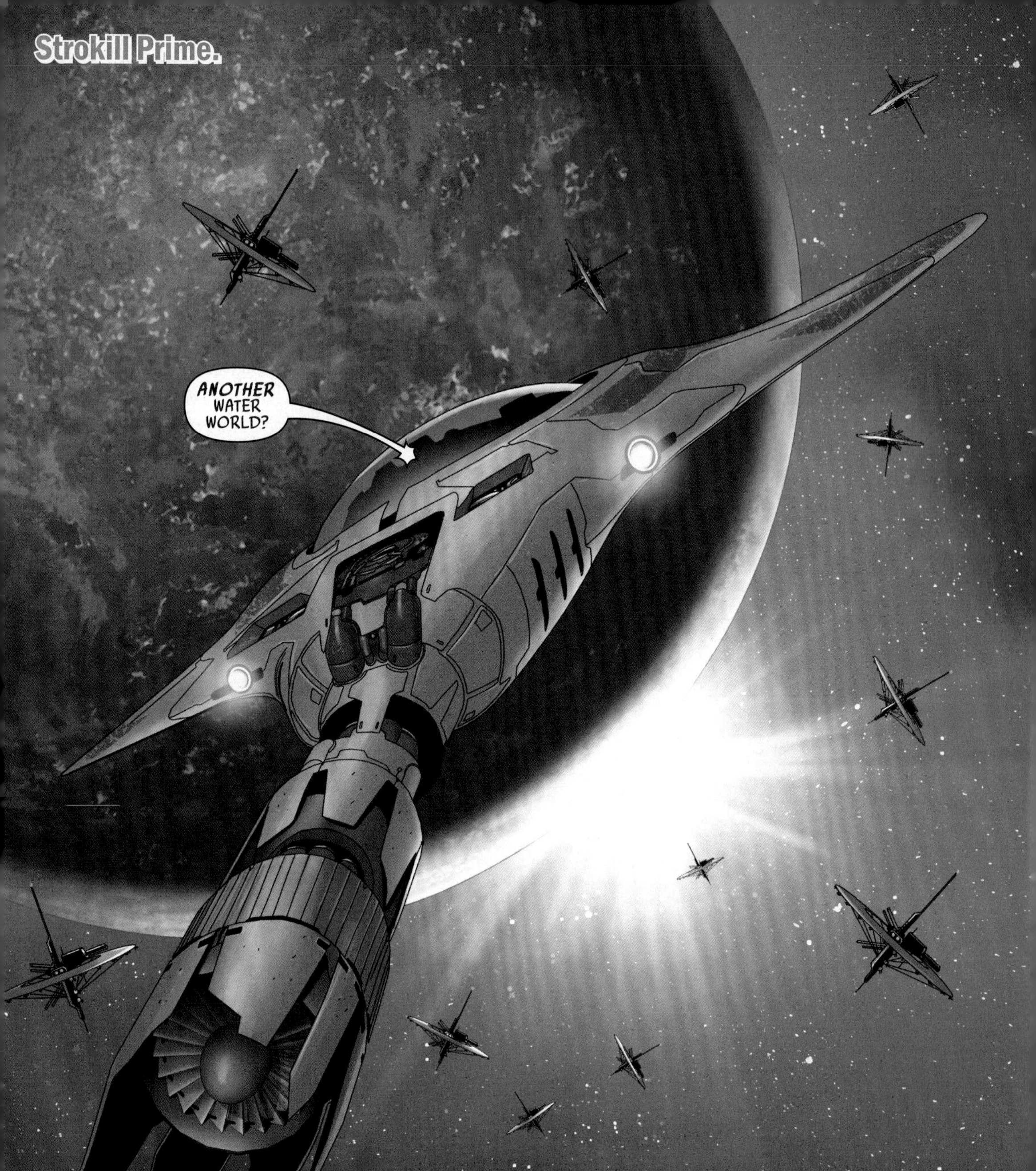
Strokill Prime.
ANOTHER WATER WORLD?

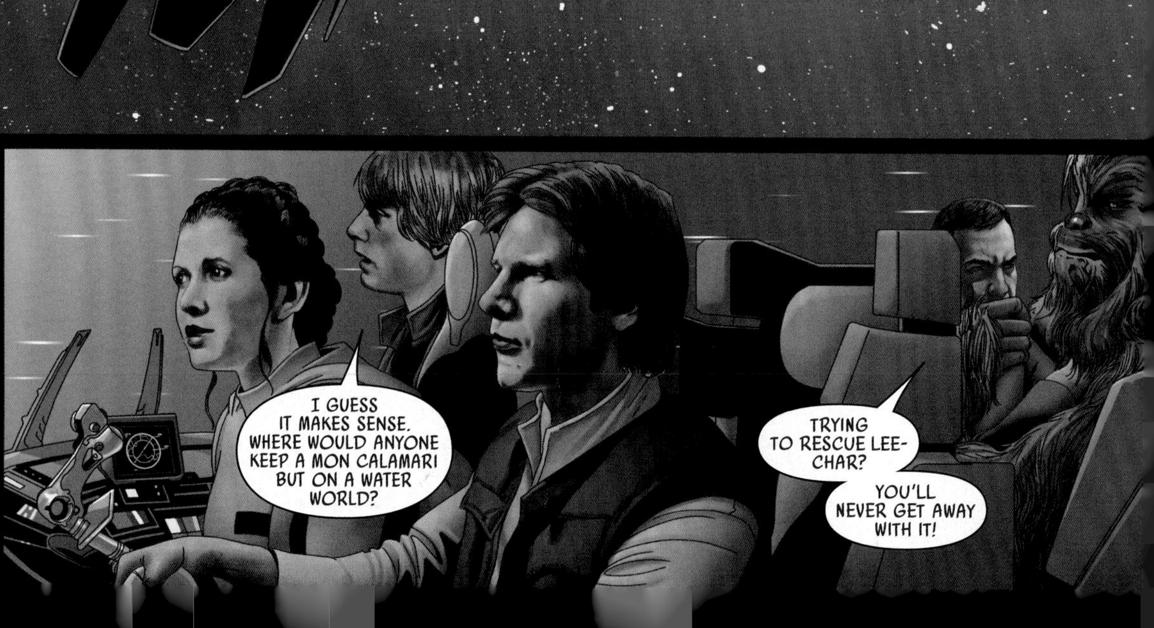
I GUESS IT MAKES SENSE. WHERE WOULD ANYONE KEEP A MON CALAMARI BUT ON A WATER WORLD?
TRYING TO RESCUE LEE-CHAR?
YOU'LL NEVER GET AWAY WITH IT!

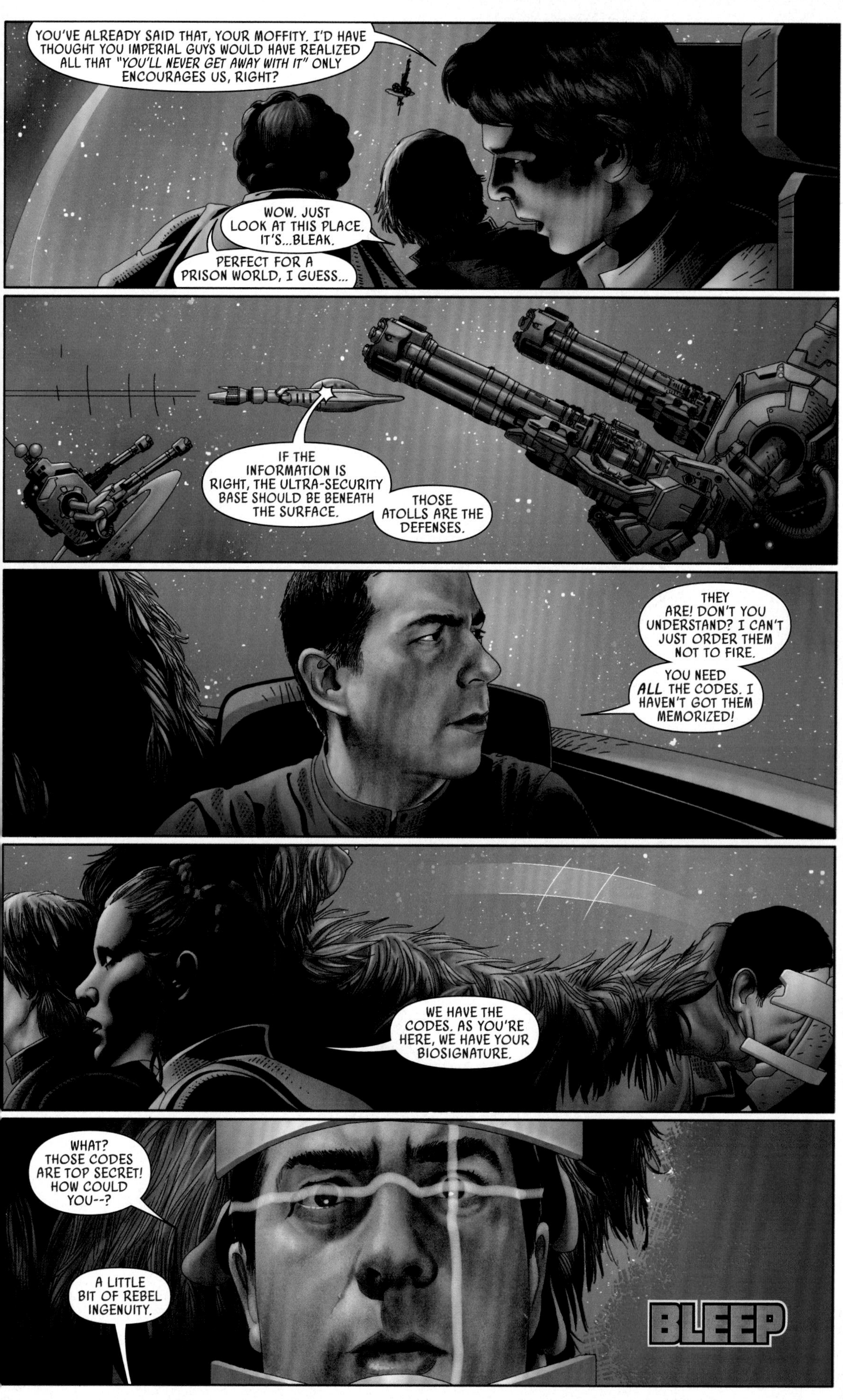

YOU'VE ALREADY SAID THAT, YOUR MOFFITY. I'D HAVE THOUGHT YOU IMPERIAL GUYS WOULD HAVE REALIZED ALL THAT "YOU'LL NEVER GET AWAY WITH IT" ONLY ENCOURAGES US, RIGHT?
WOW. JUST LOOK AT THIS PLACE. IT'S...BLEAK.
PERFECT FOR A PRISON WORLD, I GUESS...
IF THE INFORMATION IS RIGHT, THE ULTRA-SECURITY BASE SHOULD BE BENEATH THE SURFACE.
THOSE ATOLLS ARE THE DEFENSES.
THEY ARE! DON'T YOU UNDERSTAND? I CAN'T JUST ORDER THEM NOT TO FIRE.
YOU NEED ALL THE CODES. I HAVEN'T GOT THEM MEMORIZED!
WE HAVE THE CODES. AS YOU'RE HERE, WE HAVE YOUR BIOSIGNATURE.
WHAT? THOSE CODES ARE TOP SECRET! HOW COULD YOU--?
A LITTLE BIT OF REBEL INGENUITY.
BLEEP

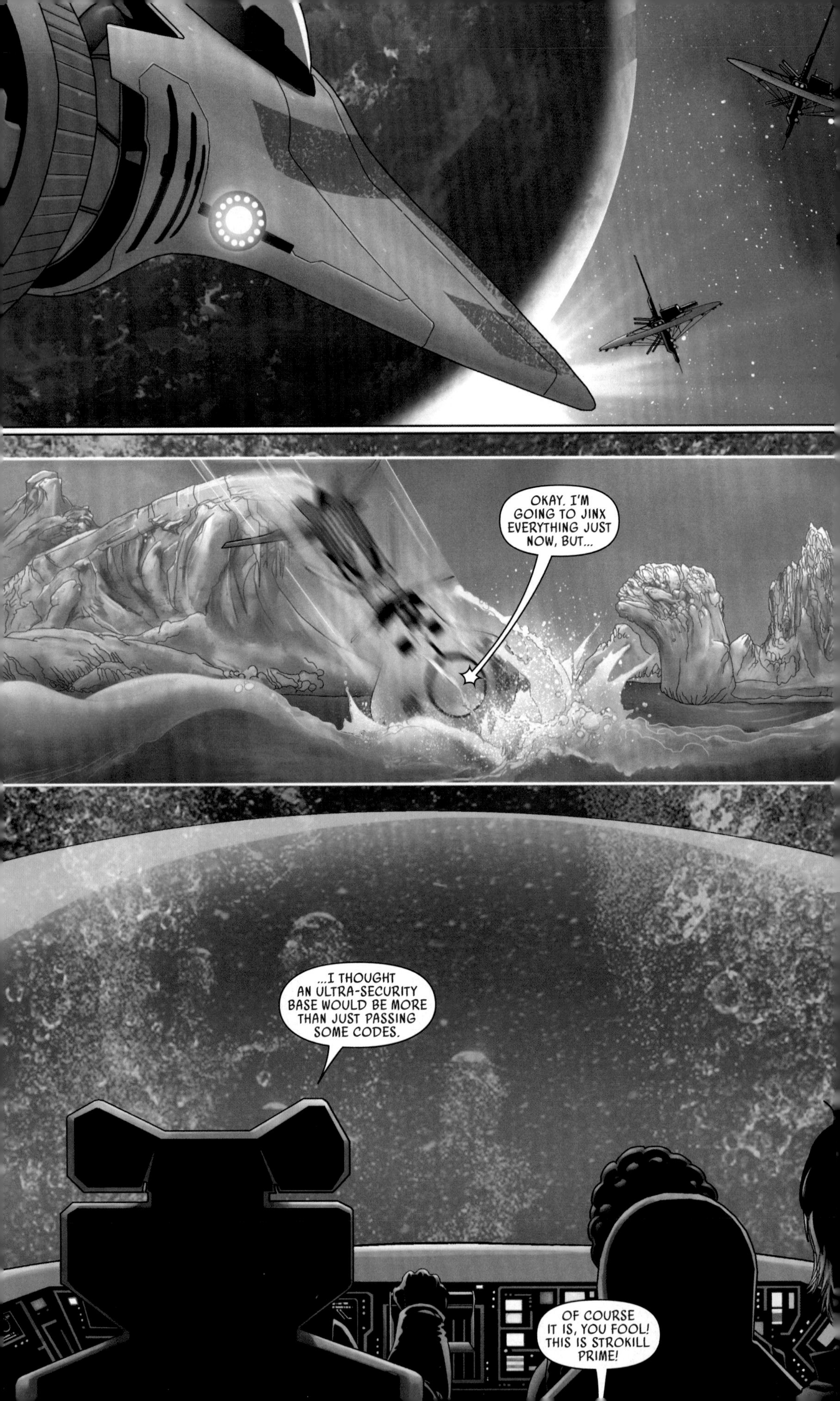
OKAY. I'M GOING TO JINX EVERYTHING JUST NOW, BUT...
...I THOUGHT AN ULTRA-SECURITY BASE WOULD BE MORE THAN JUST PASSING SOME CODES.
OF COURSE IT IS, YOU FOOL! THIS IS STROKILL PRIME!

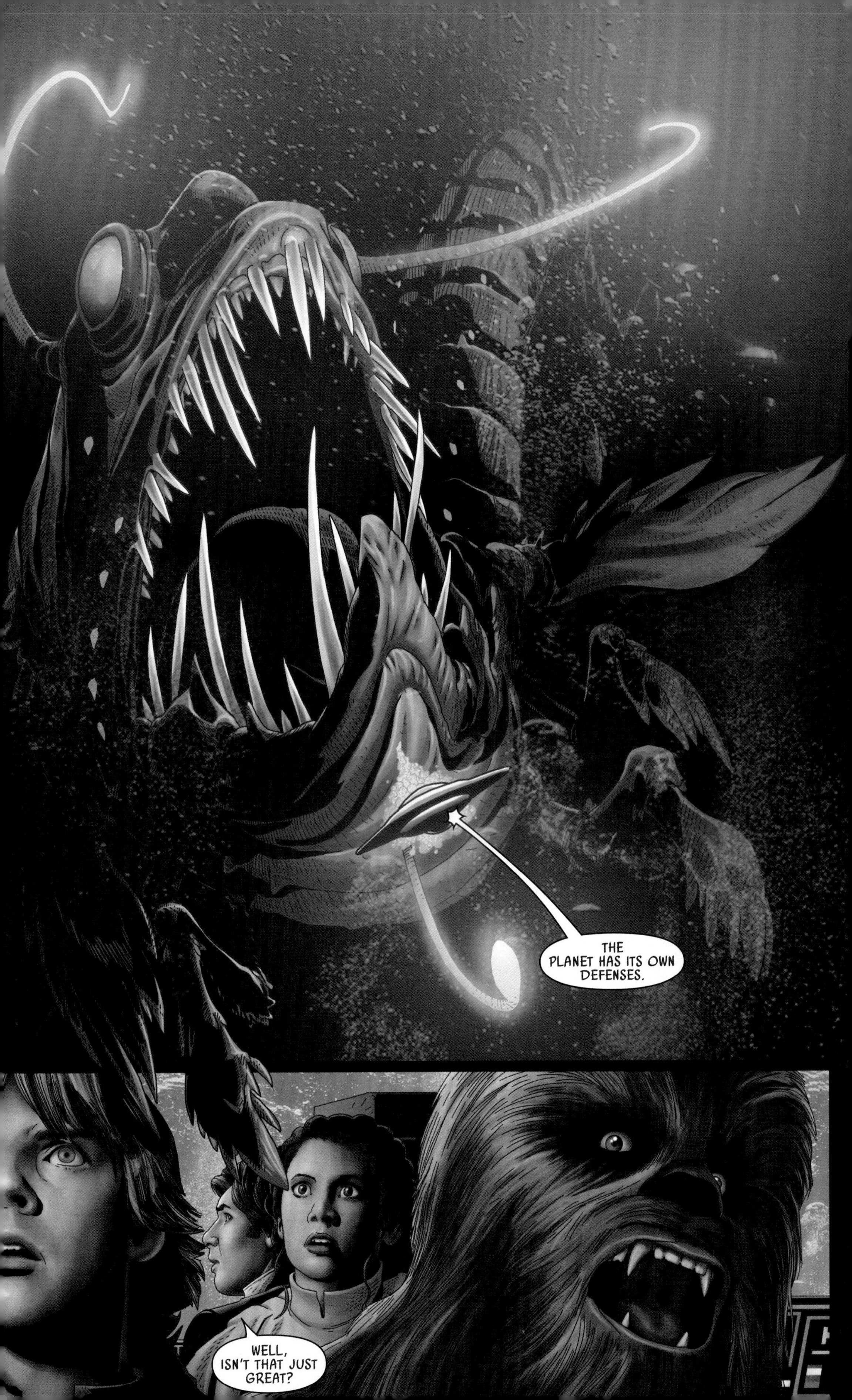
THE PLANET HAS ITS OWN DEFENSES.
WELL, ISN'T THAT JUST GREAT?

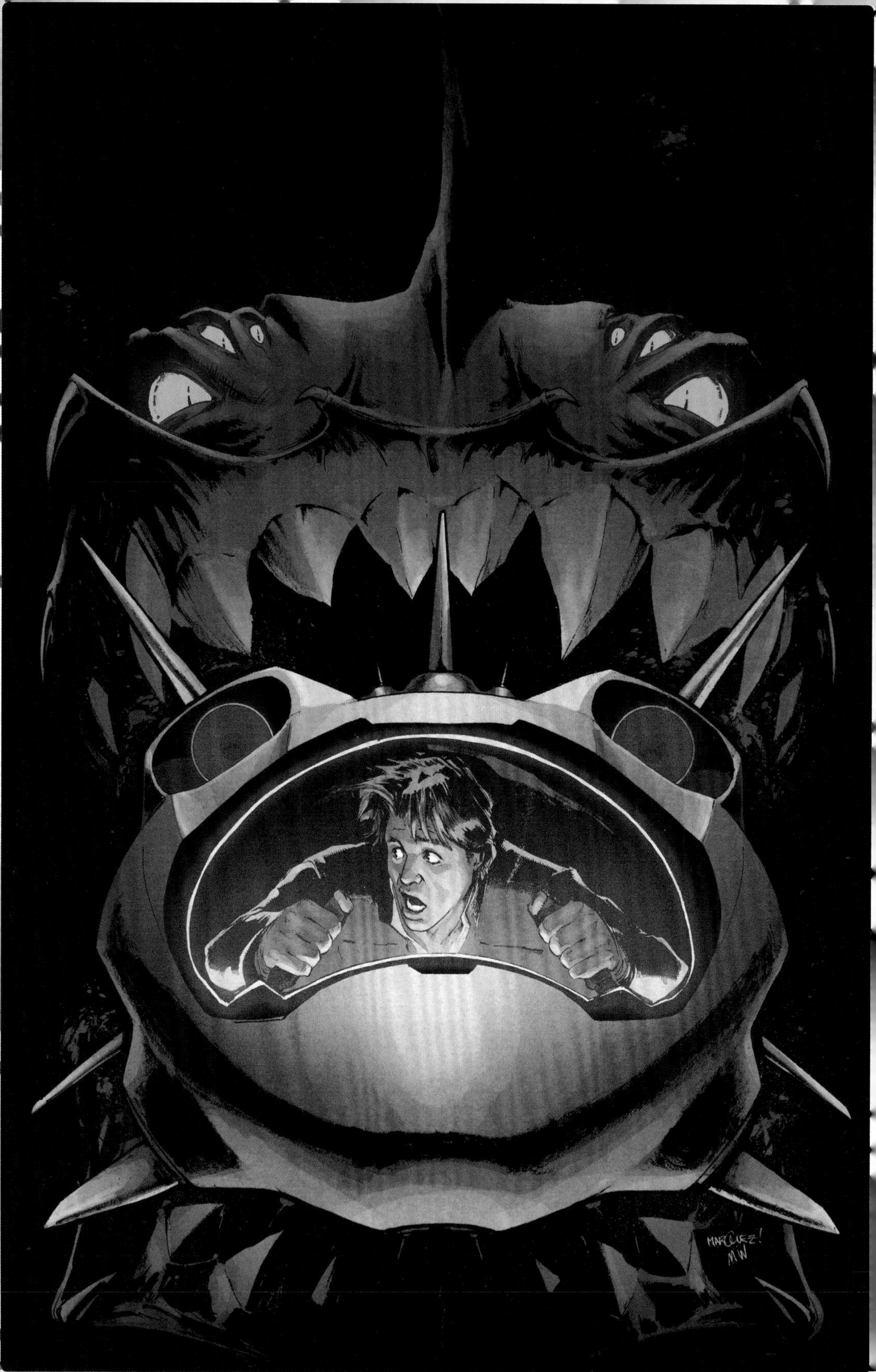
MARQUEZ!
MW

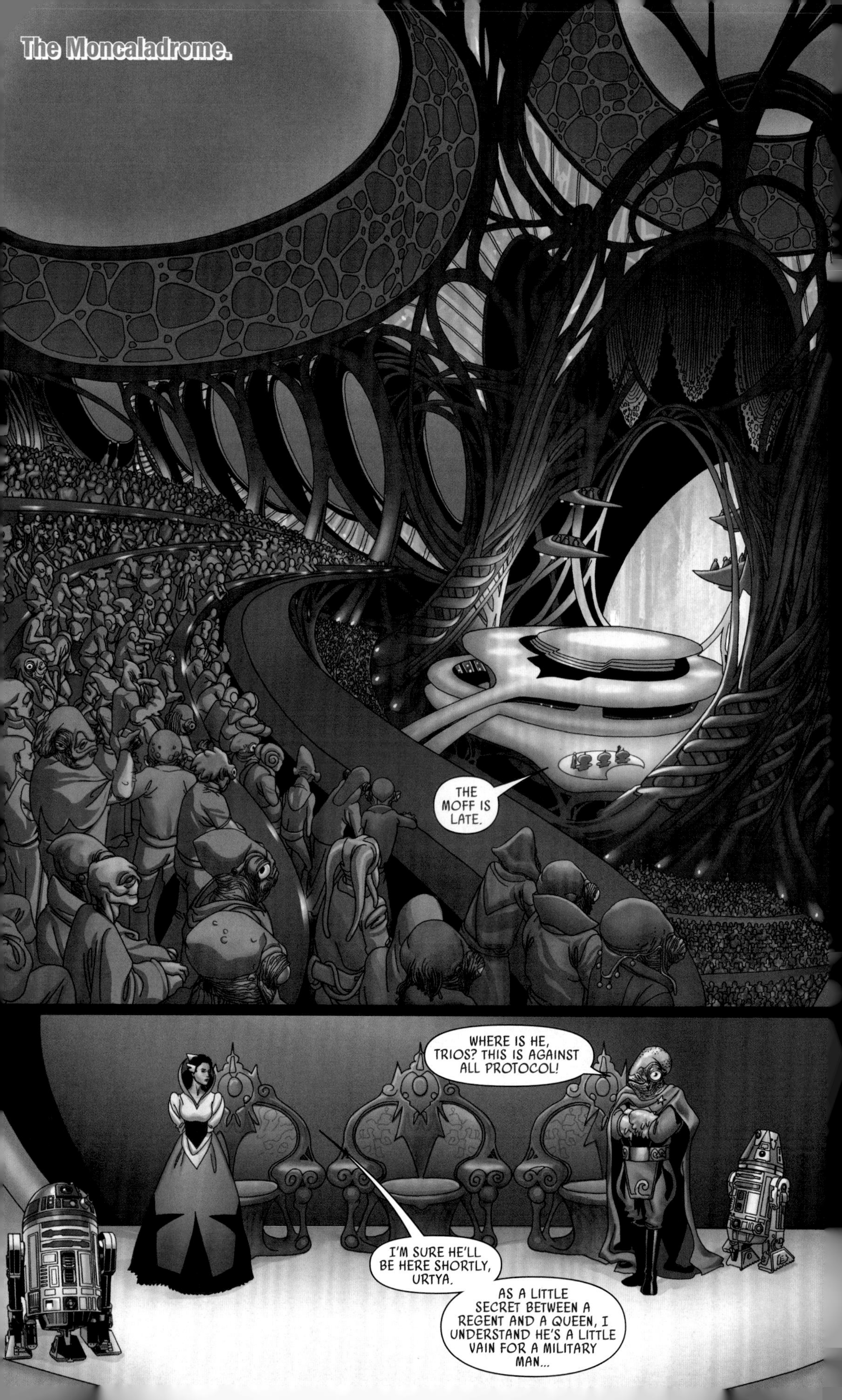
The Moncaladrome.
THE MOFF IS LATE.
WHERE IS HE, TRIOS? THIS IS AGAINST ALL PROTOCOL!
I'M SURE HE'LL BE HERE SHORTLY, URTYA.
AS A LITTLE SECRET BETWEEN A REGENT AND A QUEEN, I UNDERSTAND HE'S A LITTLE VAIN FOR A MILITARY MAN...

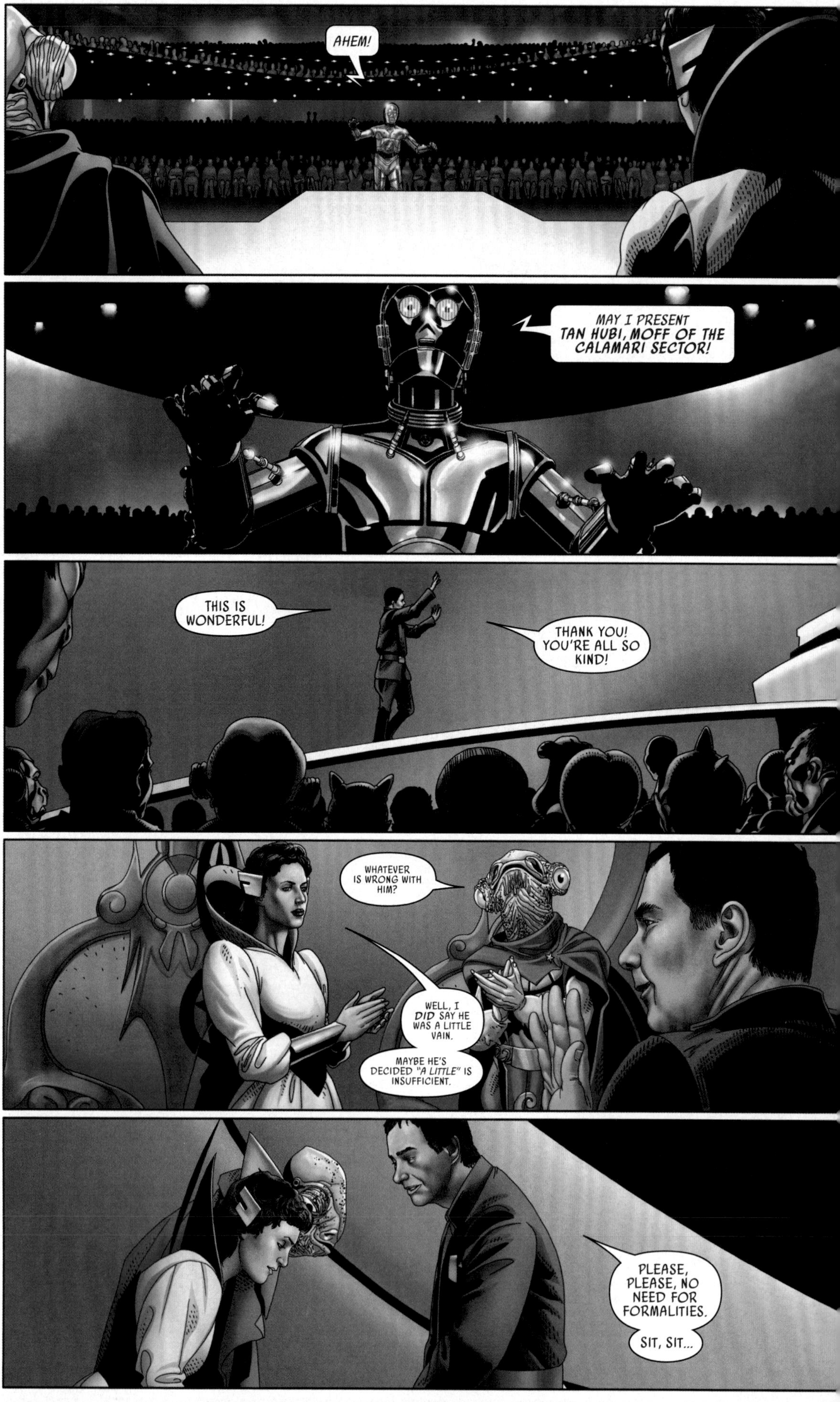
AHEM!
MAY I PRESENT TAN HUBI, MOFF OF THE CALAMARI SECTOR!
THIS IS WONDERFUL!
THANK YOU! YOU'RE ALL SO KIND!
WHATEVER IS WRONG WITH HIM?
WELL, I *DID* SAY HE WAS A LITTLE VAIN.
MAYBE HE'S DECIDED *"A LITTLE"* IS INSUFFICIENT.
PLEASE, PLEASE, NO NEED FOR FORMALITIES.
SIT, SIT...

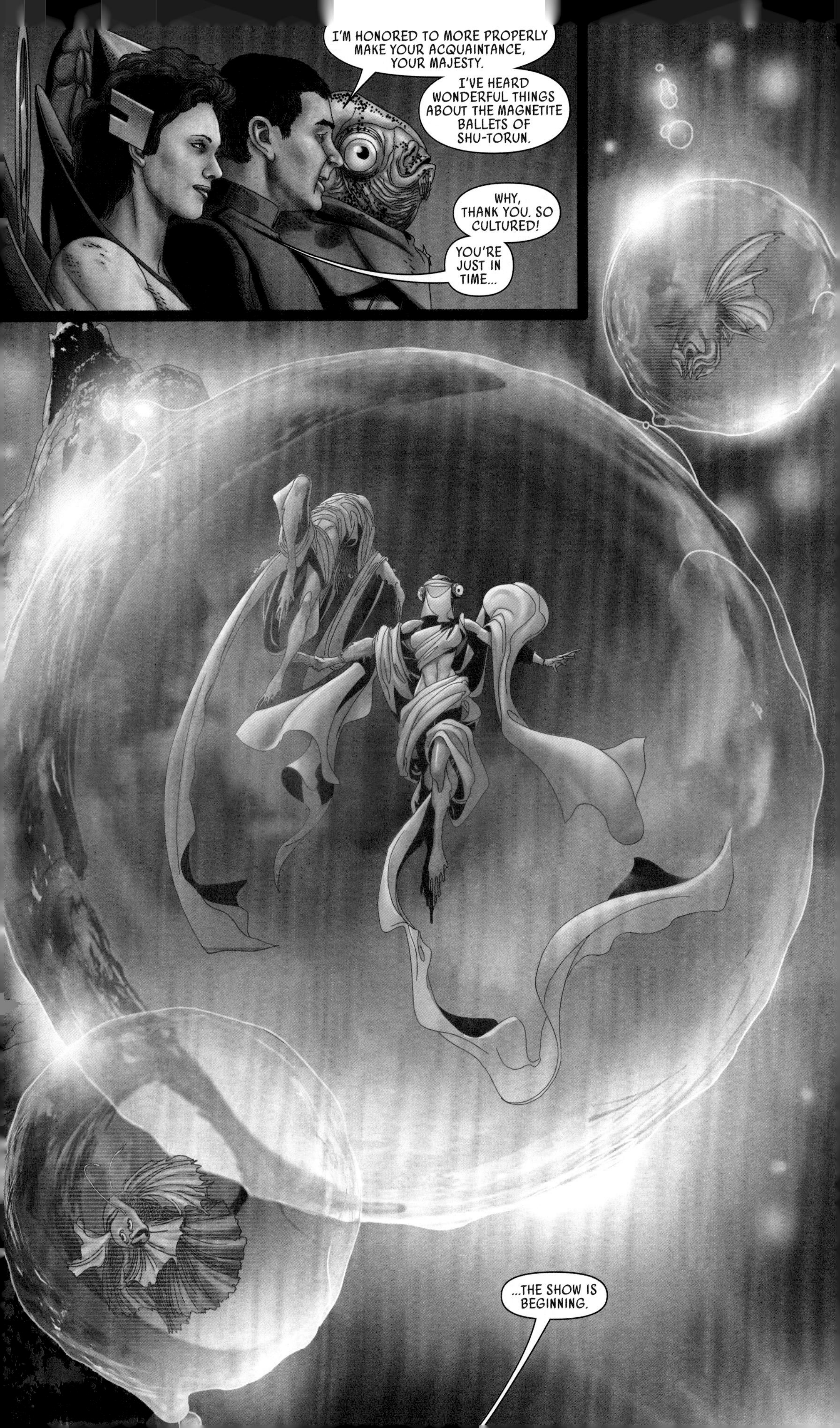
I'M HONORED TO MORE PROPERLY MAKE YOUR ACQUAINTANCE, YOUR MAJESTY.
I'VE HEARD WONDERFUL THINGS ABOUT THE MAGNETITE BALLETS OF SHU-TORUN.
WHY, THANK YOU. SO CULTURED!
YOU'RE JUST IN TIME...
...THE SHOW IS BEGINNING.

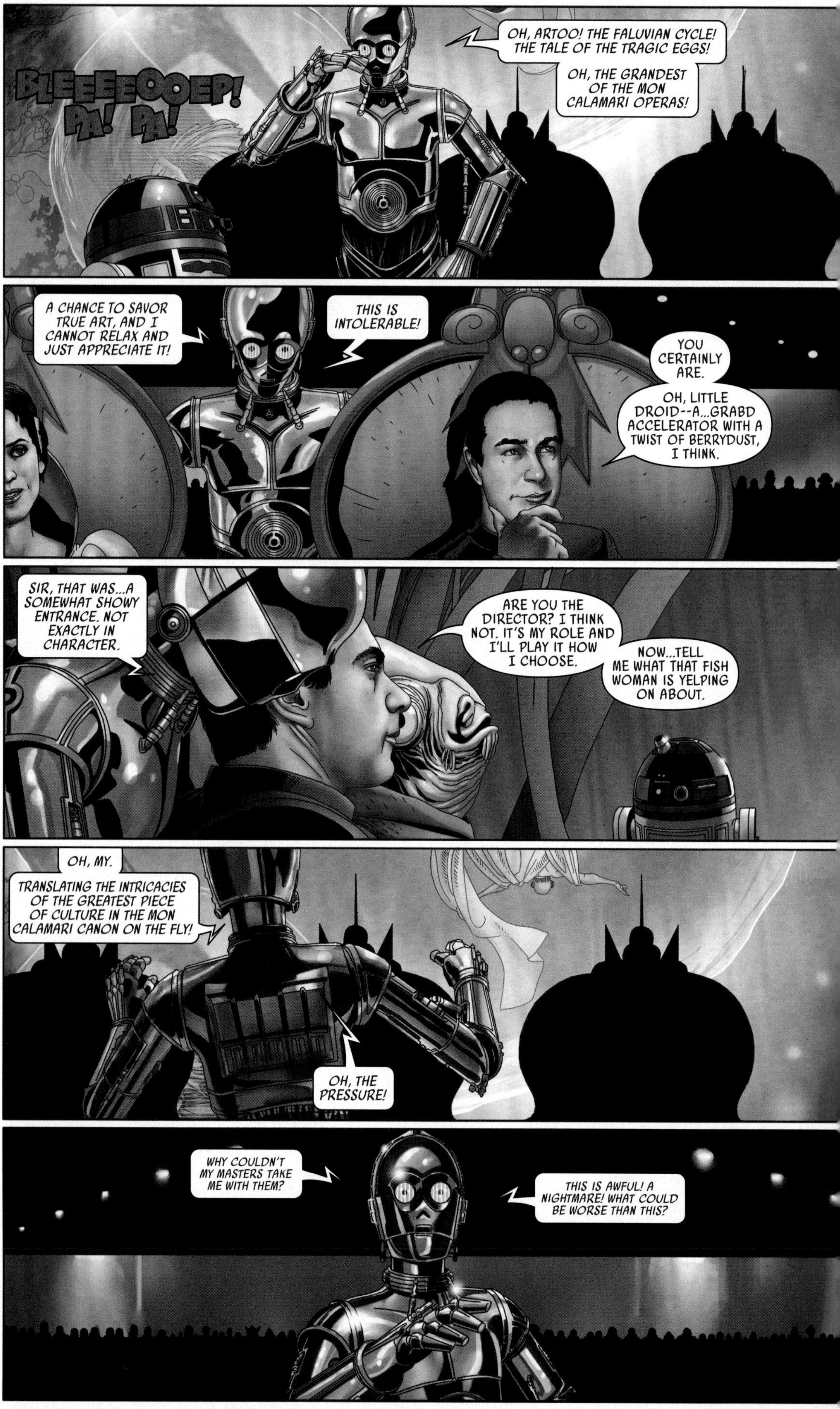

BLEEEEEOOEP! PA! PA!
OH, ARTOO! THE FALUVIAN CYCLE! THE TALE OF THE TRAGIC EGGS!
OH, THE GRANDEST OF THE MON CALAMARI OPERAS!
A CHANCE TO SAVOR TRUE ART, AND I CANNOT RELAX AND JUST APPRECIATE IT!
THIS IS INTOLERABLE!
YOU CERTAINLY ARE.
OH, LITTLE DROID--A...GRABD ACCELERATOR WITH A TWIST OF BERRYDUST, I THINK.
SIR, THAT WAS...A SOMEWHAT SHOWY ENTRANCE. NOT EXACTLY IN CHARACTER.
ARE YOU THE DIRECTOR? I THINK NOT. IT'S MY ROLE AND I'LL PLAY IT HOW I CHOOSE.
NOW...TELL ME WHAT THAT FISH WOMAN IS YELPING ON ABOUT.
OH, MY.
TRANSLATING THE INTRICACIES OF THE GREATEST PIECE OF CULTURE IN THE MON CALAMARI CANON ON THE FLY!
OH, THE PRESSURE!
WHY COULDN'T MY MASTERS TAKE ME WITH THEM?
THIS IS AWFUL! A NIGHTMARE! WHAT COULD BE WORSE THAN THIS?

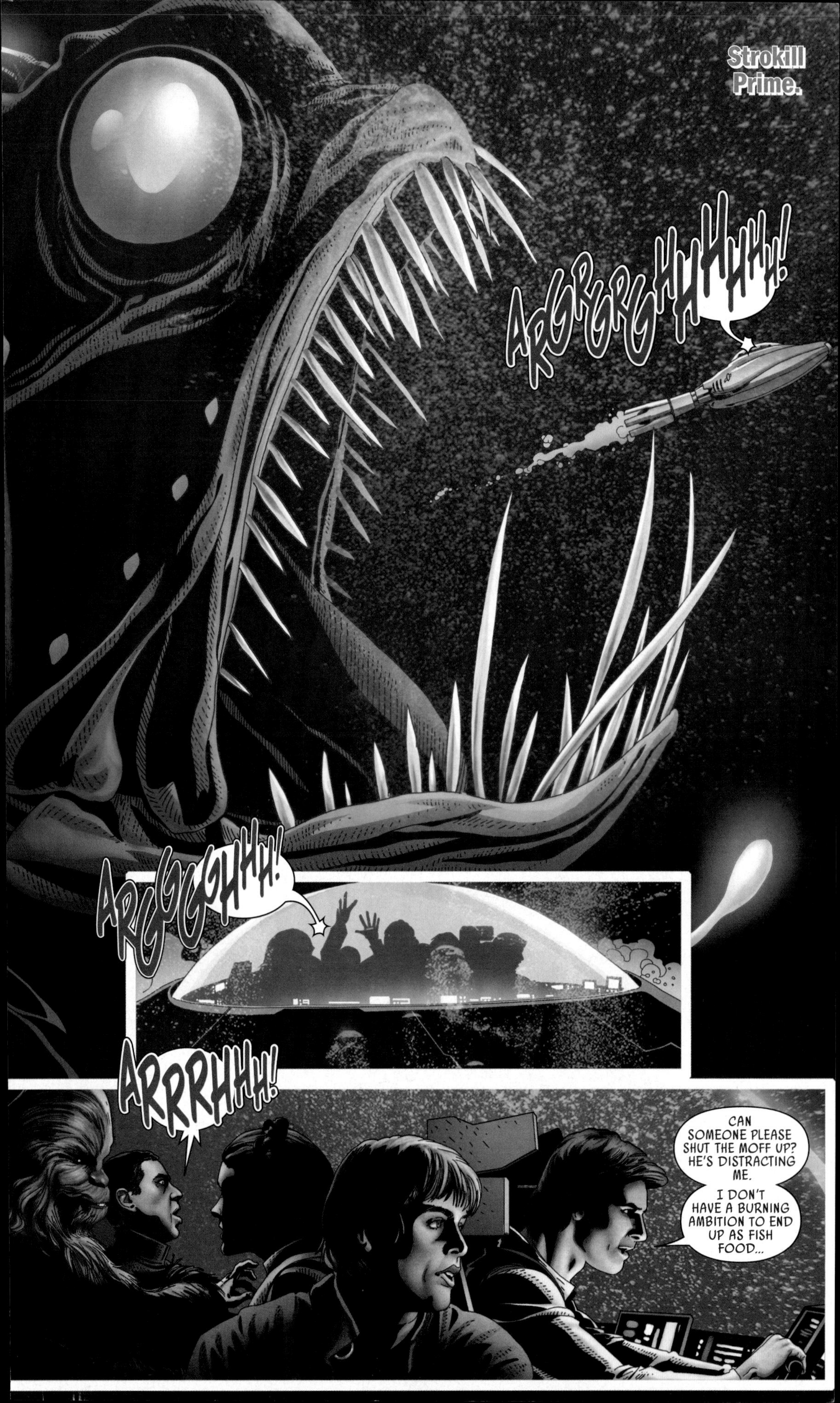
Strokill Prime.
ARGRGRGHHHHHH!
ARGGGHHH!
ARRRHHH!
CAN SOMEONE PLEASE SHUT THE MOFF UP? HE'S DISTRACTING ME.
I DON'T HAVE A BURNING AMBITION TO END UP AS FISH FOOD...

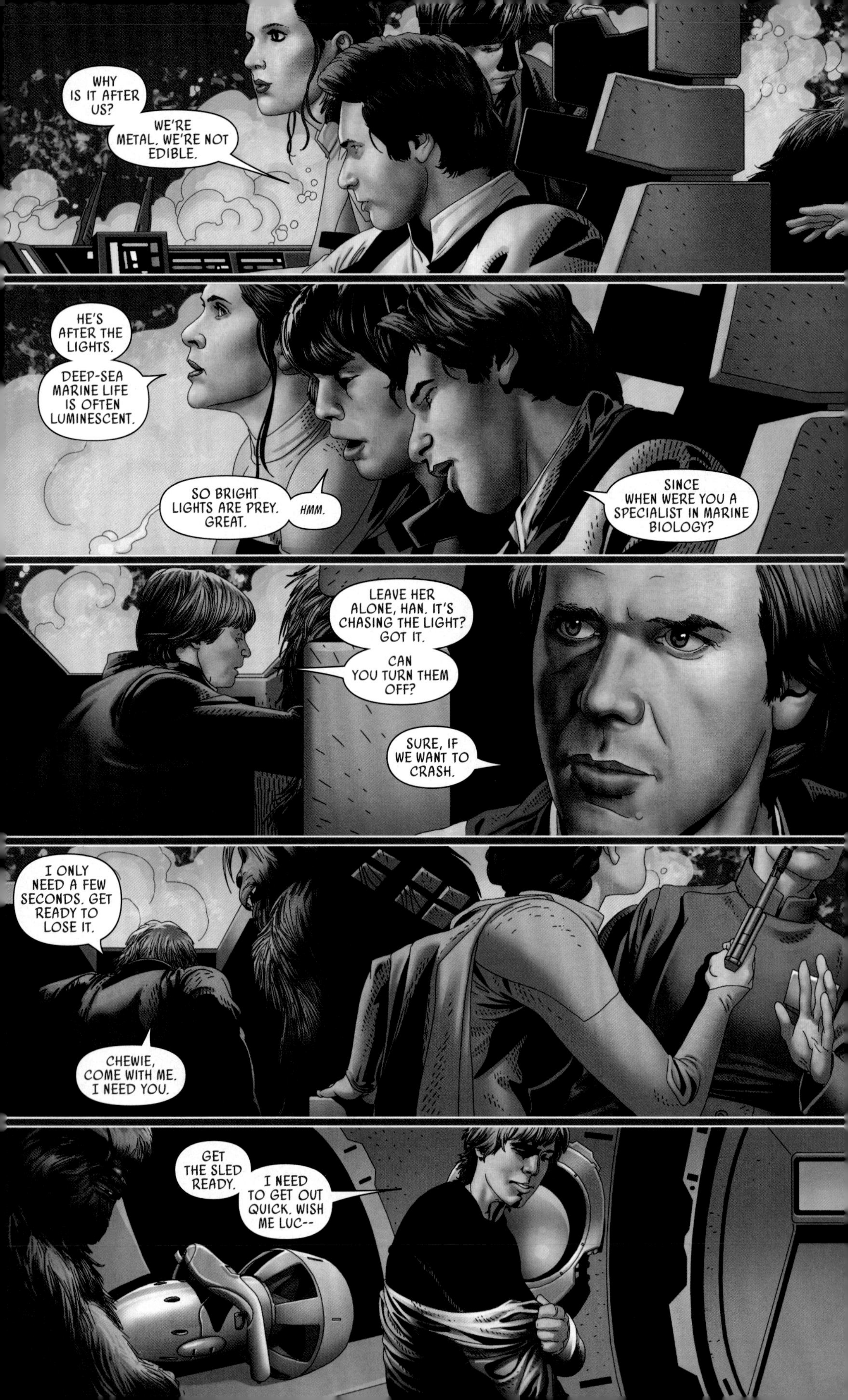
WHY IS IT AFTER US?
WE'RE METAL. WE'RE NOT EDIBLE.
HE'S AFTER THE LIGHTS.
DEEP-SEA MARINE LIFE IS OFTEN LUMINESCENT.
SO BRIGHT LIGHTS ARE PREY. GREAT.
HMM.
SINCE WHEN WERE YOU A SPECIALIST IN MARINE BIOLOGY?
LEAVE HER ALONE, HAN. IT'S CHASING THE LIGHT? GOT IT.
CAN YOU TURN THEM OFF?
SURE, IF WE WANT TO CRASH.
I ONLY NEED A FEW SECONDS. GET READY TO LOSE IT.
CHEWIE, COME WITH ME. I NEED YOU.
GET THE SLED READY.
I NEED TO GET OUT QUICK. WISH ME LUC--

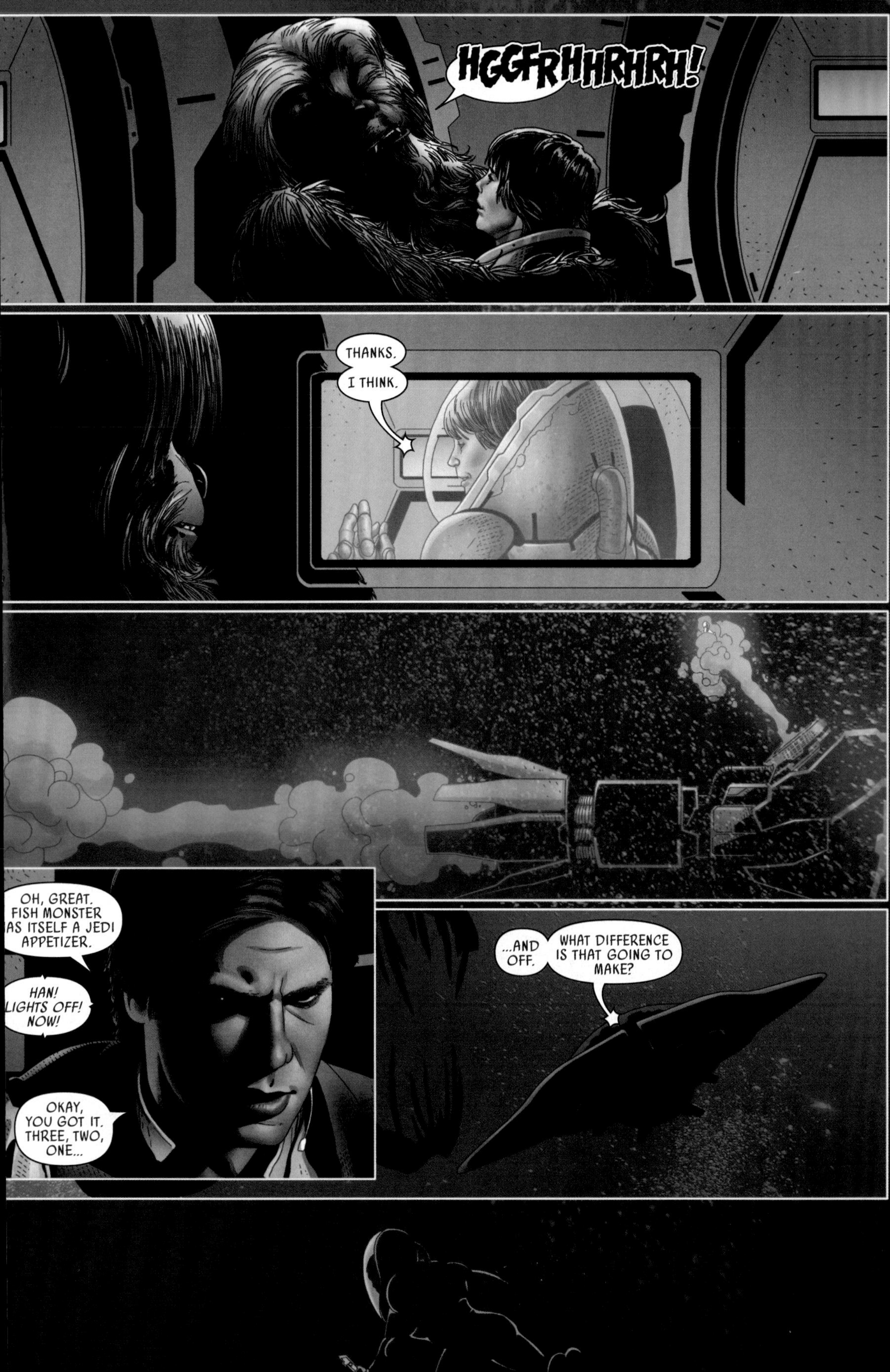
HGGFRHHRHRH!
THANKS.
I THINK.
OH, GREAT. FISH MONSTER HAS ITSELF A JEDI APPETIZER.
HAN! LIGHTS OFF! NOW!
OKAY, YOU GOT IT. THREE, TWO, ONE...
...AND OFF.
WHAT DIFFERENCE IS THAT GOING TO MAKE?

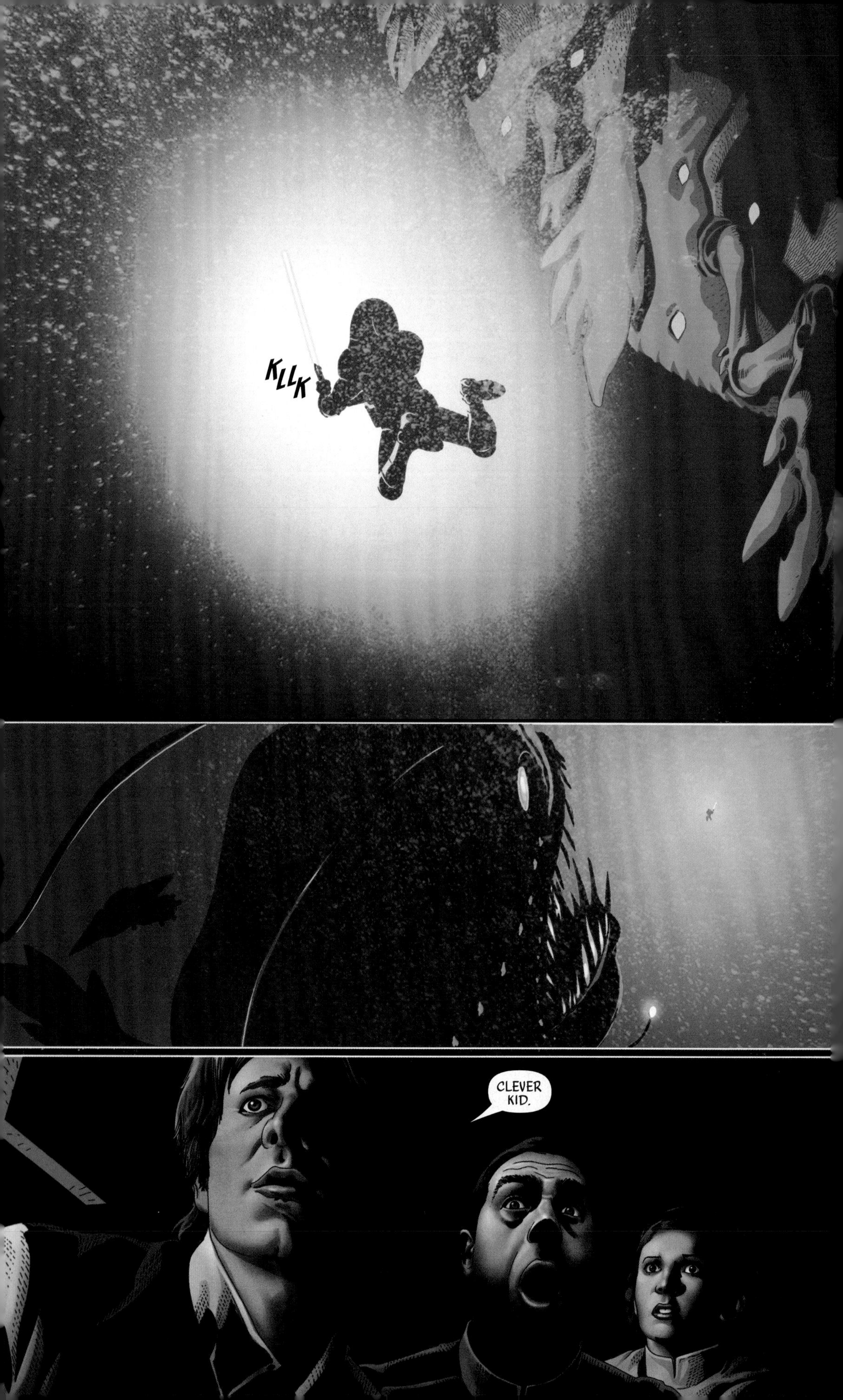
KLLK
CLEVER KID.

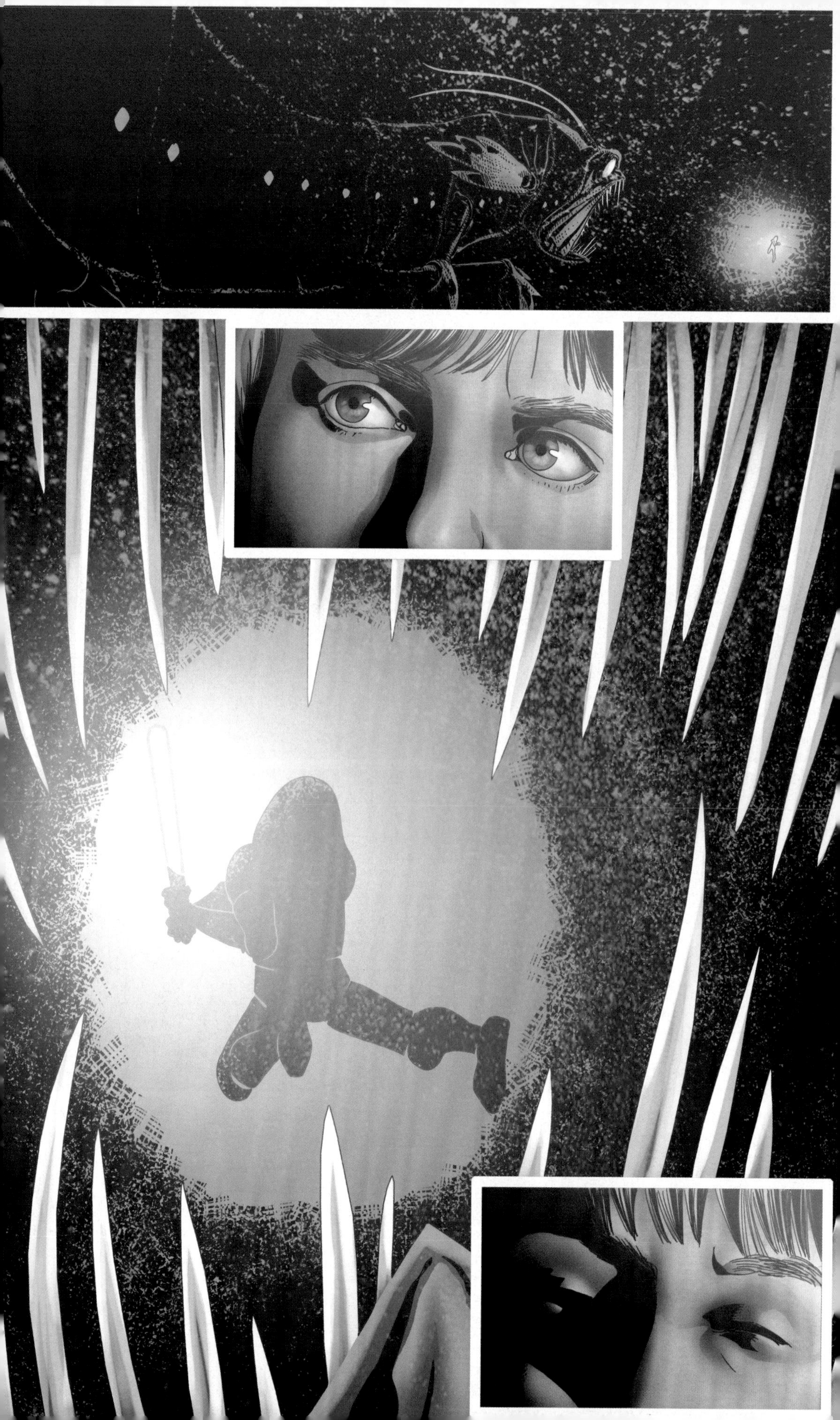

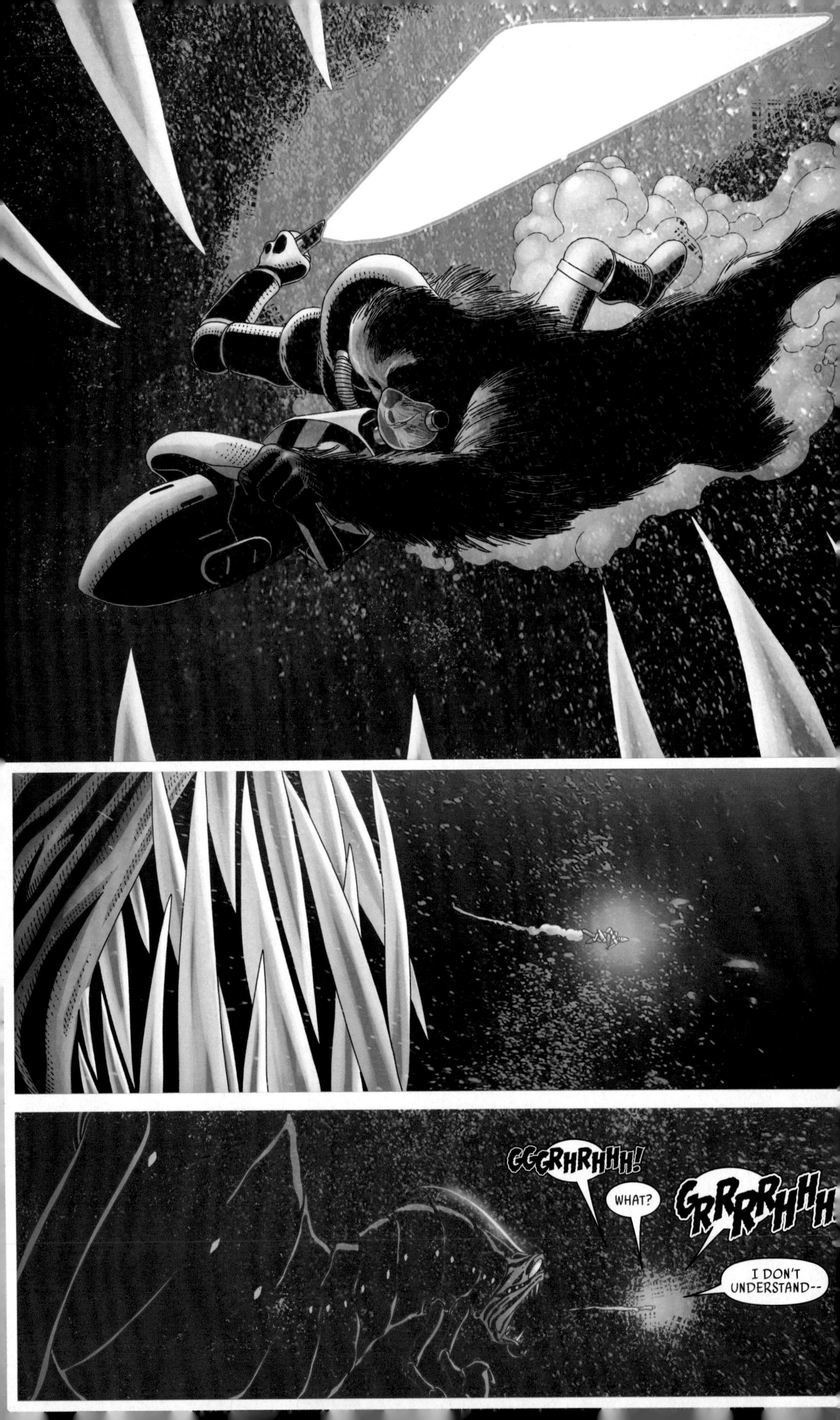
GGGRHRHHH!
WHAT?
GRRRRHHH
I DON'T UNDERSTAND--

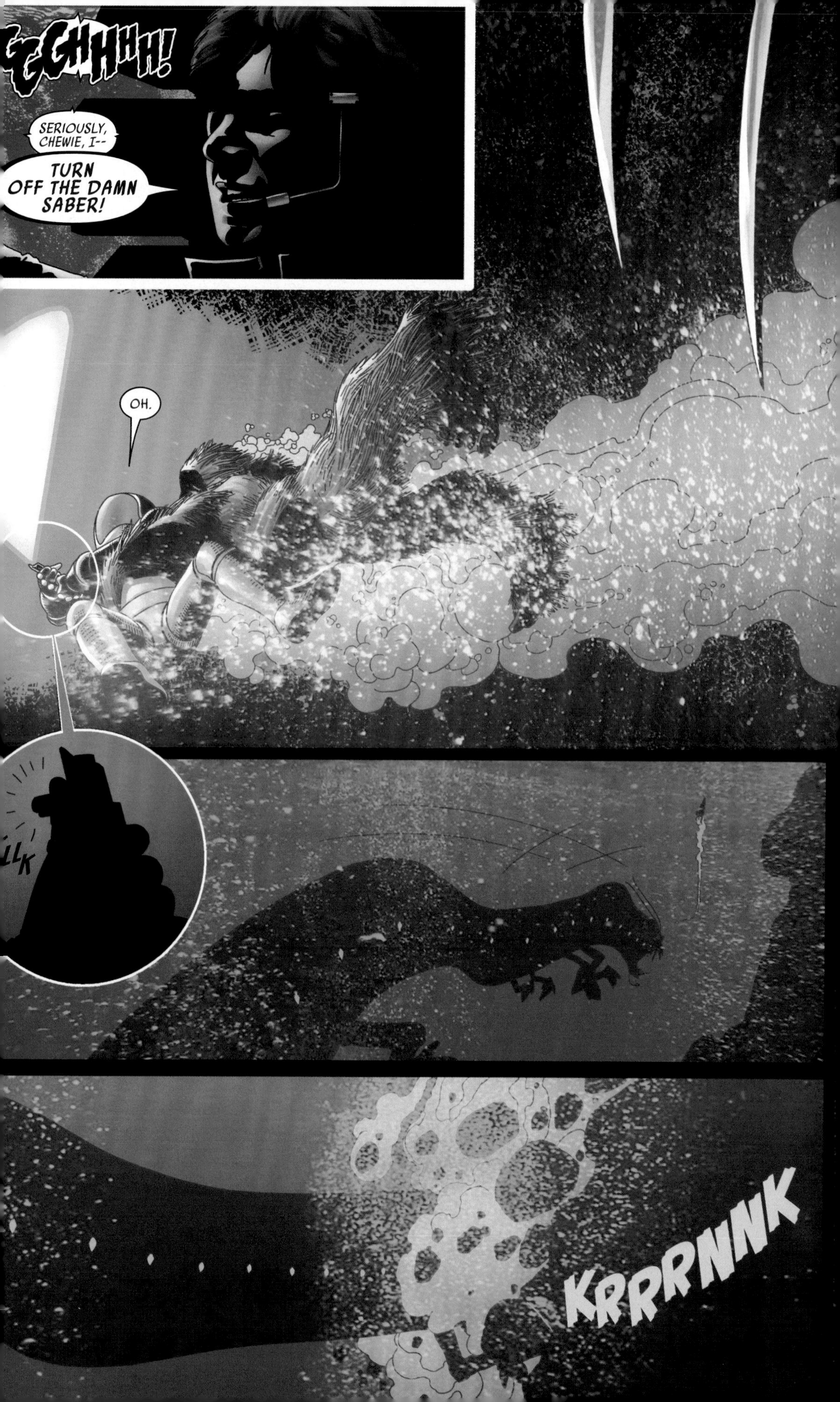

...GHHHH!
SERIOUSLY, CHEWIE, I--
TURN OFF THE DAMN SABER!
OH.
LK
KRRRNNK

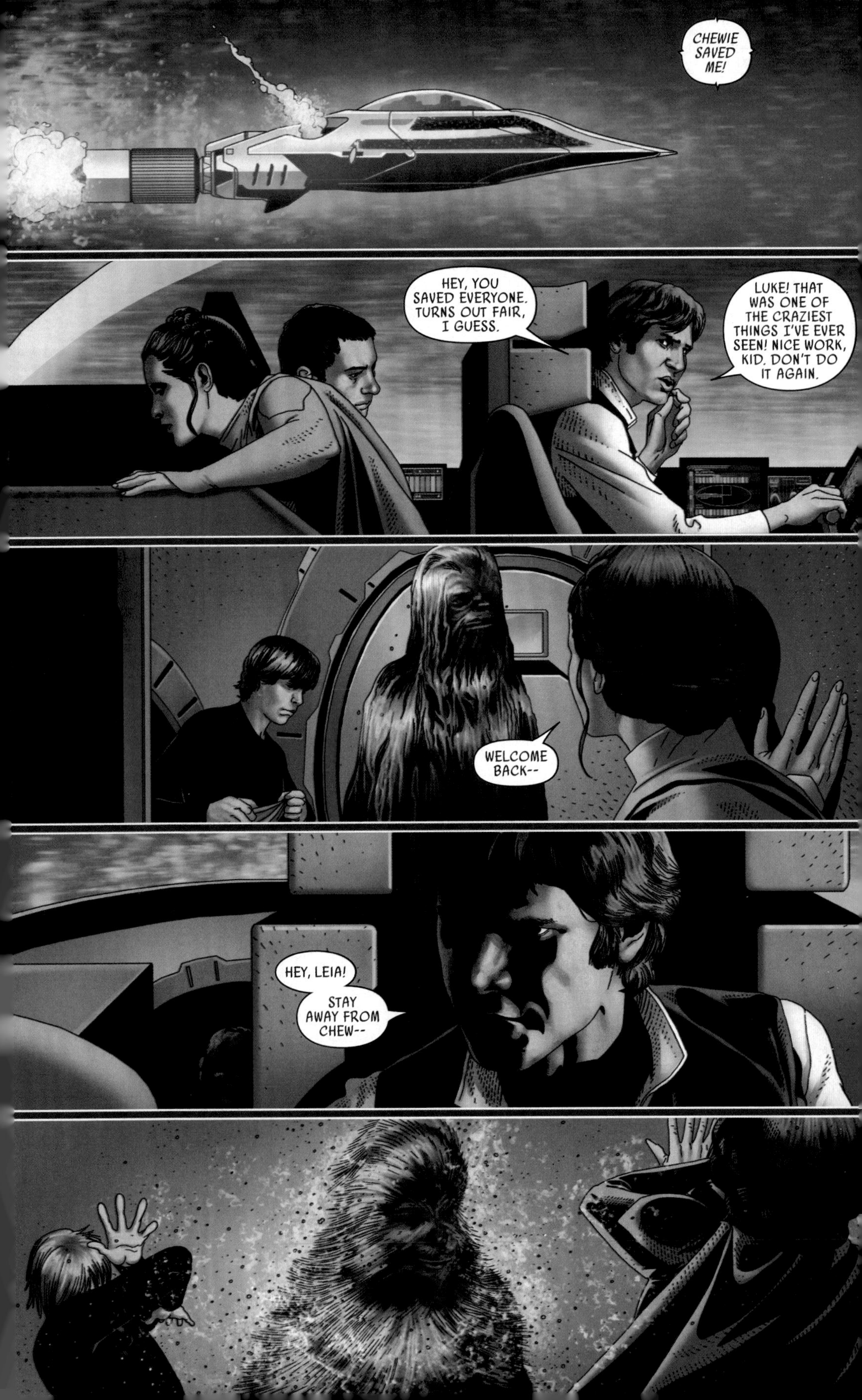
CHEWIE SAVED ME!
HEY, YOU SAVED EVERYONE. TURNS OUT FAIR, I GUESS.
LUKE! THAT WAS ONE OF THE CRAZIEST THINGS I'VE EVER SEEN! NICE WORK, KID. DON'T DO IT AGAIN.
WELCOME BACK--
HEY, LEIA!
STAY AWAY FROM CHEW--

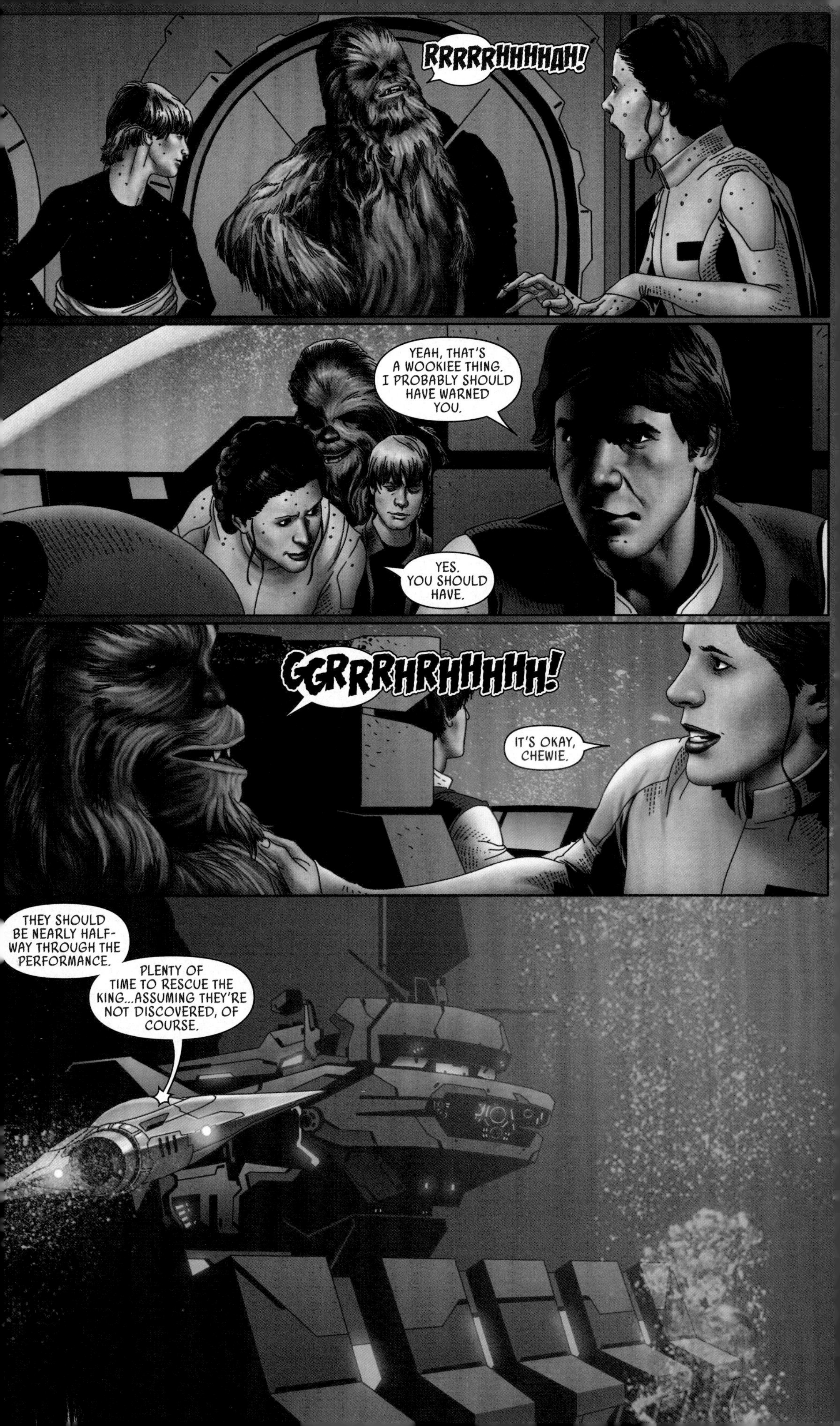
RRRRRHHHHAH!
YEAH, THAT'S A WOOKIEE THING. I PROBABLY SHOULD HAVE WARNED YOU.
YES. YOU SHOULD HAVE.
GGRRRRHRHHHHH!
IT'S OKAY, CHEWIE.
THEY SHOULD BE NEARLY HALF-WAY THROUGH THE PERFORMANCE.
PLENTY OF TIME TO RESCUE THE KING...ASSUMING THEY'RE NOT DISCOVERED, OF COURSE.

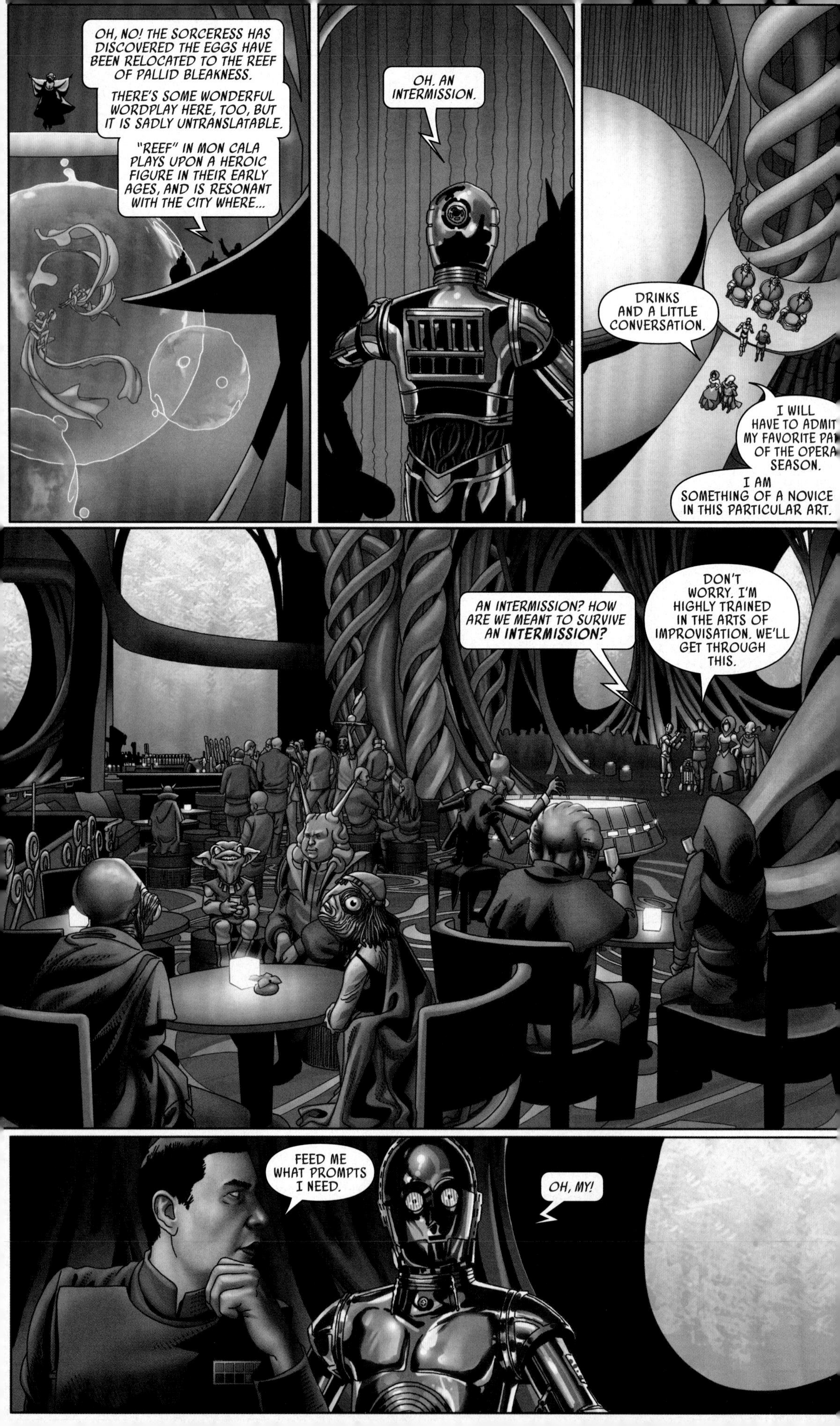
OH, NO! THE SORCERESS HAS DISCOVERED THE EGGS HAVE BEEN RELOCATED TO THE REEF OF PALLID BLEAKNESS.
THERE'S SOME WONDERFUL WORDPLAY HERE, TOO, BUT IT IS SADLY UNTRANSLATABLE.
"REEF" IN MON CALA PLAYS UPON A HEROIC FIGURE IN THEIR EARLY AGES, AND IS RESONANT WITH THE CITY WHERE...
OH. AN INTERMISSION.
DRINKS AND A LITTLE CONVERSATION.
I WILL HAVE TO ADMIT MY FAVORITE PA OF THE OPERA SEASON.
I AM SOMETHING OF A NOVICE IN THIS PARTICULAR ART.
AN INTERMISSION? HOW ARE WE MEANT TO SURVIVE AN INTERMISSION?
DON'T WORRY. I'M HIGHLY TRAINED IN THE ARTS OF IMPROVISATION. WE'LL GET THROUGH THIS.
FEED ME WHAT PROMPTS I NEED.
OH, MY!

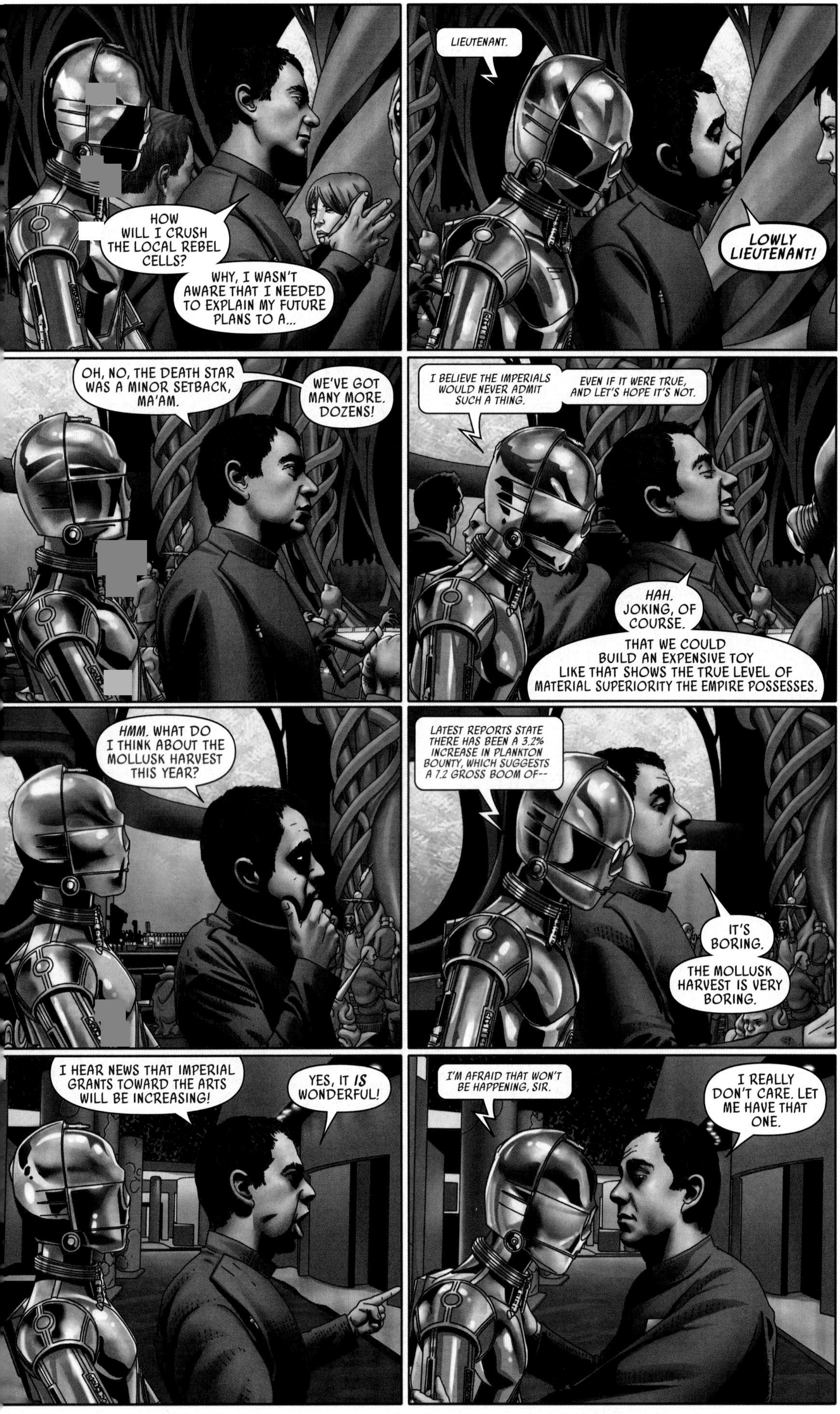
HOW WILL I CRUSH THE LOCAL REBEL CELLS?
WHY, I WASN'T AWARE THAT I NEEDED TO EXPLAIN MY FUTURE PLANS TO A...
LIEUTENANT.
LOWLY LIEUTENANT!
OH, NO, THE DEATH STAR WAS A MINOR SETBACK, MA'AM.
WE'VE GOT MANY MORE. DOZENS!
I BELIEVE THE IMPERIALS WOULD NEVER ADMIT SUCH A THING.
EVEN IF IT WERE TRUE, AND LET'S HOPE IT'S NOT.
HAH. JOKING, OF COURSE.
THAT WE COULD BUILD AN EXPENSIVE TOY LIKE THAT SHOWS THE TRUE LEVEL OF MATERIAL SUPERIORITY THE EMPIRE POSSESSES.
HMM. WHAT DO I THINK ABOUT THE MOLLUSK HARVEST THIS YEAR?
LATEST REPORTS STATE THERE HAS BEEN A 3.2% INCREASE IN PLANKTON BOUNTY, WHICH SUGGESTS A 7.2 GROSS BOOM OF--
IT'S BORING.
THE MOLLUSK HARVEST IS VERY BORING.
I HEAR NEWS THAT IMPERIAL GRANTS TOWARD THE ARTS WILL BE INCREASING!
YES, IT *IS* WONDERFUL!
I'M AFRAID THAT WON'T BE HAPPENING, SIR.
I REALLY DON'T CARE. LET ME HAVE THAT ONE.

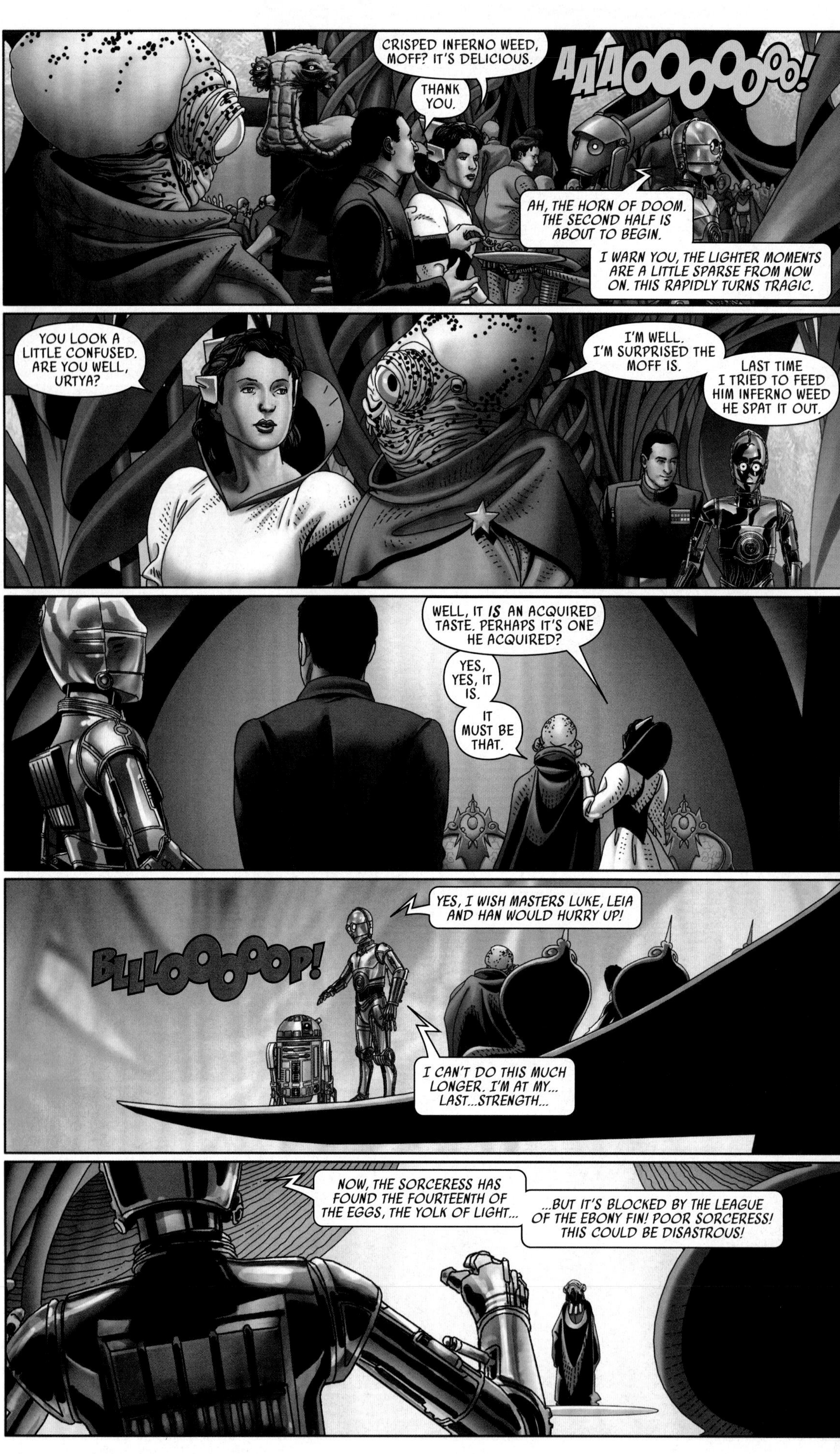
CRISPED INFERNO WEED, MOFF? IT'S DELICIOUS.
THANK YOU.
AAAOOOOOOoo!
AH, THE HORN OF DOOM. THE SECOND HALF IS ABOUT TO BEGIN.
I WARN YOU, THE LIGHTER MOMENTS ARE A LITTLE SPARSE FROM NOW ON. THIS RAPIDLY TURNS TRAGIC.
YOU LOOK A LITTLE CONFUSED. ARE YOU WELL, URTYA?
I'M WELL. I'M SURPRISED THE MOFF IS.
LAST TIME I TRIED TO FEED HIM INFERNO WEED HE SPAT IT OUT.
WELL, IT *IS* AN ACQUIRED TASTE. PERHAPS IT'S ONE HE ACQUIRED?
YES, YES, IT IS.
IT MUST BE THAT.
YES, I WISH MASTERS LUKE, LEIA AND HAN WOULD HURRY UP!
BLLLOOOOOOP!
I CAN'T DO THIS MUCH LONGER. I'M AT MY... LAST...STRENGTH...
NOW, THE SORCERESS HAS FOUND THE FOURTEENTH OF THE EGGS, THE YOLK OF LIGHT...
...BUT IT'S BLOCKED BY THE LEAGUE OF THE EBONY FIN! POOR SORCERESS! THIS COULD BE DISASTROUS!

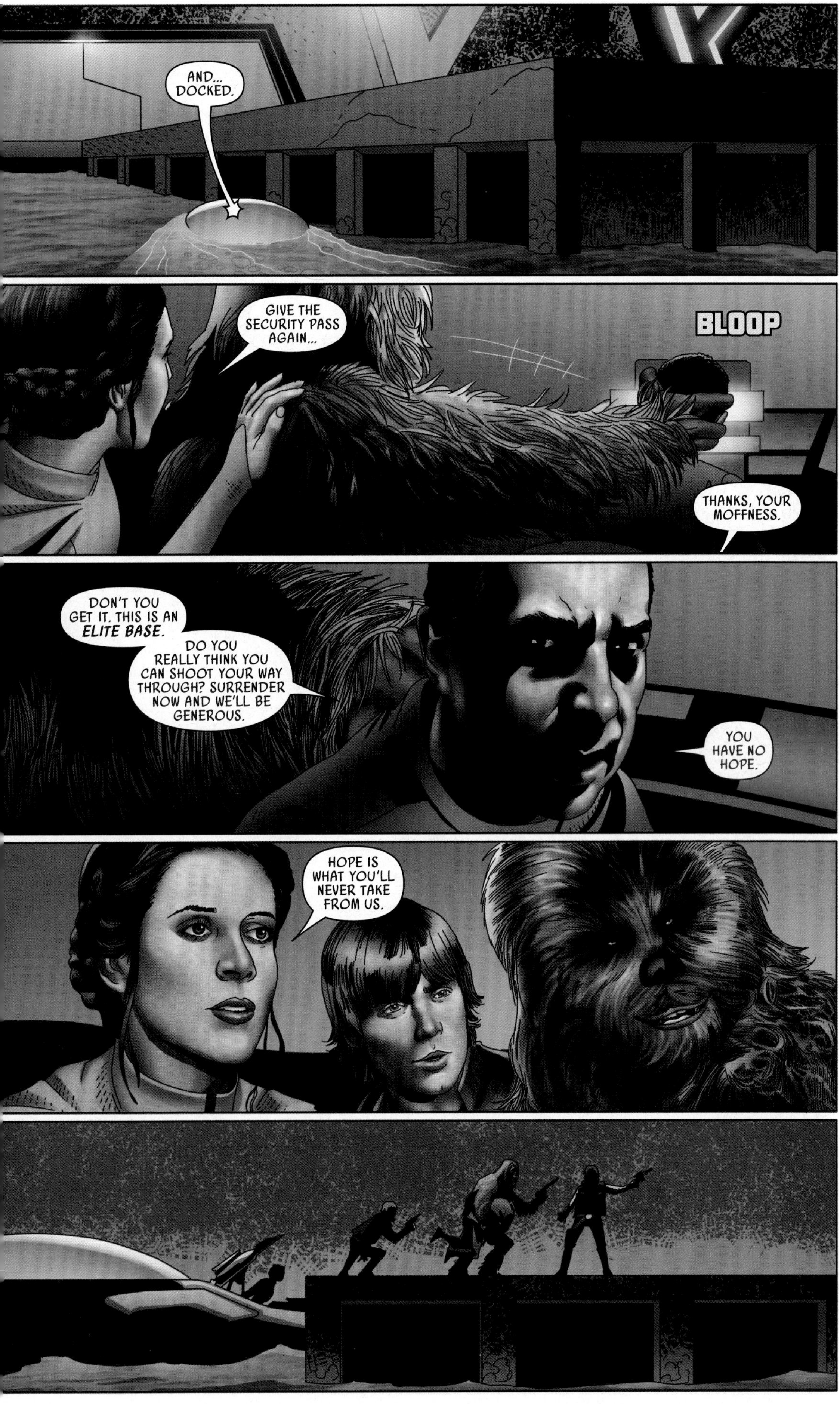
AND... DOCKED.
GIVE THE SECURITY PASS AGAIN...
BLOOP
THANKS, YOUR MOFFNESS.
DON'T YOU GET IT. THIS IS AN *ELITE BASE*.
DO YOU REALLY THINK YOU CAN SHOOT YOUR WAY THROUGH? SURRENDER NOW AND WE'LL BE GENEROUS.
YOU HAVE NO HOPE.
HOPE IS WHAT YOU'LL NEVER TAKE FROM US.

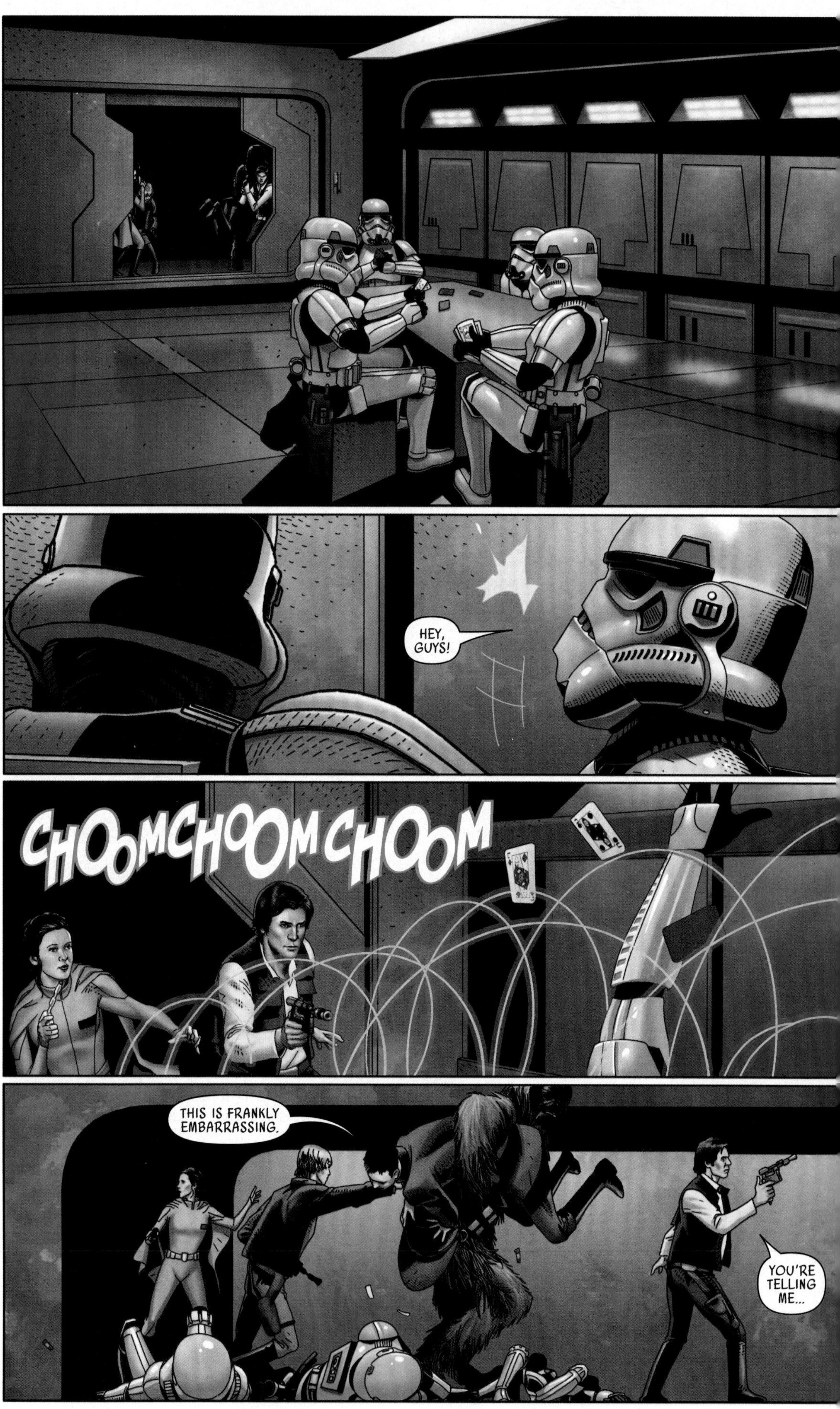
HEY, GUYS!
CHOOMCHOOMCHOOM
THIS IS FRANKLY EMBARRASSING.
YOU'RE TELLING ME...

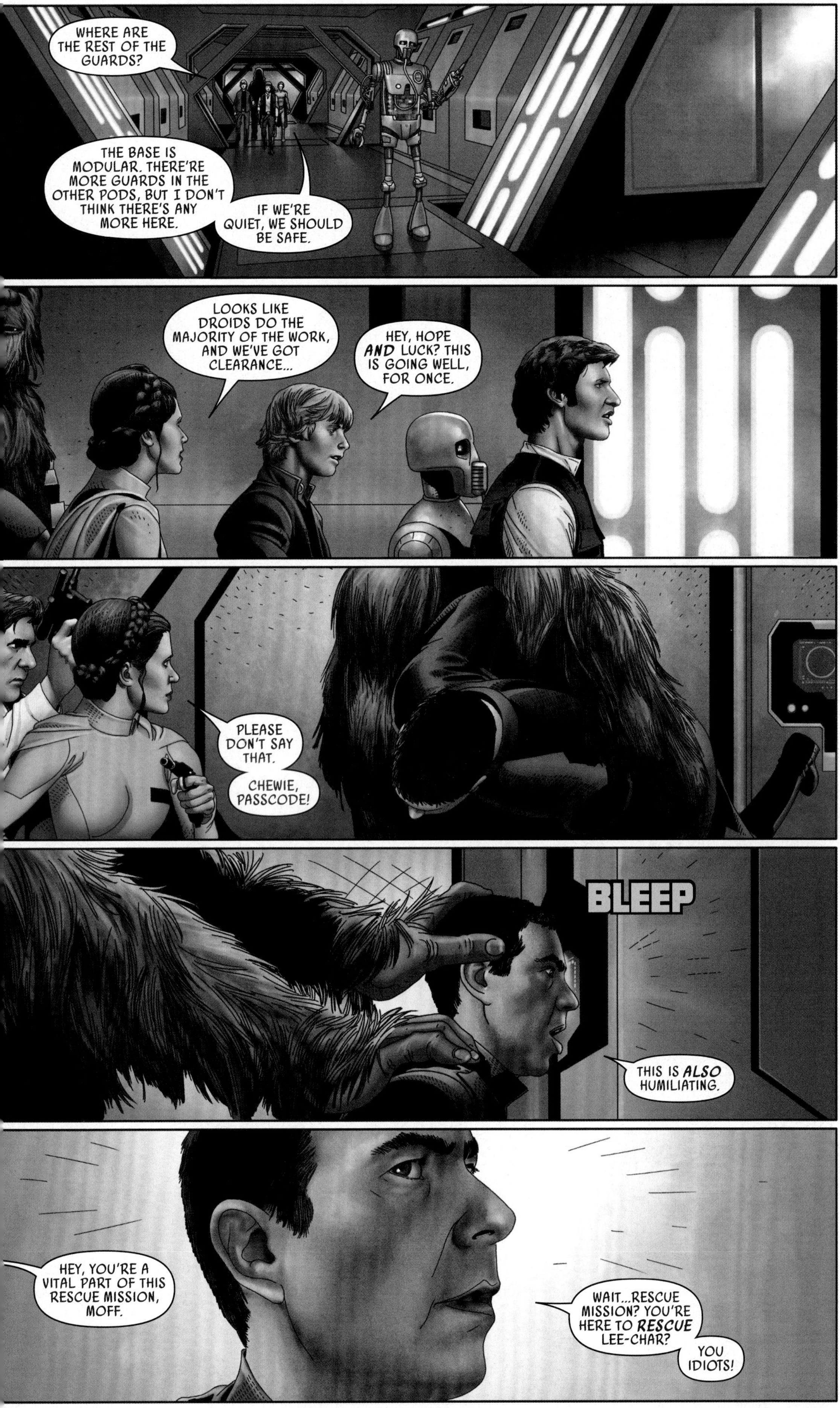
WHERE ARE THE REST OF THE GUARDS?
THE BASE IS MODULAR. THERE'RE MORE GUARDS IN THE OTHER PODS, BUT I DON'T THINK THERE'S ANY MORE HERE.
IF WE'RE QUIET, WE SHOULD BE SAFE.
LOOKS LIKE DROIDS DO THE MAJORITY OF THE WORK, AND WE'VE GOT CLEARANCE...
HEY, HOPE AND LUCK? THIS IS GOING WELL, FOR ONCE.
PLEASE DON'T SAY THAT.
CHEWIE, PASSCODE!
BLEEP
THIS IS ALSO HUMILIATING.
HEY, YOU'RE A VITAL PART OF THIS RESCUE MISSION, MOFF.
WAIT...RESCUE MISSION? YOU'RE HERE TO RESCUE LEE-CHAR?
YOU IDIOTS!

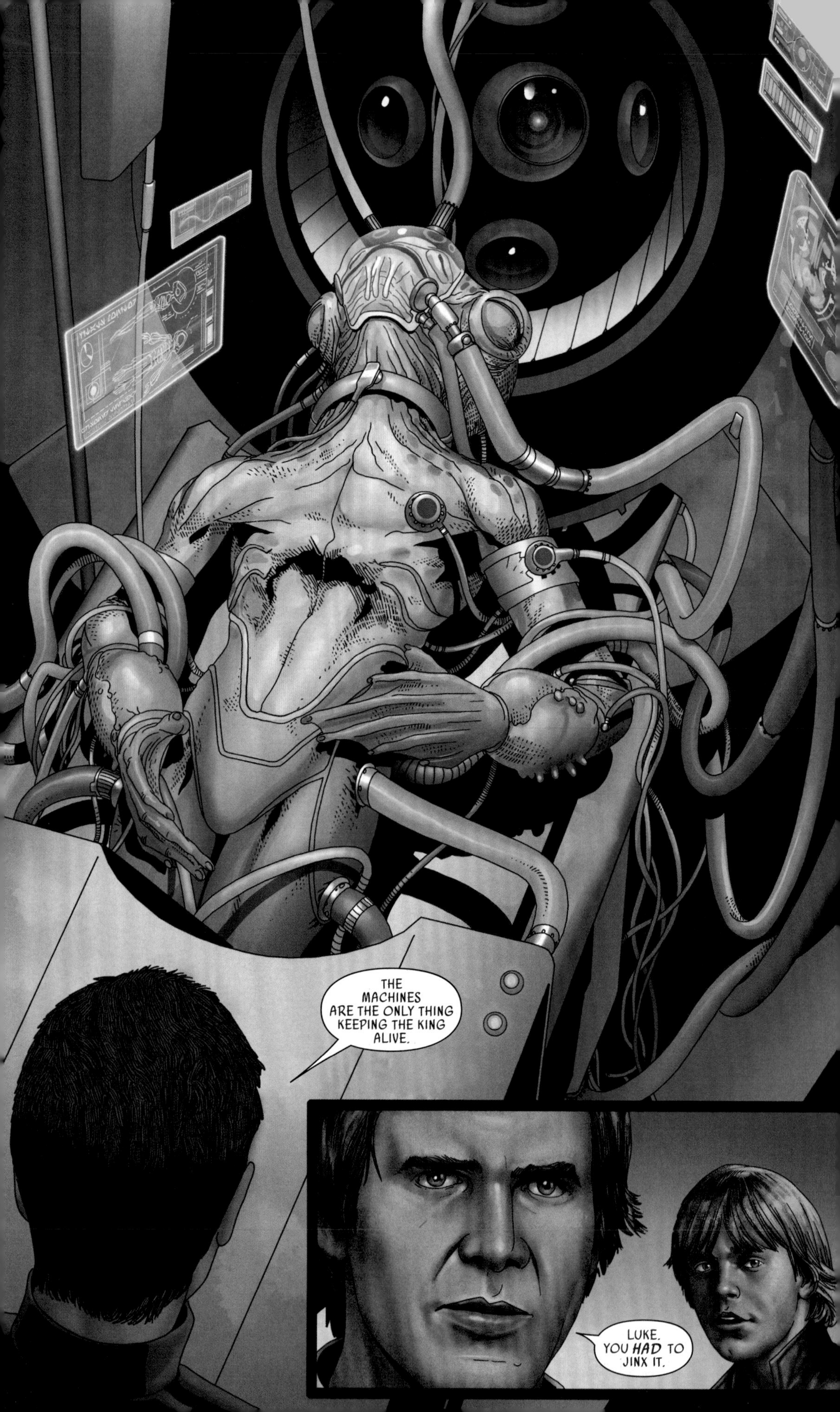
THE MACHINES ARE THE ONLY THING KEEPING THE KING ALIVE.
LUKE. YOU HAD TO JINX IT.

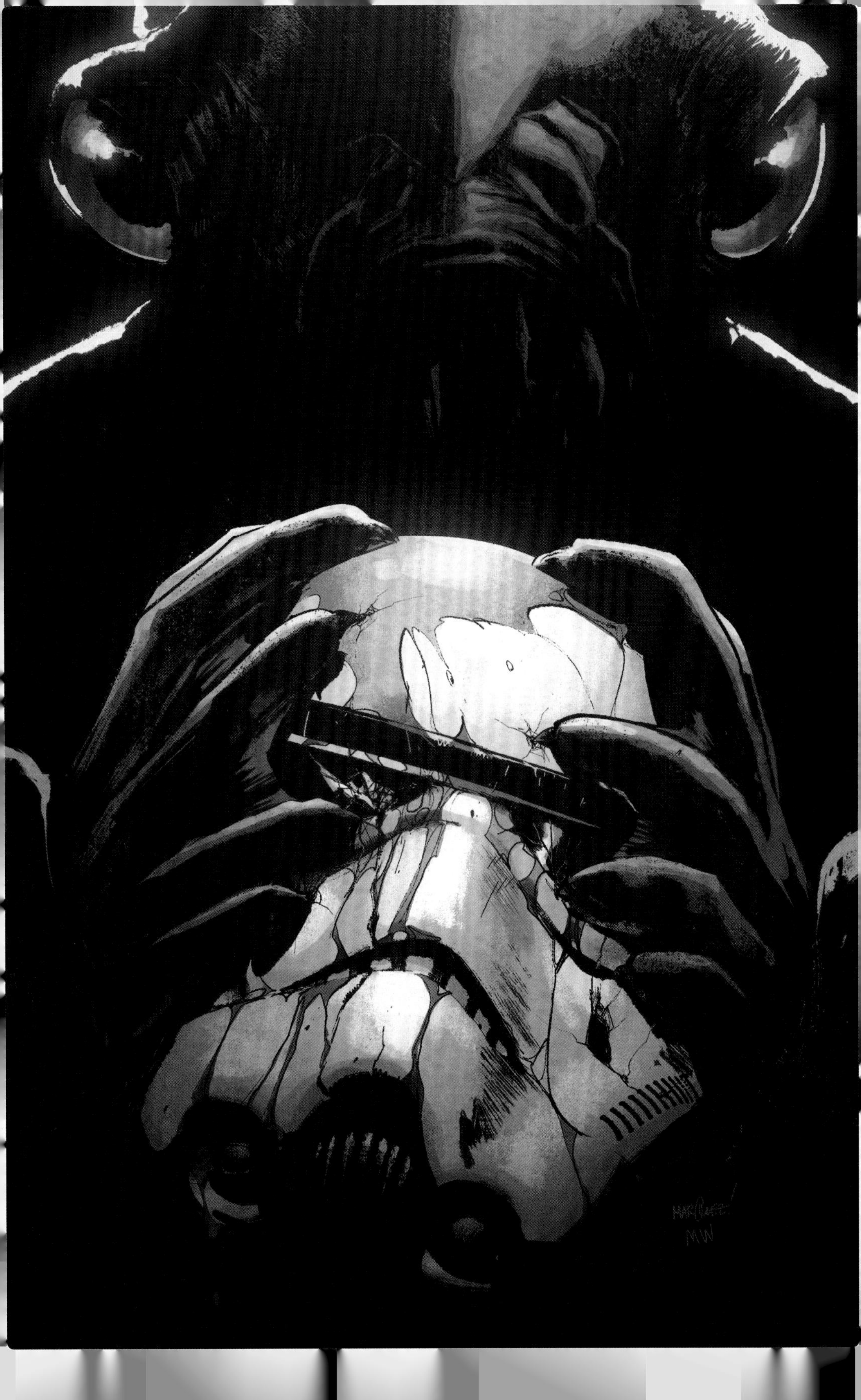

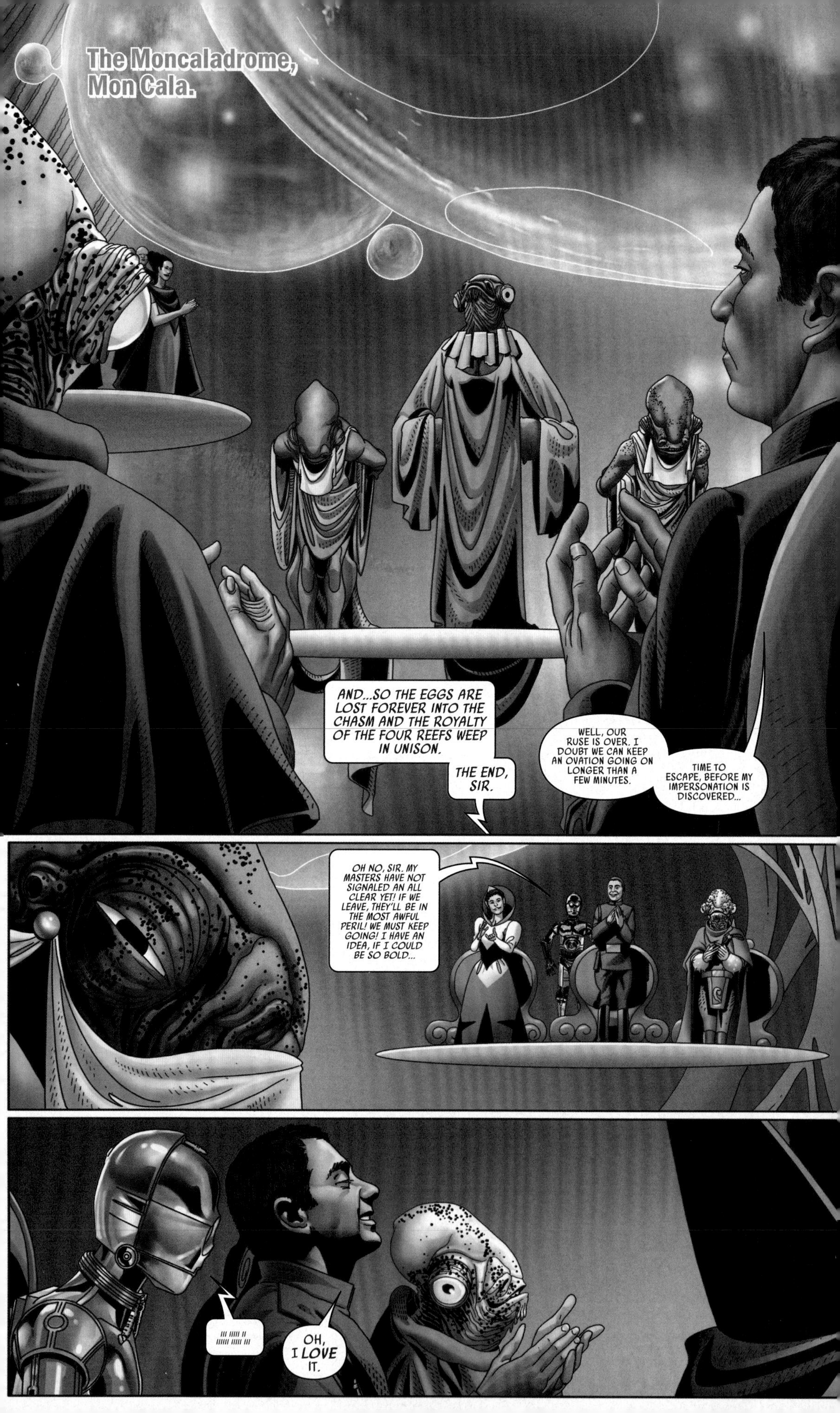
The Moncaladrome, Mon Cala.
AND...SO THE EGGS ARE LOST FOREVER INTO THE CHASM AND THE ROYALTY OF THE FOUR REEFS WEEP IN UNISON.
THE END, SIR.
WELL, OUR RUSE IS OVER. I DOUBT WE CAN KEEP AN OVATION GOING ON LONGER THAN A FEW MINUTES.
TIME TO ESCAPE, BEFORE MY IMPERSONATION IS DISCOVERED...
OH NO, SIR. MY MASTERS HAVE NOT SIGNALED AN ALL CLEAR YET! IF WE LEAVE, THEY'LL BE IN THE MOST AWFUL PERIL! WE MUST KEEP GOING! I HAVE AN IDEA, IF I COULD BE SO BOLD...
OH, I LOVE IT.

THIS IS FAR TOO EARLY TO END THE FIRST NIGHT OF THE SEASON!

URTYA! A FLYER TO THE STAGE FOR ME AND MY DROIDS.

I... I...

WELL, OF COURSE, MOFF.

LET ME HELP YOUR COMPANION...

OOF.

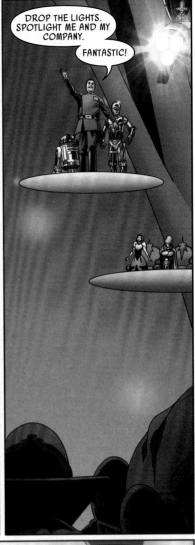

DROP THE LIGHTS. SPOTLIGHT ME AND MY COMPANY.

FANTASTIC!

THIS IS AN OUTRAGE--

HE'S THE MOFF! LEAVE HIM BE!

TO END THIS EVENING, WE WILL HAVE A RECITAL FROM THE POET-PLAYWRIGHT MOOBIAN TAX! SPECIFICALLY, THE GRAND ROMANCE OF AMON DAAK. WE WILL BE PERFORMING THE WORK UNABRIDGED.

I WILL TAKE THE ROLE OF PRINCESS-WARRIOR ARTHONI...

...AND MY DROID WILL TAKE THE ROLE OF THE URCHIN TURNED DEMAGOGUE PANAI!

BLLEEEPPP?!

PLEASE, ARTOO. DON'T DISTRACT ME.

THIS COULD BE MY BIG BREAK.

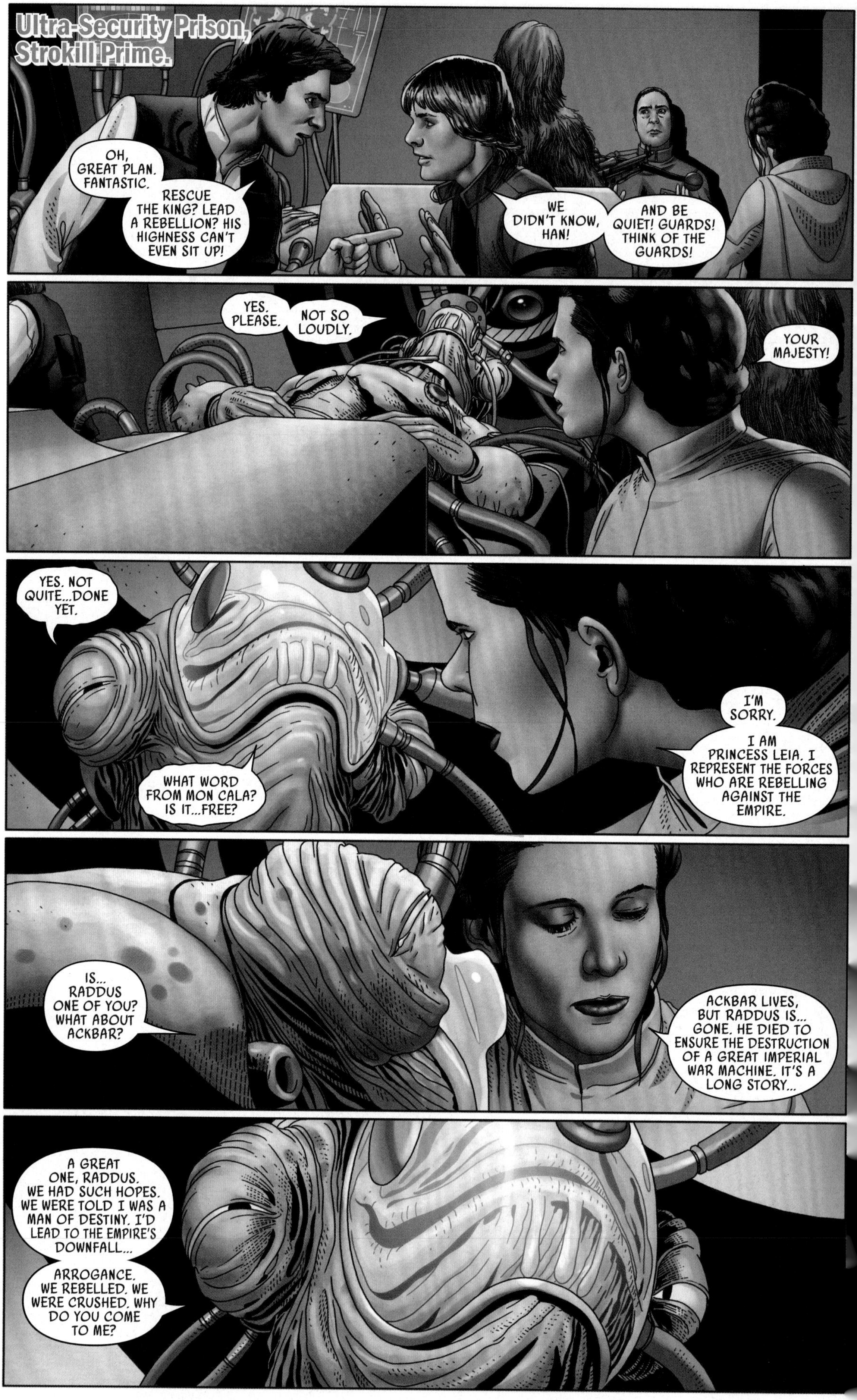
Ultra-Security Prison, Strokill Prime.
OH, GREAT PLAN. FANTASTIC.
RESCUE THE KING? LEAD A REBELLION? HIS HIGHNESS CAN'T EVEN SIT UP!
WE DIDN'T KNOW, HAN!
AND BE QUIET! GUARDS! THINK OF THE GUARDS!
YES. PLEASE.
NOT SO LOUDLY.
YOUR MAJESTY!
YES. NOT QUITE...DONE YET.
I'M SORRY.
I AM PRINCESS LEIA. I REPRESENT THE FORCES WHO ARE REBELLING AGAINST THE EMPIRE.
WHAT WORD FROM MON CALA? IS IT...FREE?
IS... RADDUS ONE OF YOU? WHAT ABOUT ACKBAR?
ACKBAR LIVES, BUT RADDUS IS... GONE. HE DIED TO ENSURE THE DESTRUCTION OF A GREAT IMPERIAL WAR MACHINE. IT'S A LONG STORY...
A GREAT ONE, RADDUS. WE HAD SUCH HOPES. WE WERE TOLD I WAS A MAN OF DESTINY. I'D LEAD TO THE EMPIRE'S DOWNFALL...
ARROGANCE. WE REBELLED. WE WERE CRUSHED. WHY DO YOU COME TO ME?

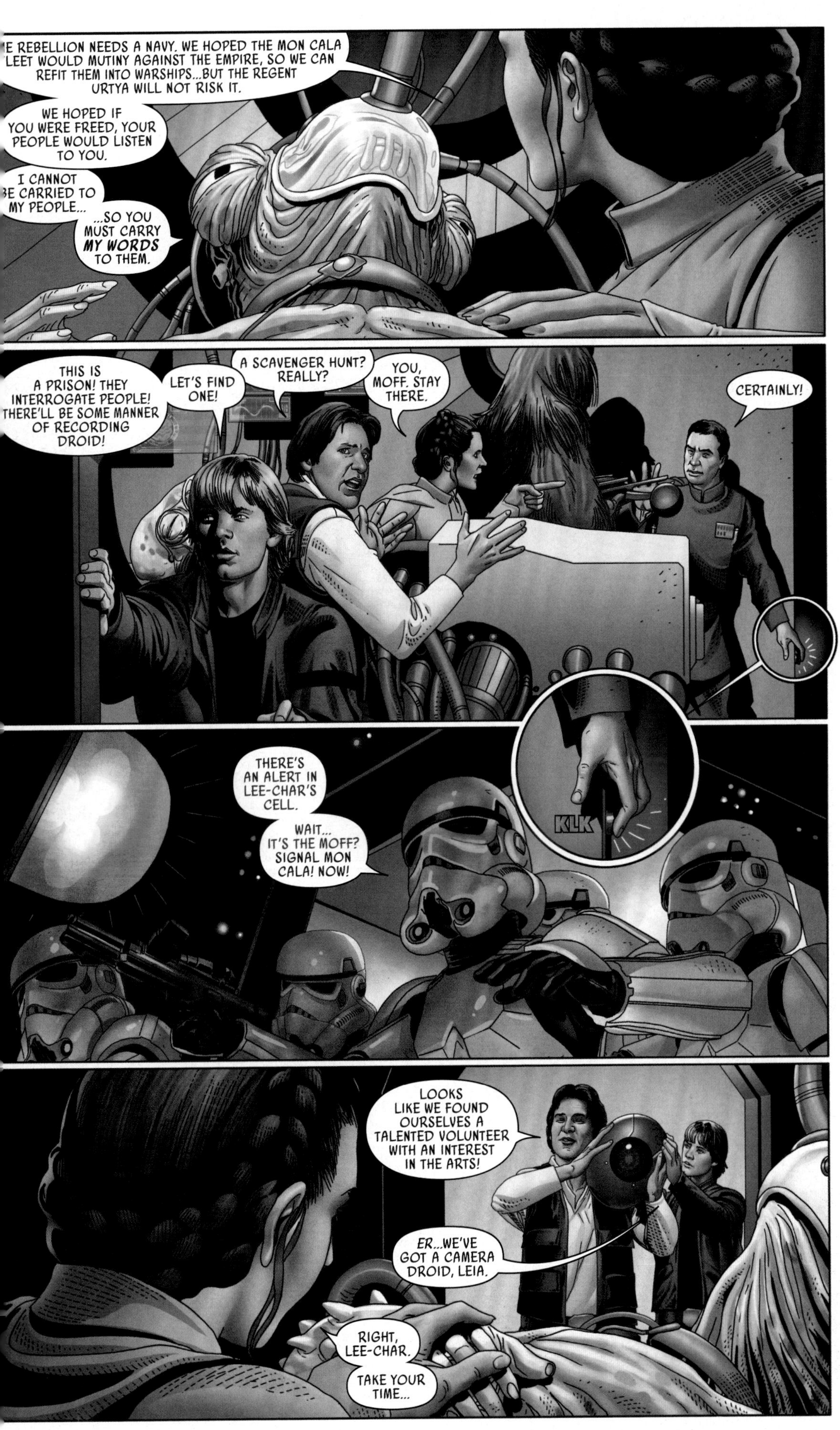
E REBELLION NEEDS A NAVY. WE HOPED THE MON CALA LEET WOULD MUTINY AGAINST THE EMPIRE, SO WE CAN REFIT THEM INTO WARSHIPS...BUT THE REGENT URTYA WILL NOT RISK IT.
WE HOPED IF YOU WERE FREED, YOUR PEOPLE WOULD LISTEN TO YOU.
I CANNOT BE CARRIED TO MY PEOPLE...
...SO YOU MUST CARRY *MY WORDS* TO THEM.
THIS IS A PRISON! THEY INTERROGATE PEOPLE! THERE'LL BE SOME MANNER OF RECORDING DROID!
LET'S FIND ONE!
A SCAVENGER HUNT? REALLY?
YOU, MOFF. STAY THERE.
CERTAINLY!
KLK
THERE'S AN ALERT IN LEE-CHAR'S CELL.
WAIT... IT'S THE MOFF? SIGNAL MON CALA! NOW!
LOOKS LIKE WE FOUND OURSELVES A TALENTED VOLUNTEER WITH AN INTEREST IN THE ARTS!
ER...WE'VE GOT A CAMERA DROID, LEIA.
RIGHT, LEE-CHAR.
TAKE YOUR TIME...

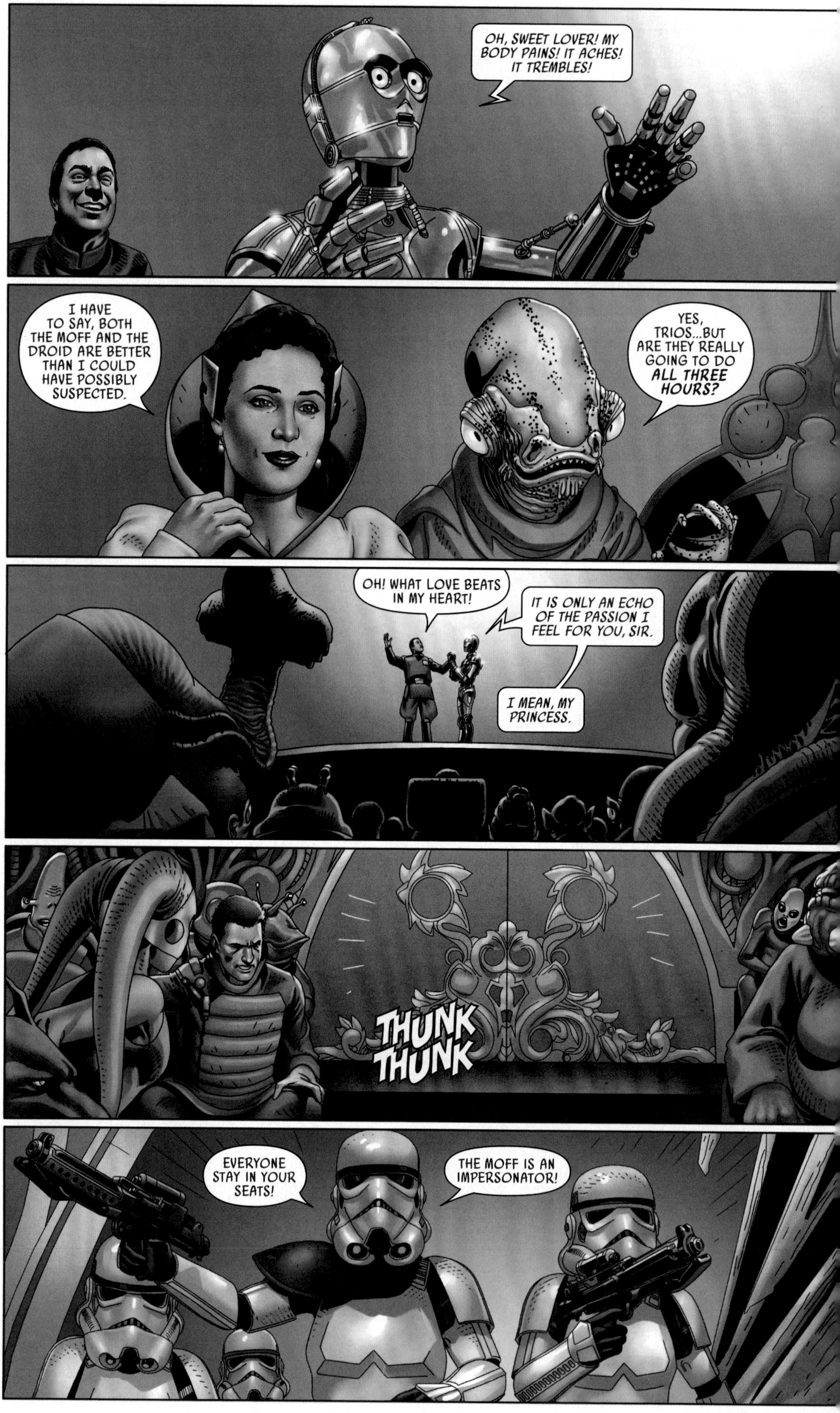
OH, SWEET LOVER! MY BODY PAINS! IT ACHES! IT TREMBLES!
I HAVE TO SAY, BOTH THE MOFF AND THE DROID ARE BETTER THAN I COULD HAVE POSSIBLY SUSPECTED.
YES, TRIOS...BUT ARE THEY REALLY GOING TO DO ALL THREE HOURS?
OH! WHAT LOVE BEATS IN MY HEART!
IT IS ONLY AN ECHO OF THE PASSION I FEEL FOR YOU, SIR.
I MEAN, MY PRINCESS.
THUNK THUNK
EVERYONE STAY IN YOUR SEATS!
THE MOFF IS AN IMPERSONATOR!

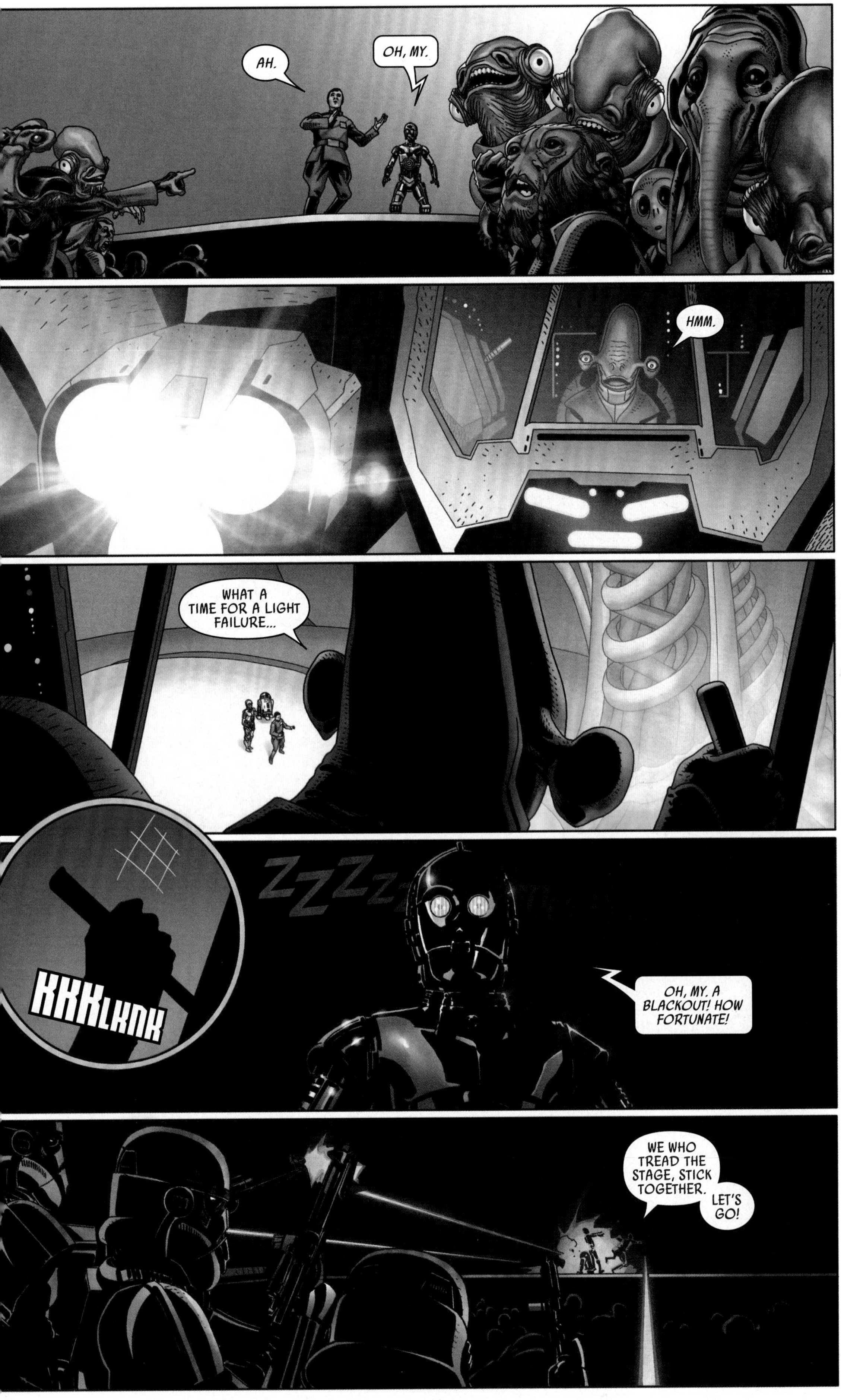
AH.
OH, MY.
HMM.
WHAT A TIME FOR A LIGHT FAILURE...
KKKLKNK
ZZZZZ
OH, MY. A BLACKOUT! HOW FORTUNATE!
WE WHO TREAD THE STAGE, STICK TOGETHER.
LET'S GO!

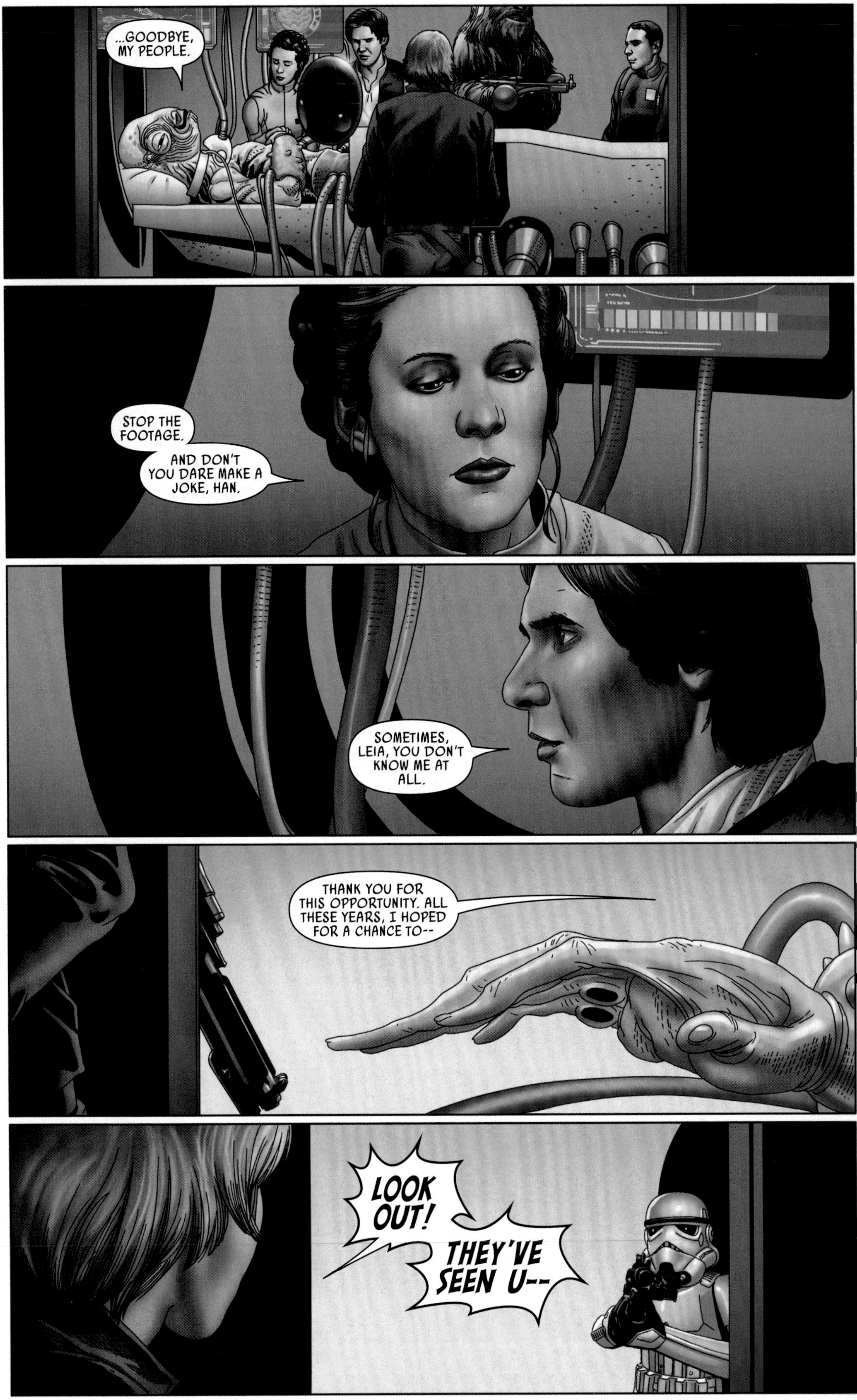
...GOODBYE, MY PEOPLE.
STOP THE FOOTAGE.
AND DON'T YOU DARE MAKE A JOKE, HAN.
SOMETIMES, LEIA, YOU DON'T KNOW ME AT ALL.
THANK YOU FOR THIS OPPORTUNITY. ALL THESE YEARS, I HOPED FOR A CHANCE TO--
LOOK OUT!
THEY'VE SEEN U--

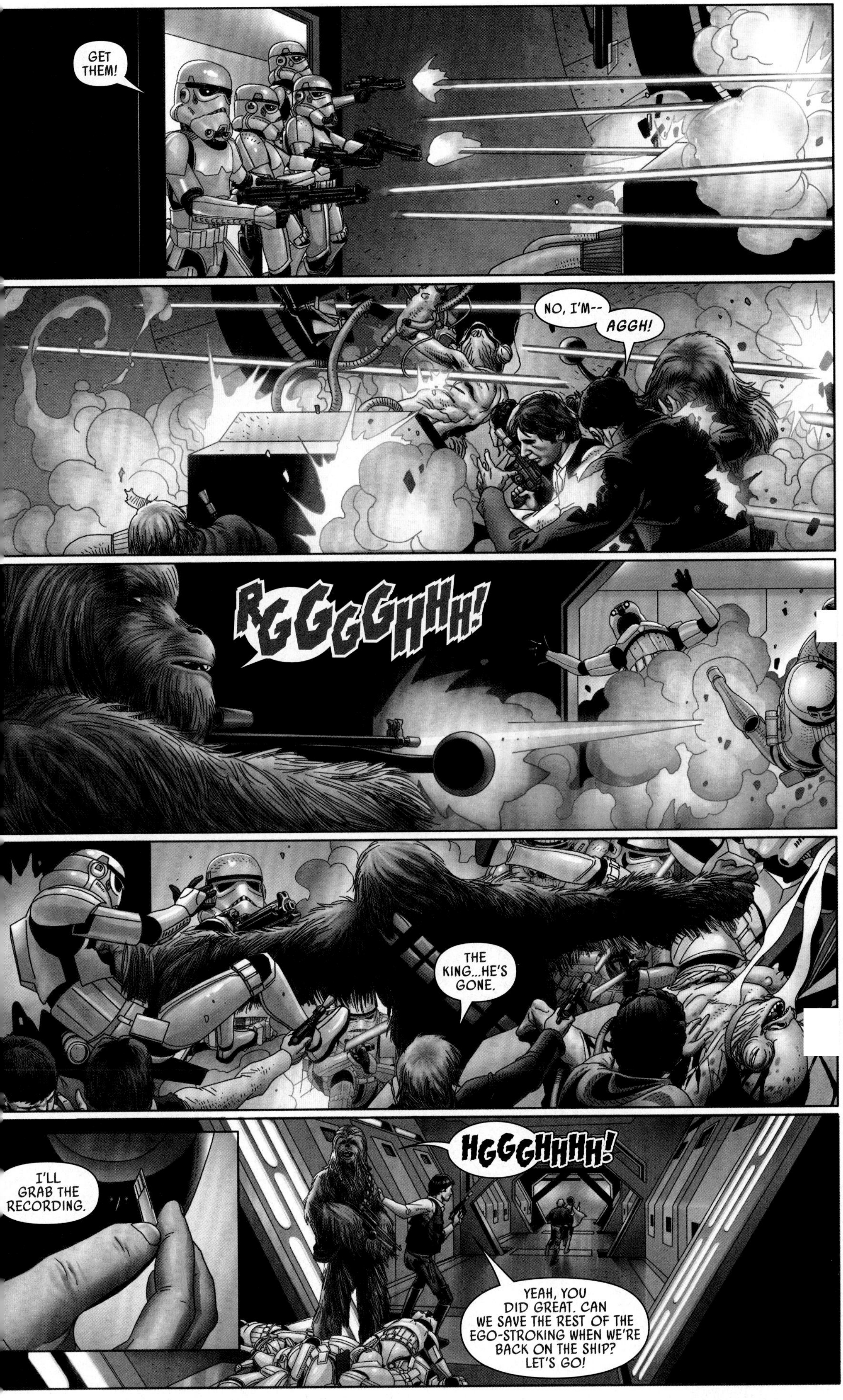
GET THEM!
NO, I'M--
AGGH!
RGGGGHHH!
THE KING...HE'S GONE.
I'LL GRAB THE RECORDING.
HGGGHHHH!
YEAH, YOU DID GREAT. CAN WE SAVE THE REST OF THE EGO-STROKING WHEN WE'RE BACK ON THE SHIP? LET'S GO!

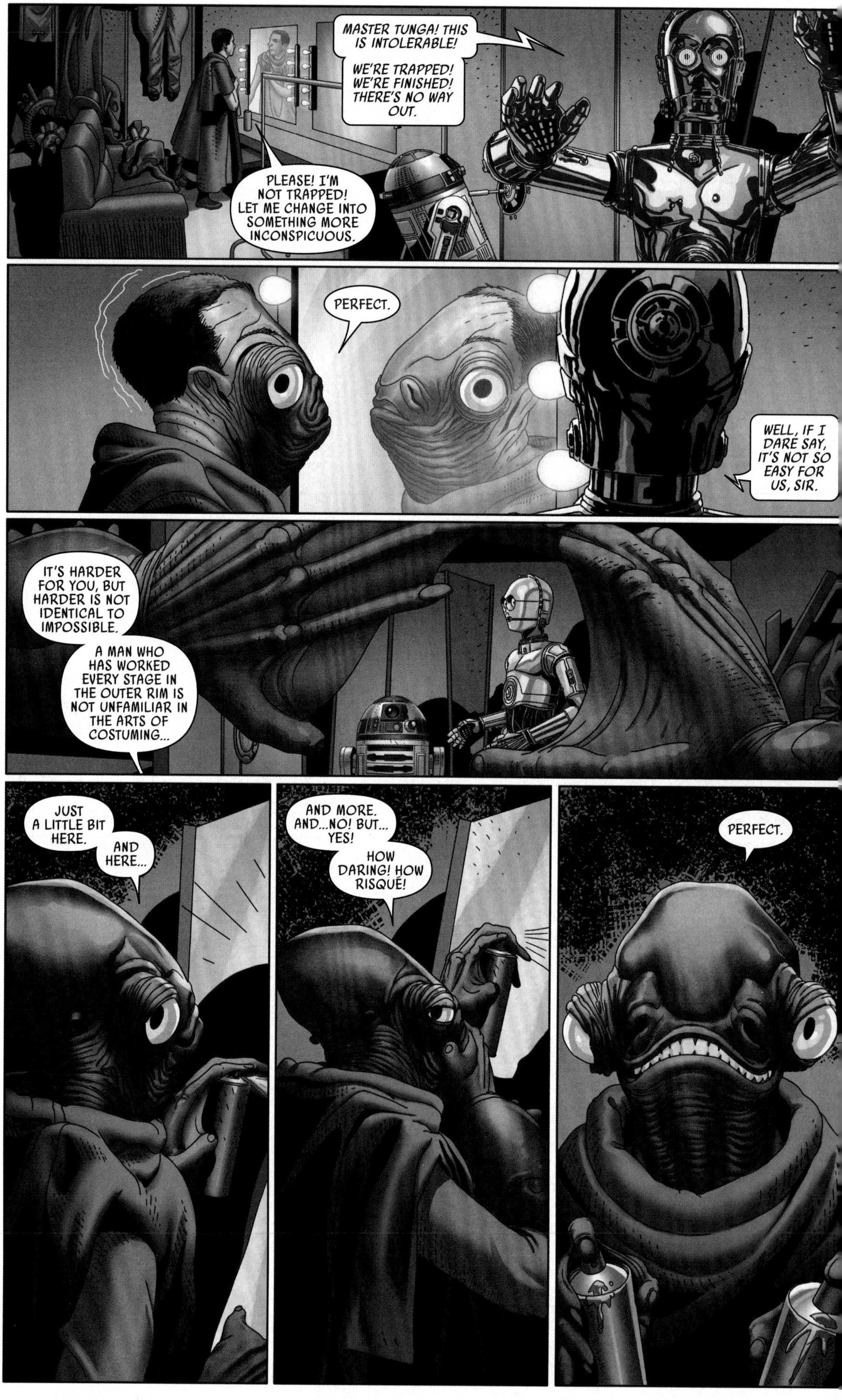
MASTER TUNGA! THIS IS INTOLERABLE!
WE'RE TRAPPED! WE'RE FINISHED! THERE'S NO WAY OUT.
PLEASE! I'M NOT TRAPPED! LET ME CHANGE INTO SOMETHING MORE INCONSPICUOUS.
PERFECT.
WELL, IF I DARE SAY, IT'S NOT SO EASY FOR US, SIR.
IT'S HARDER FOR YOU, BUT HARDER IS NOT IDENTICAL TO IMPOSSIBLE.
A MAN WHO HAS WORKED EVERY STAGE IN THE OUTER RIM IS NOT UNFAMILIAR IN THE ARTS OF COSTUMING...
JUST A LITTLE BIT HERE.
AND HERE...
AND MORE. AND...NO! BUT... YES!
HOW DARING! HOW RISQUÉ!
PERFECT.

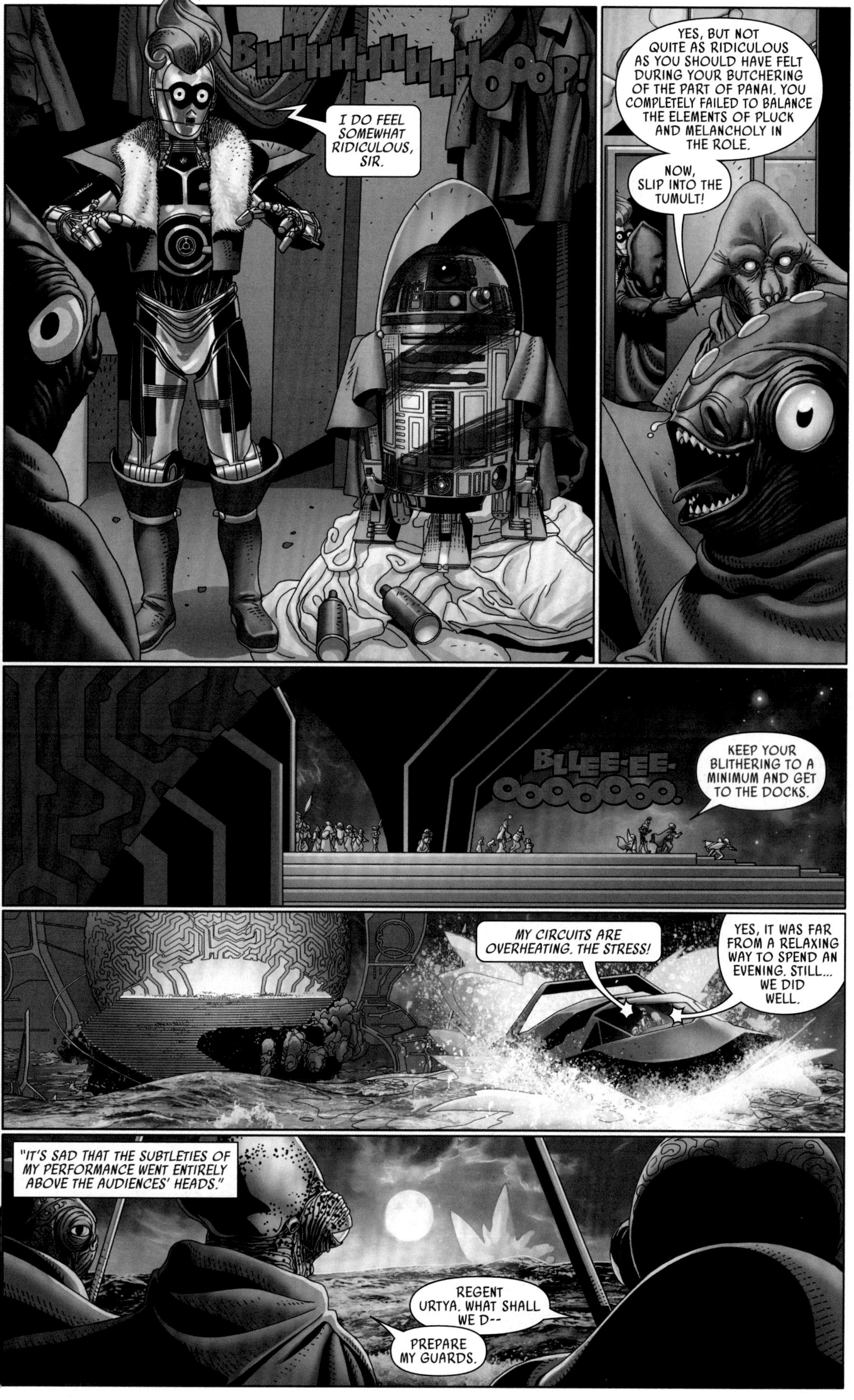
BHHHHHHHHHHOOOOP!
I DO FEEL SOMEWHAT RIDICULOUS, SIR.
YES, BUT NOT QUITE AS RIDICULOUS AS YOU SHOULD HAVE FELT DURING YOUR BUTCHERING OF THE PART OF PANAI. YOU COMPLETELY FAILED TO BALANCE THE ELEMENTS OF PLUCK AND MELANCHOLY IN THE ROLE.
NOW, SLIP INTO THE TUMULT!
BLLEE-EE-OOOOOOO.
KEEP YOUR BLITHERING TO A MINIMUM AND GET TO THE DOCKS.
MY CIRCUITS ARE OVERHEATING. THE STRESS!
YES, IT WAS FAR FROM A RELAXING WAY TO SPEND AN EVENING. STILL... WE DID WELL.
"IT'S SAD THAT THE SUBTLETIES OF MY PERFORMANCE WENT ENTIRELY ABOVE THE AUDIENCES' HEADS."
REGENT URTYA. WHAT SHALL WE D--
PREPARE MY GUARDS.

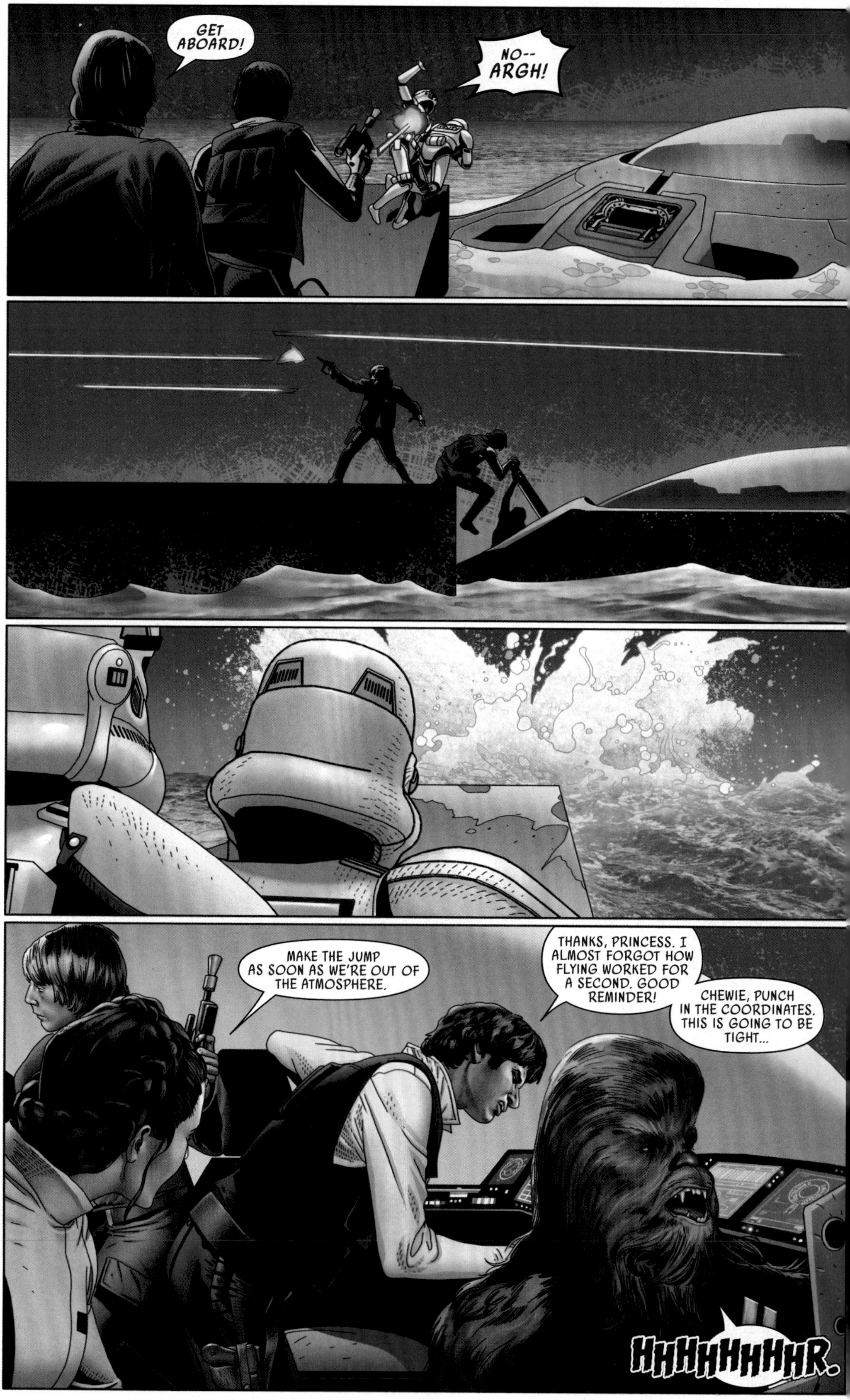

GET ABOARD!
NO-- ARGH!
MAKE THE JUMP AS SOON AS WE'RE OUT OF THE ATMOSPHERE.
THANKS, PRINCESS. I ALMOST FORGOT HOW FLYING WORKED FOR A SECOND. GOOD REMINDER!
CHEWIE, PUNCH IN THE COORDINATES. THIS IS GOING TO BE TIGHT...
HHHHHHHHR.

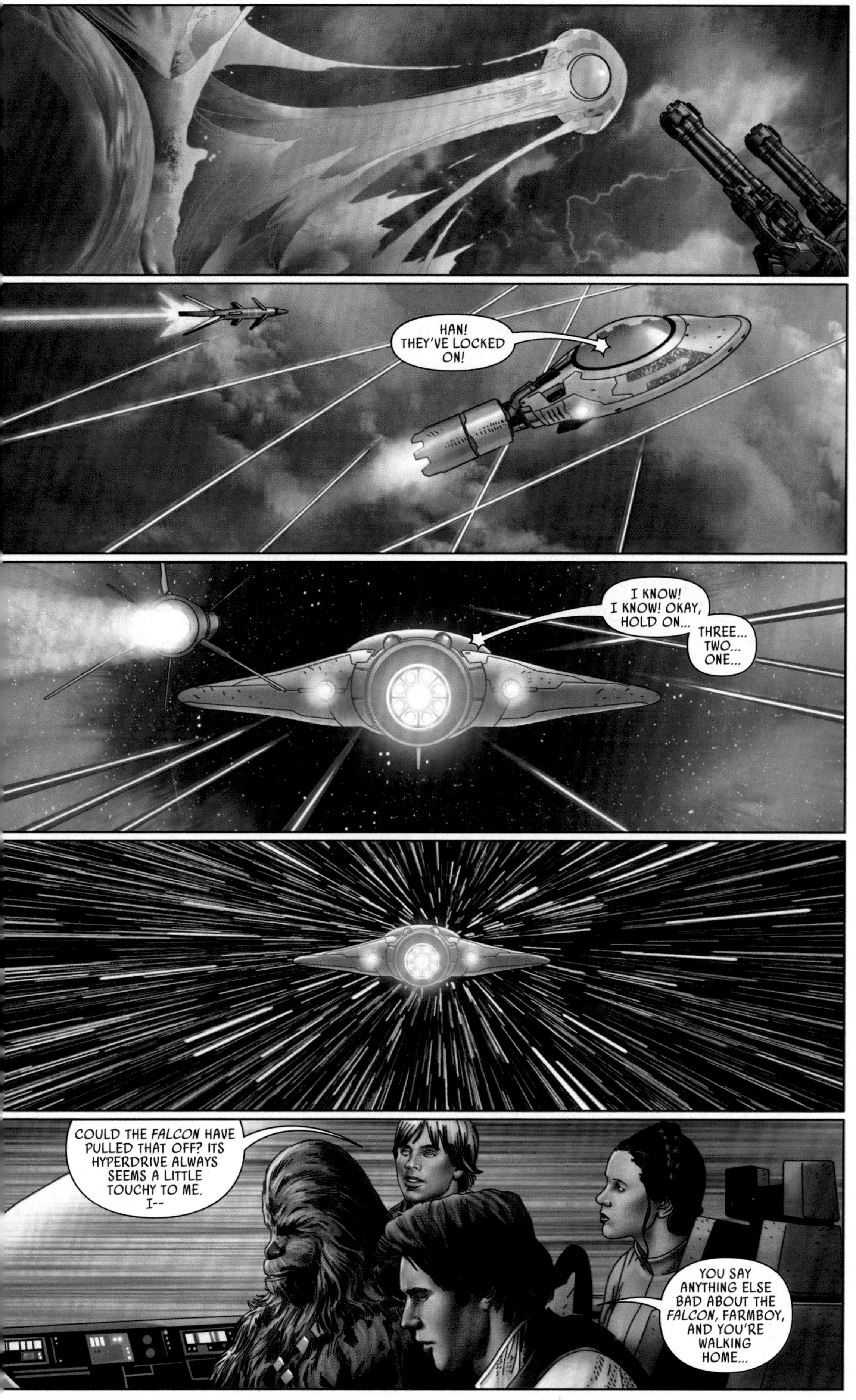
HAN! THEY'VE LOCKED ON!
I KNOW! I KNOW! OKAY, HOLD ON... THREE... TWO... ONE...
COULD THE *FALCON* HAVE PULLED THAT OFF? ITS HYPERDRIVE ALWAYS SEEMS A LITTLE TOUCHY TO ME. I--
YOU SAY ANYTHING ELSE BAD ABOUT THE *FALCON*, FARMBOY, AND YOU'RE WALKING HOME...

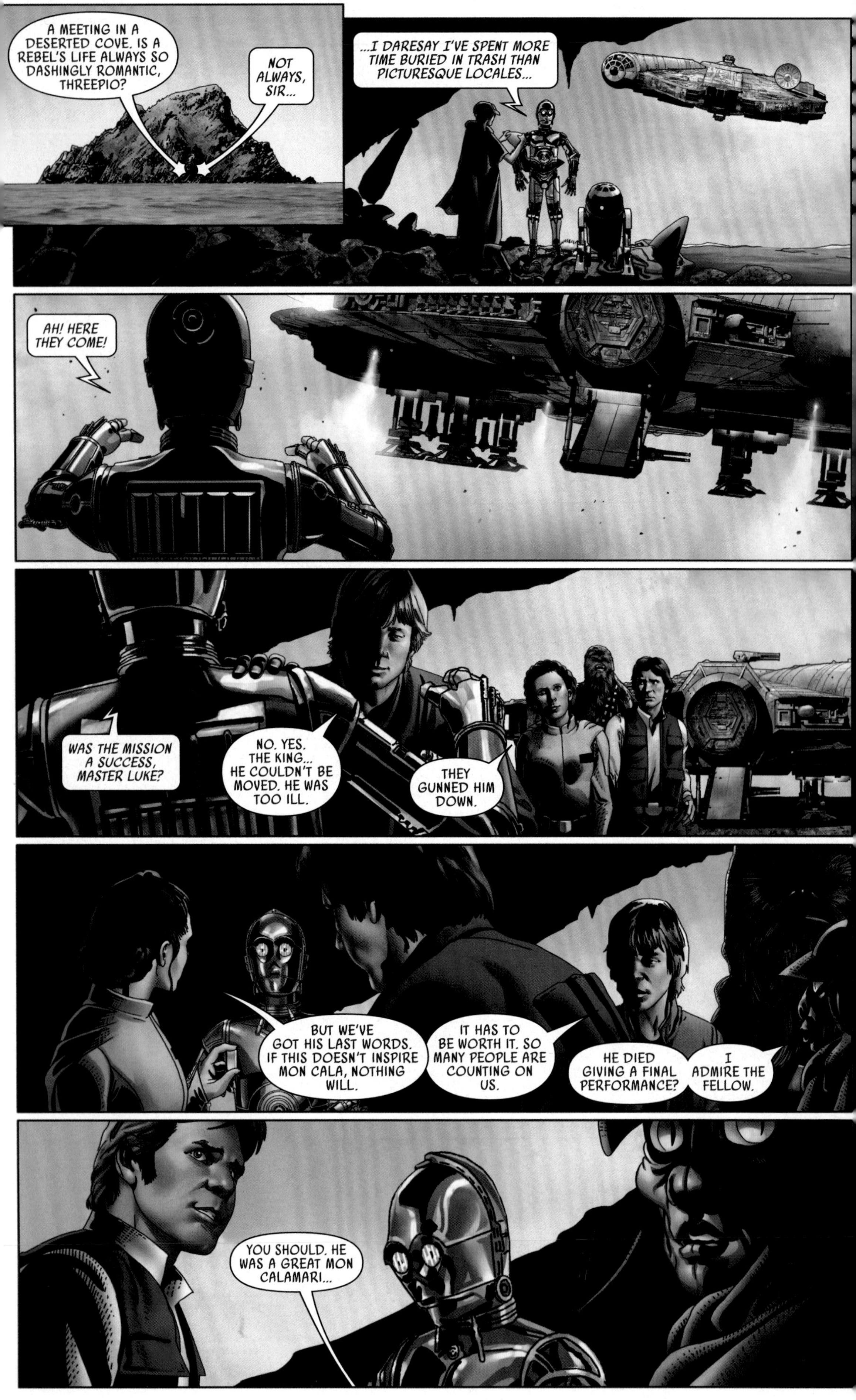
A MEETING IN A DESERTED COVE. IS A REBEL'S LIFE ALWAYS SO DASHINGLY ROMANTIC, THREEPIO?
NOT ALWAYS, SIR...
...I DARESAY I'VE SPENT MORE TIME BURIED IN TRASH THAN PICTURESQUE LOCALES...
AH! HERE THEY COME!
WAS THE MISSION A SUCCESS, MASTER LUKE?
NO. YES. THE KING... HE COULDN'T BE MOVED. HE WAS TOO ILL.
THEY GUNNED HIM DOWN.
BUT WE'VE GOT HIS LAST WORDS. IF THIS DOESN'T INSPIRE MON CALA, NOTHING WILL.
IT HAS TO BE WORTH IT. SO MANY PEOPLE ARE COUNTING ON US.
HE DIED GIVING A FINAL PERFORMANCE?
I ADMIRE THE FELLOW.
YOU SHOULD. HE WAS A GREAT MON CALAMARI...

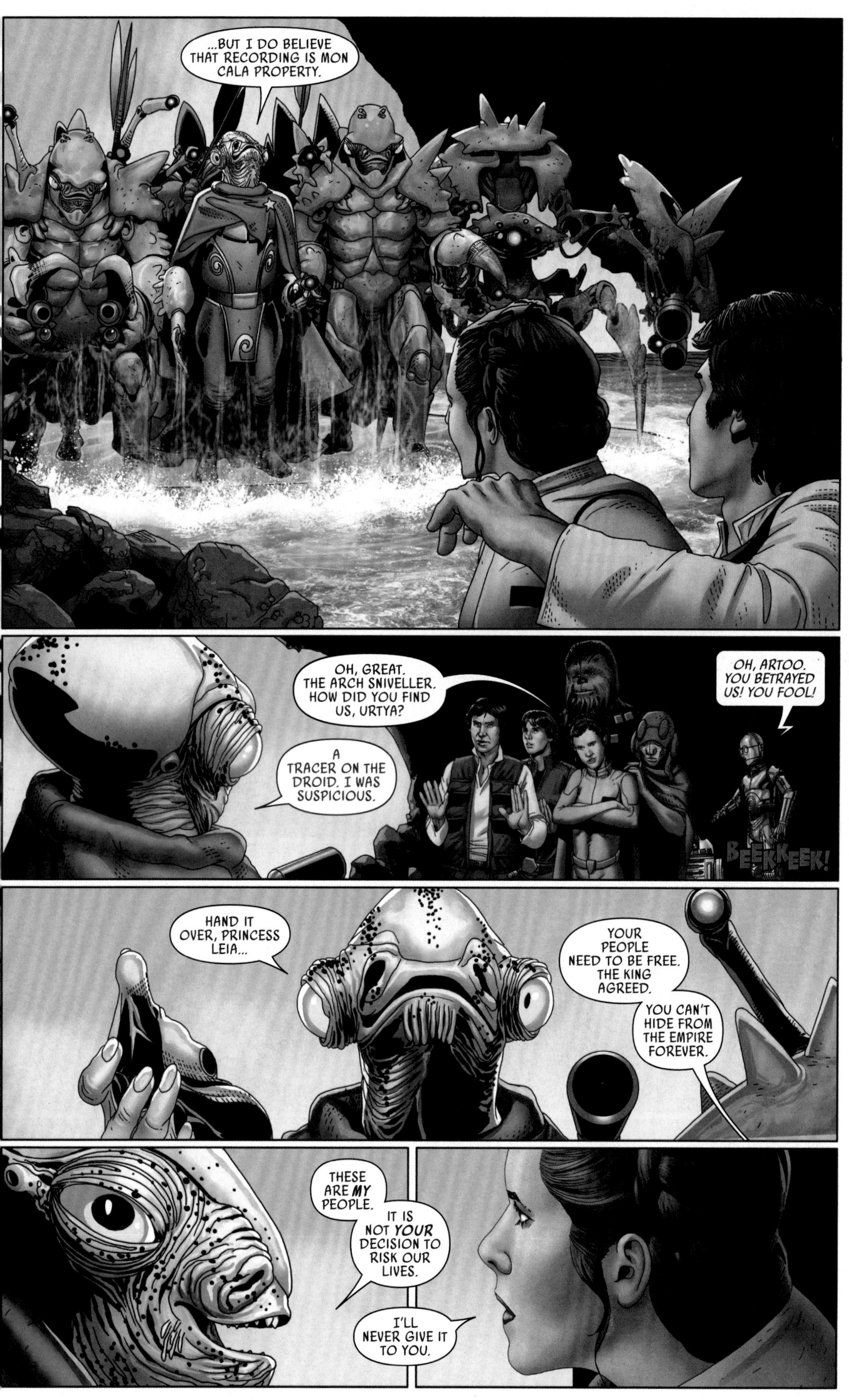

...BUT I DO BELIEVE THAT RECORDING IS MON CALA PROPERTY.
OH, GREAT. THE ARCH SNIVELLER. HOW DID YOU FIND US, URTYA?
A TRACER ON THE DROID. I WAS SUSPICIOUS.
OH, ARTOO. YOU BETRAYED US! YOU FOOL!
BEEKKEEK!
HAND IT OVER, PRINCESS LEIA...
YOUR PEOPLE NEED TO BE FREE. THE KING AGREED.
YOU CAN'T HIDE FROM THE EMPIRE FOREVER.
THESE ARE MY PEOPLE.
IT IS NOT YOUR DECISION TO RISK OUR LIVES.
I'LL NEVER GIVE IT TO YOU.

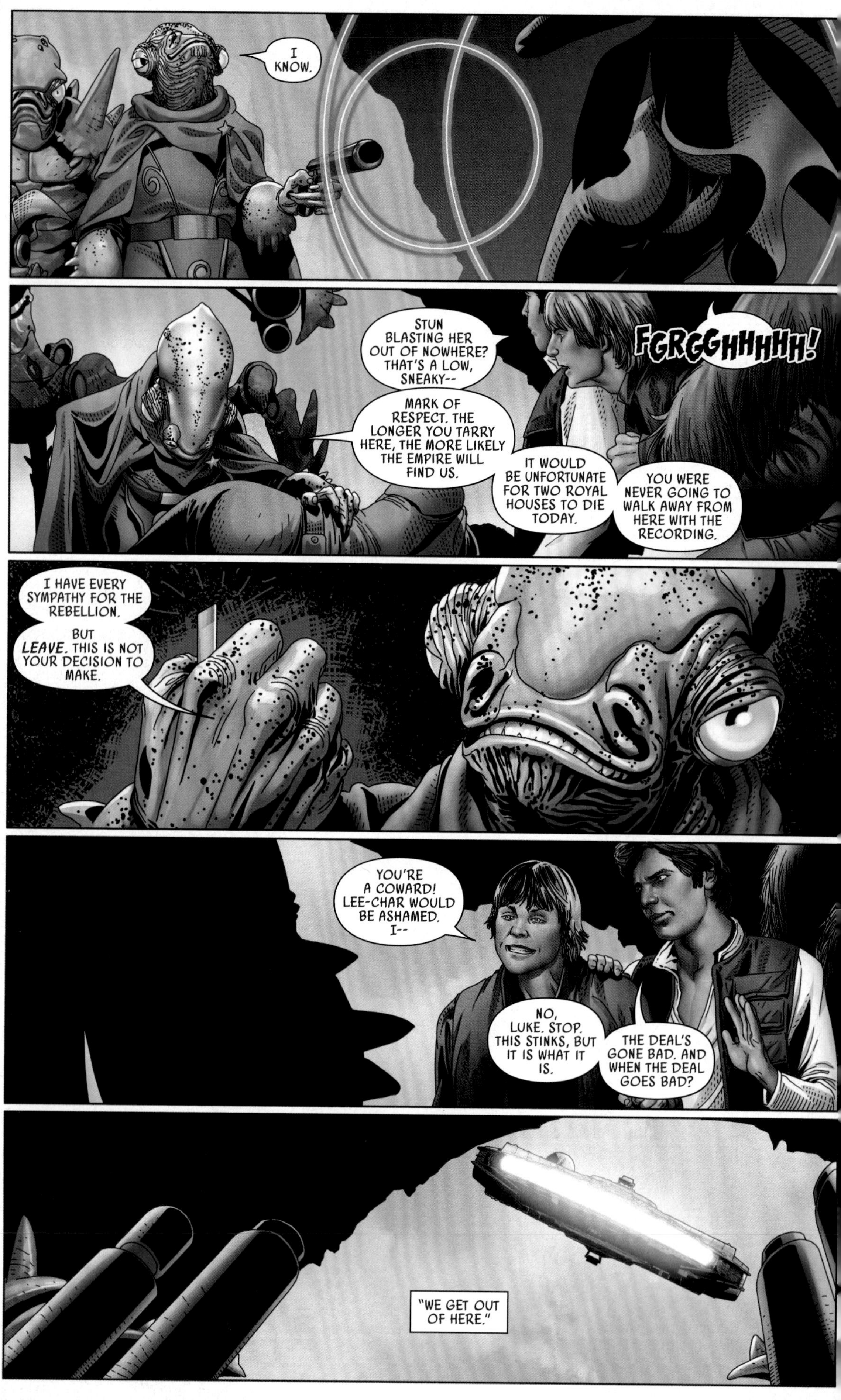
I KNOW.
STUN BLASTING HER OUT OF NOWHERE? THAT'S A LOW, SNEAKY--
FGRGGHHHHH!
MARK OF RESPECT. THE LONGER YOU TARRY HERE, THE MORE LIKELY THE EMPIRE WILL FIND US.
IT WOULD BE UNFORTUNATE FOR TWO ROYAL HOUSES TO DIE TODAY.
YOU WERE NEVER GOING TO WALK AWAY FROM HERE WITH THE RECORDING.
I HAVE EVERY SYMPATHY FOR THE REBELLION.
BUT LEAVE. THIS IS NOT YOUR DECISION TO MAKE.
YOU'RE A COWARD! LEE-CHAR WOULD BE ASHAMED. I--
NO, LUKE. STOP. THIS STINKS, BUT IT IS WHAT IT IS.
THE DEAL'S GONE BAD. AND WHEN THE DEAL GOES BAD?
"WE GET OUT OF HERE."

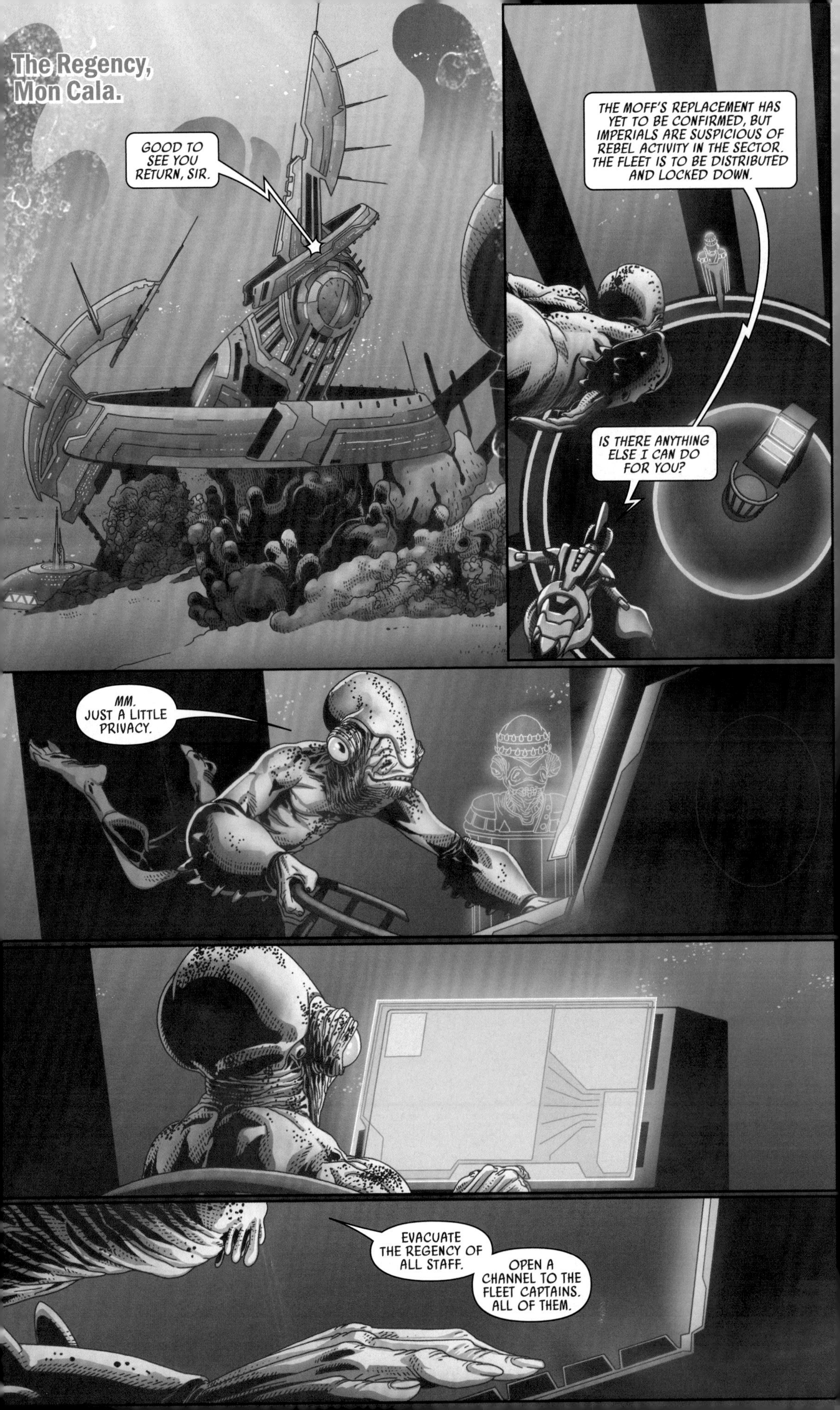
The Regency, Mon Cala.
GOOD TO SEE YOU RETURN, SIR.
THE MOFF'S REPLACEMENT HAS YET TO BE CONFIRMED, BUT IMPERIALS ARE SUSPICIOUS OF REBEL ACTIVITY IN THE SECTOR. THE FLEET IS TO BE DISTRIBUTED AND LOCKED DOWN.
IS THERE ANYTHING ELSE I CAN DO FOR YOU?
MM. JUST A LITTLE PRIVACY.
EVACUATE THE REGENCY OF ALL STAFF.
OPEN A CHANNEL TO THE FLEET CAPTAINS. ALL OF THEM.

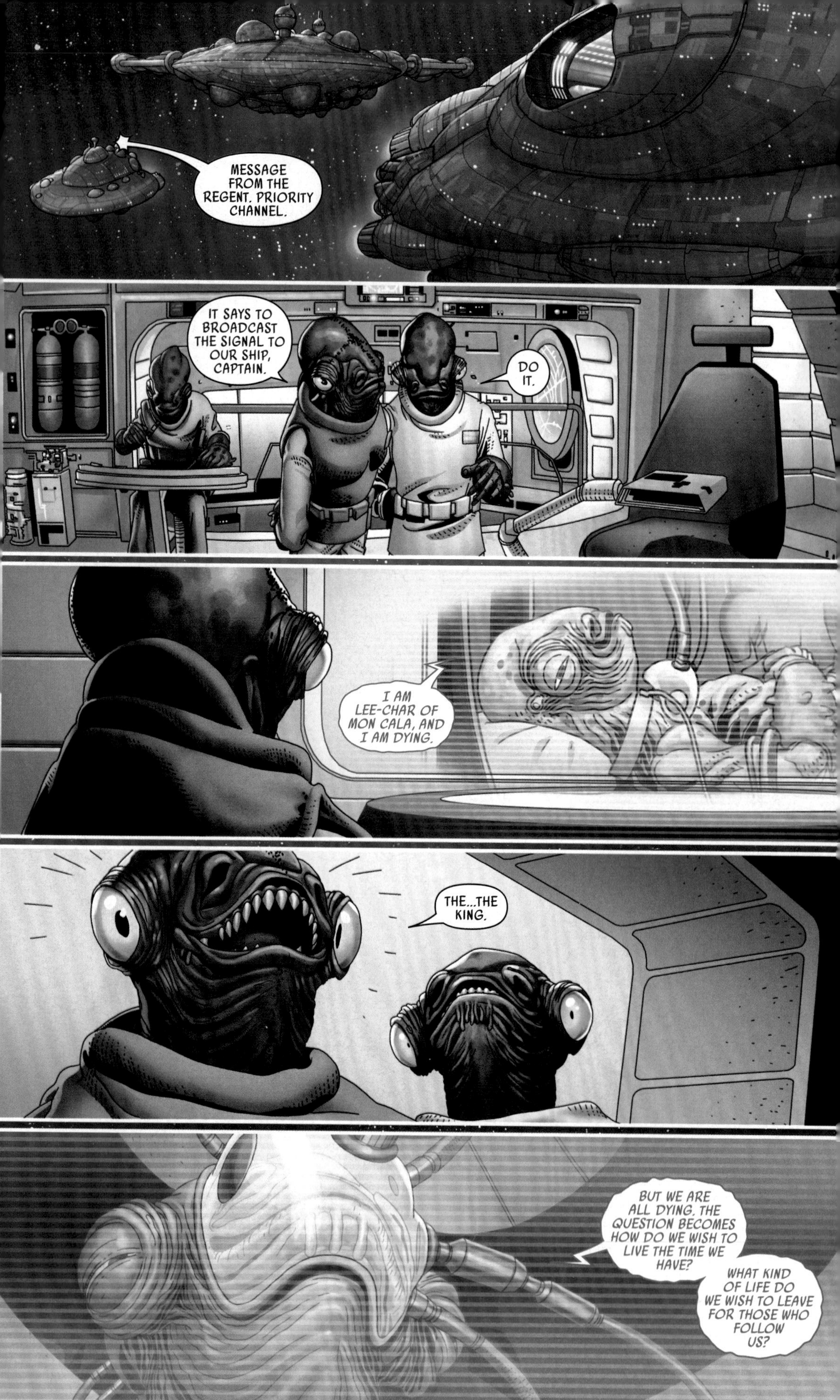
MESSAGE FROM THE REGENT. PRIORITY CHANNEL.
IT SAYS TO BROADCAST THE SIGNAL TO OUR SHIP, CAPTAIN.
DO IT.
I AM LEE-CHAR OF MON CALA, AND I AM DYING.
THE...THE KING.
BUT WE ARE ALL DYING. THE QUESTION BECOMES HOW DO WE WISH TO LIVE THE TIME WE HAVE?
WHAT KIND OF LIFE DO WE WISH TO LEAVE FOR THOSE WHO FOLLOW US?

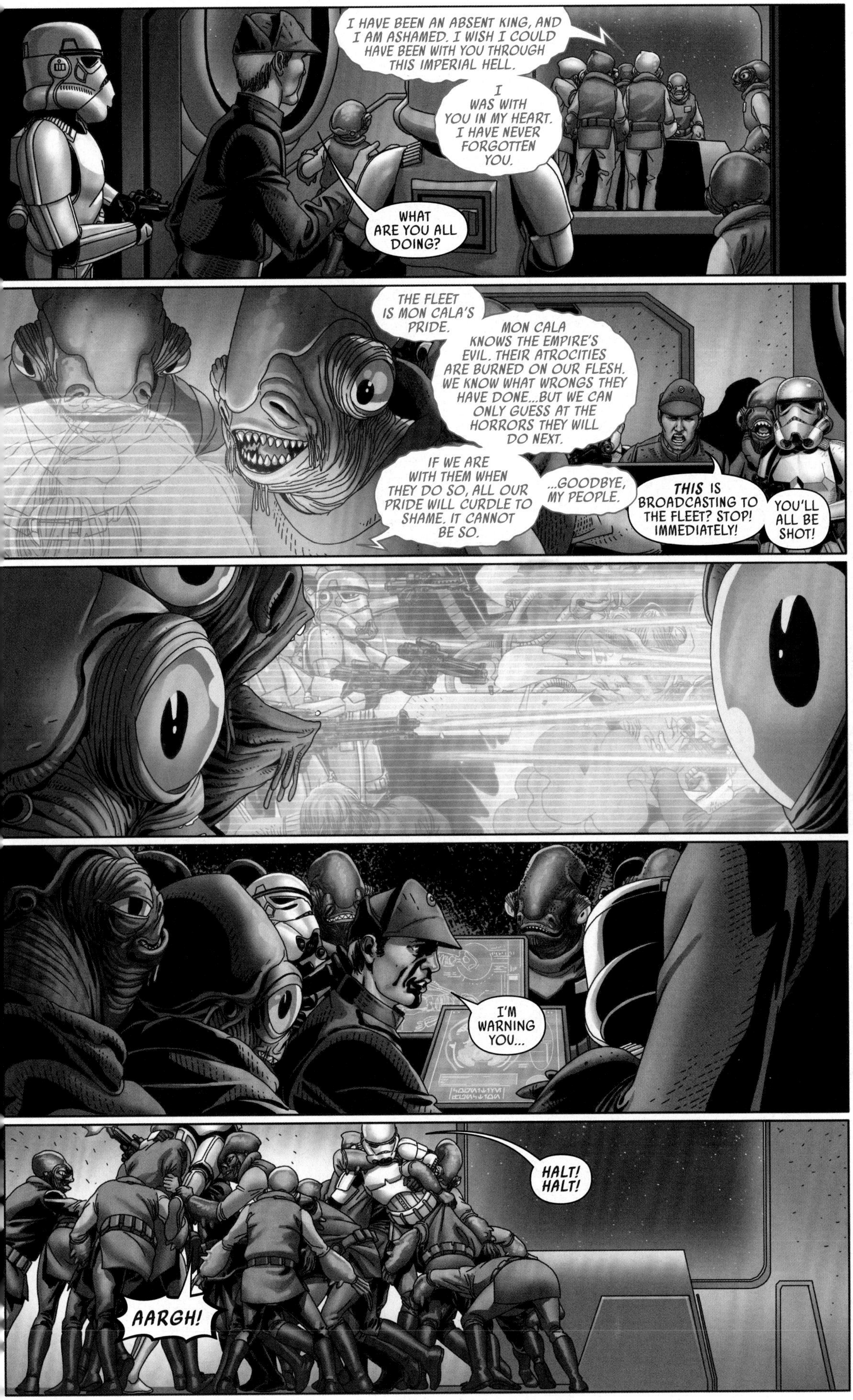
I HAVE BEEN AN ABSENT KING, AND I AM ASHAMED. I WISH I COULD HAVE BEEN WITH YOU THROUGH THIS IMPERIAL HELL.
I WAS WITH YOU IN MY HEART. I HAVE NEVER FORGOTTEN YOU.
WHAT ARE YOU ALL DOING?
THE FLEET IS MON CALA'S PRIDE.
MON CALA KNOWS THE EMPIRE'S EVIL. THEIR ATROCITIES ARE BURNED ON OUR FLESH. WE KNOW WHAT WRONGS THEY HAVE DONE...BUT WE CAN ONLY GUESS AT THE HORRORS THEY WILL DO NEXT.
IF WE ARE WITH THEM WHEN THEY DO SO, ALL OUR PRIDE WILL CURDLE TO SHAME. IT CANNOT BE SO.
...GOODBYE, MY PEOPLE.
THIS IS BROADCASTING TO THE FLEET? STOP! IMMEDIATELY!
YOU'LL ALL BE SHOT!
I'M WARNING YOU...
HALT! HALT!
AARGH!

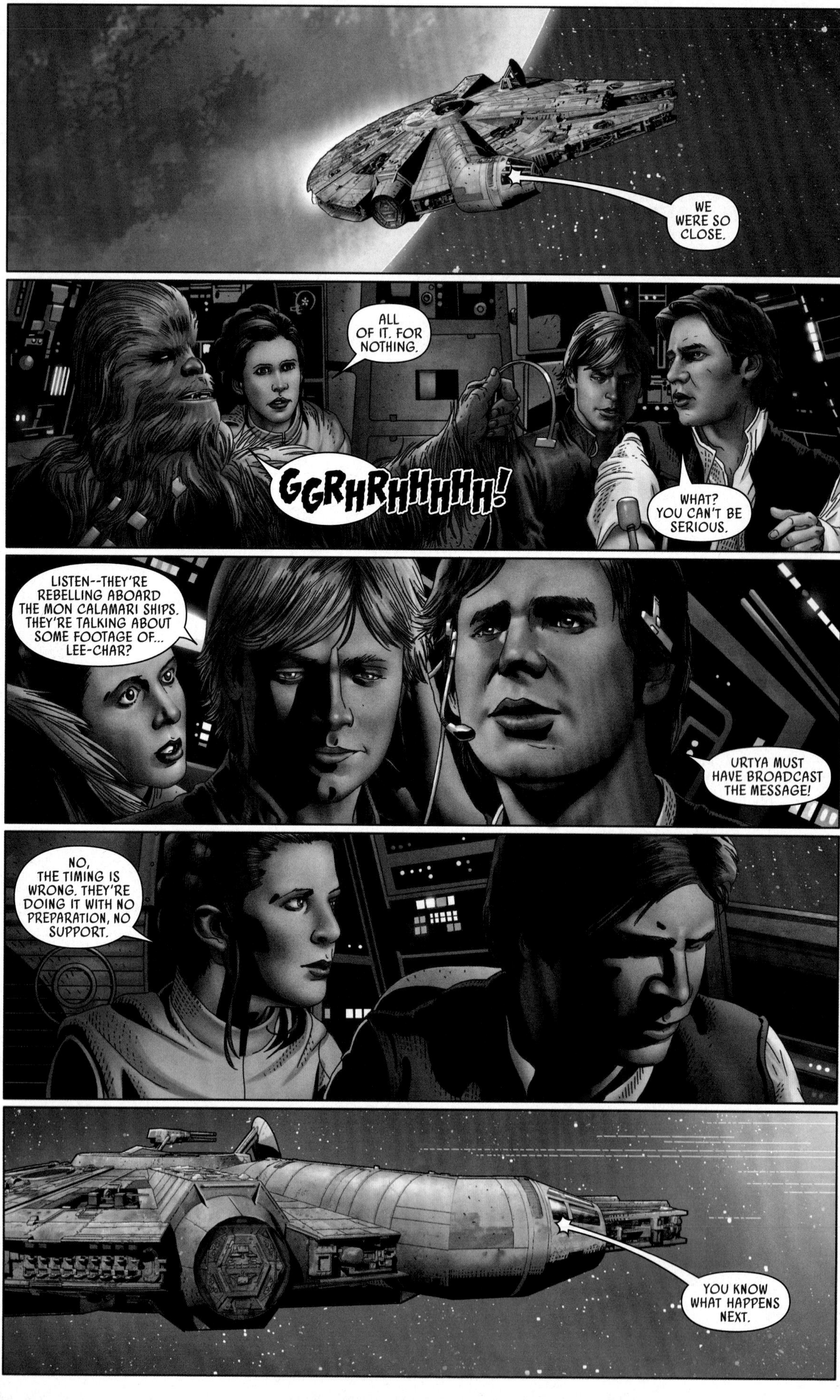
WE WERE SO CLOSE.
ALL OF IT. FOR NOTHING.
GGRHRHHHHH!
WHAT? YOU CAN'T BE SERIOUS.
LISTEN--THEY'RE REBELLING ABOARD THE MON CALAMARI SHIPS. THEY'RE TALKING ABOUT SOME FOOTAGE OF... LEE-CHAR?
URTYA MUST HAVE BROADCAST THE MESSAGE!
NO, THE TIMING IS WRONG. THEY'RE DOING IT WITH NO PREPARATION, NO SUPPORT.
YOU KNOW WHAT HAPPENS NEXT.

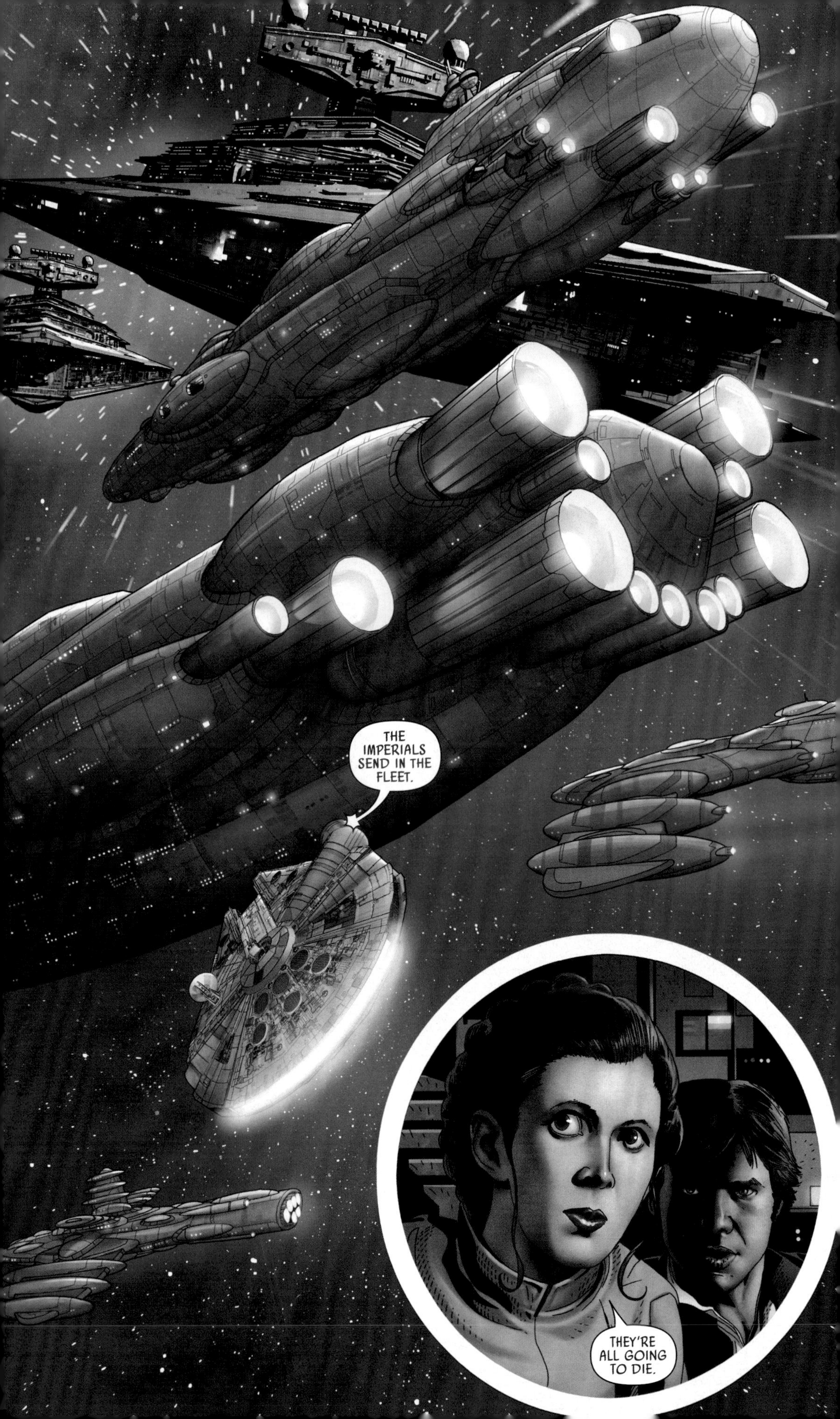
THE IMPERIALS SEND IN THE FLEET.
THEY'RE ALL GOING TO DIE.

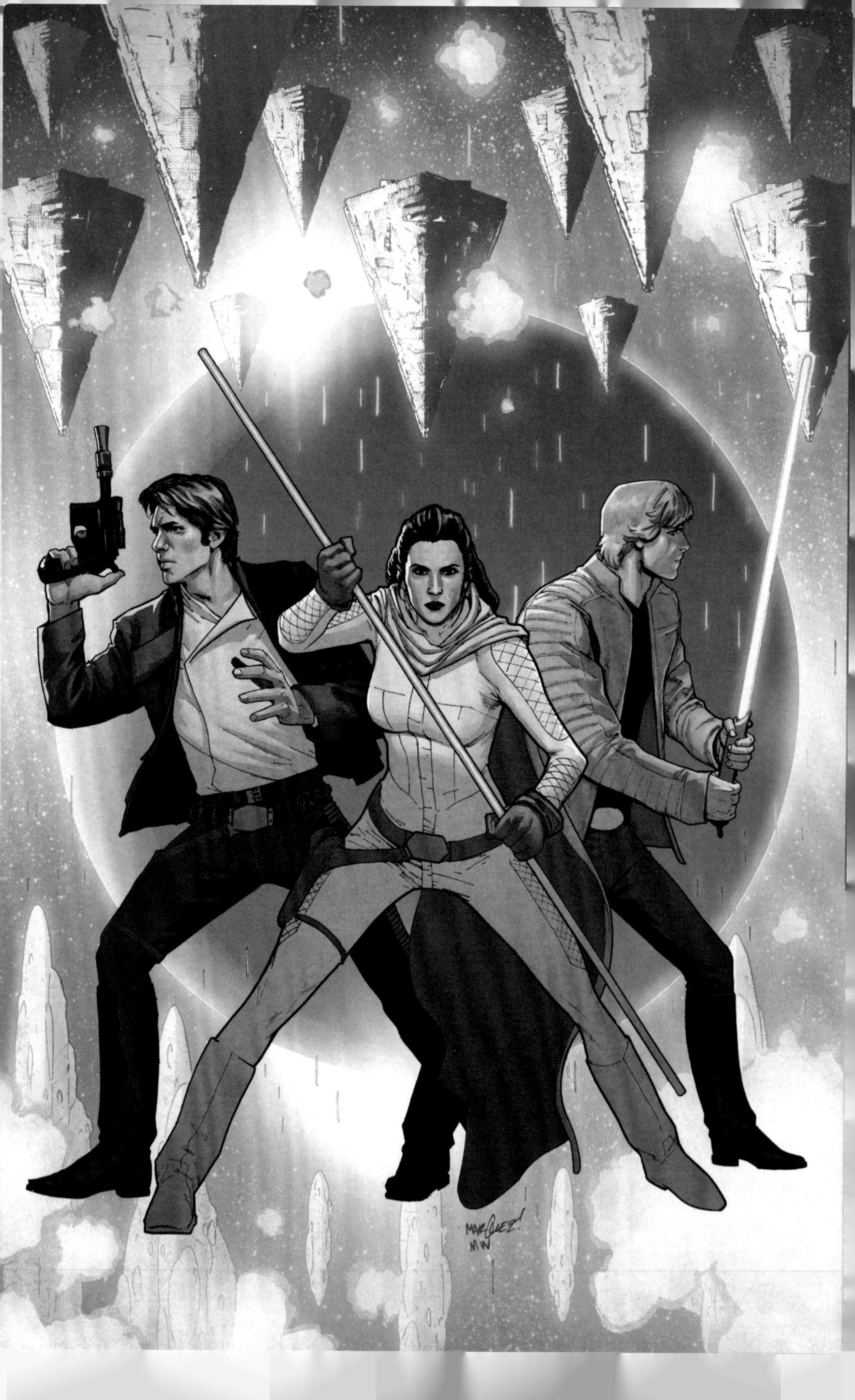

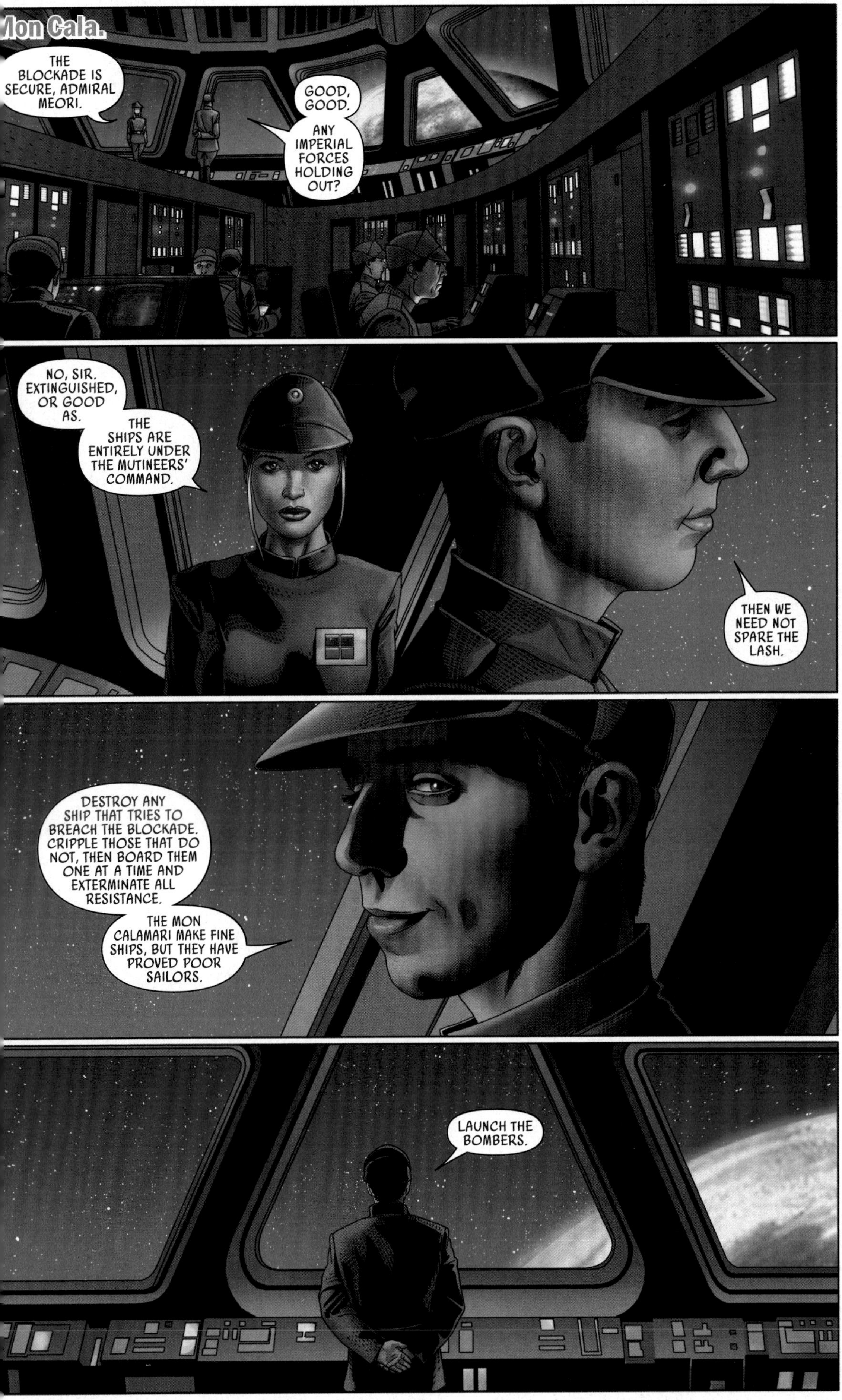

Mon Cala.
THE BLOCKADE IS SECURE, ADMIRAL MEORI.
GOOD, GOOD.
ANY IMPERIAL FORCES HOLDING OUT?
NO, SIR. EXTINGUISHED, OR GOOD AS.
THE SHIPS ARE ENTIRELY UNDER THE MUTINEERS' COMMAND.
THEN WE NEED NOT SPARE THE LASH.
DESTROY ANY SHIP THAT TRIES TO BREACH THE BLOCKADE. CRIPPLE THOSE THAT DO NOT, THEN BOARD THEM ONE AT A TIME AND EXTERMINATE ALL RESISTANCE.
THE MON CALAMARI MAKE FINE SHIPS, BUT THEY HAVE PROVED POOR SAILORS.
LAUNCH THE BOMBERS.

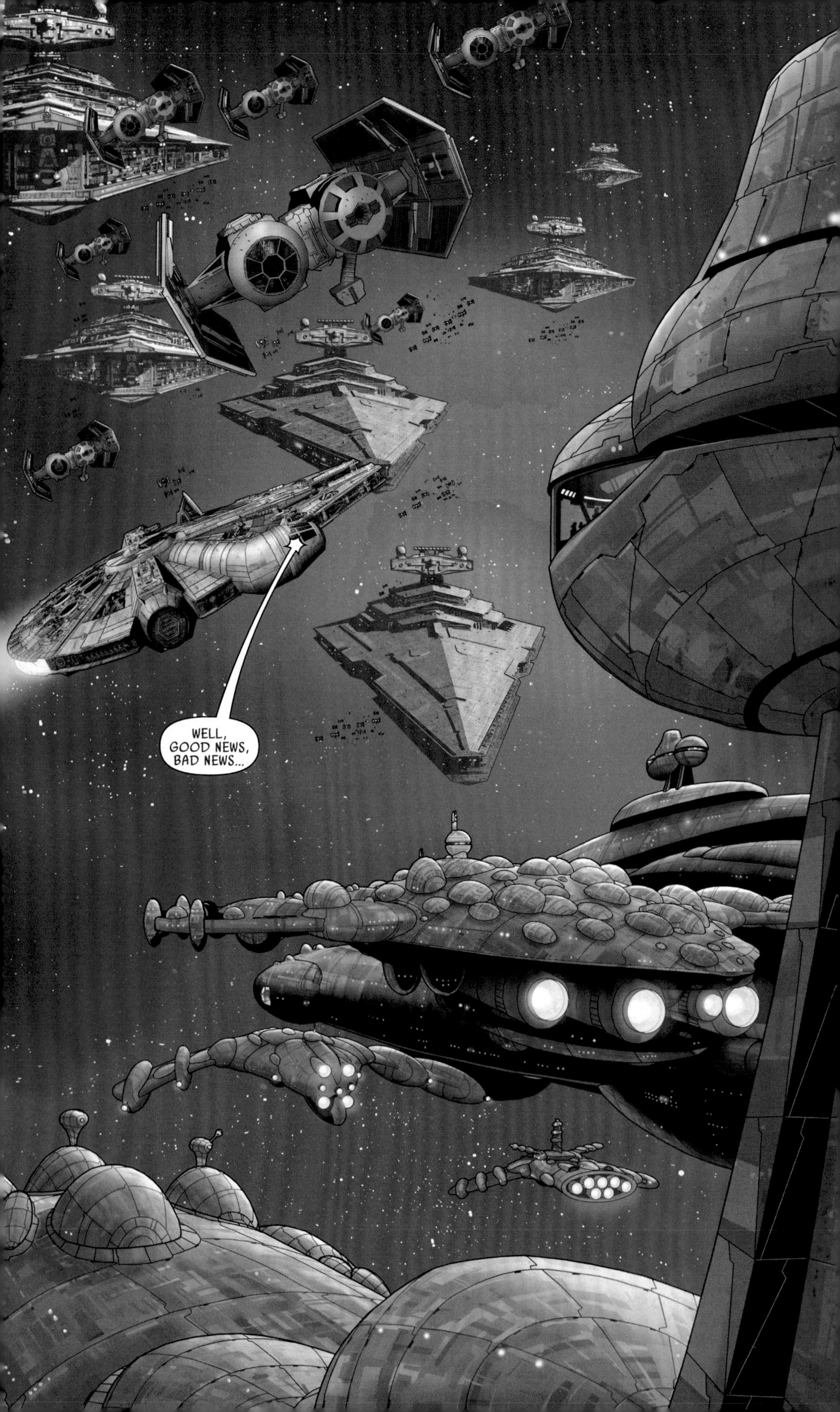
WELL, GOOD NEWS, BAD NEWS...

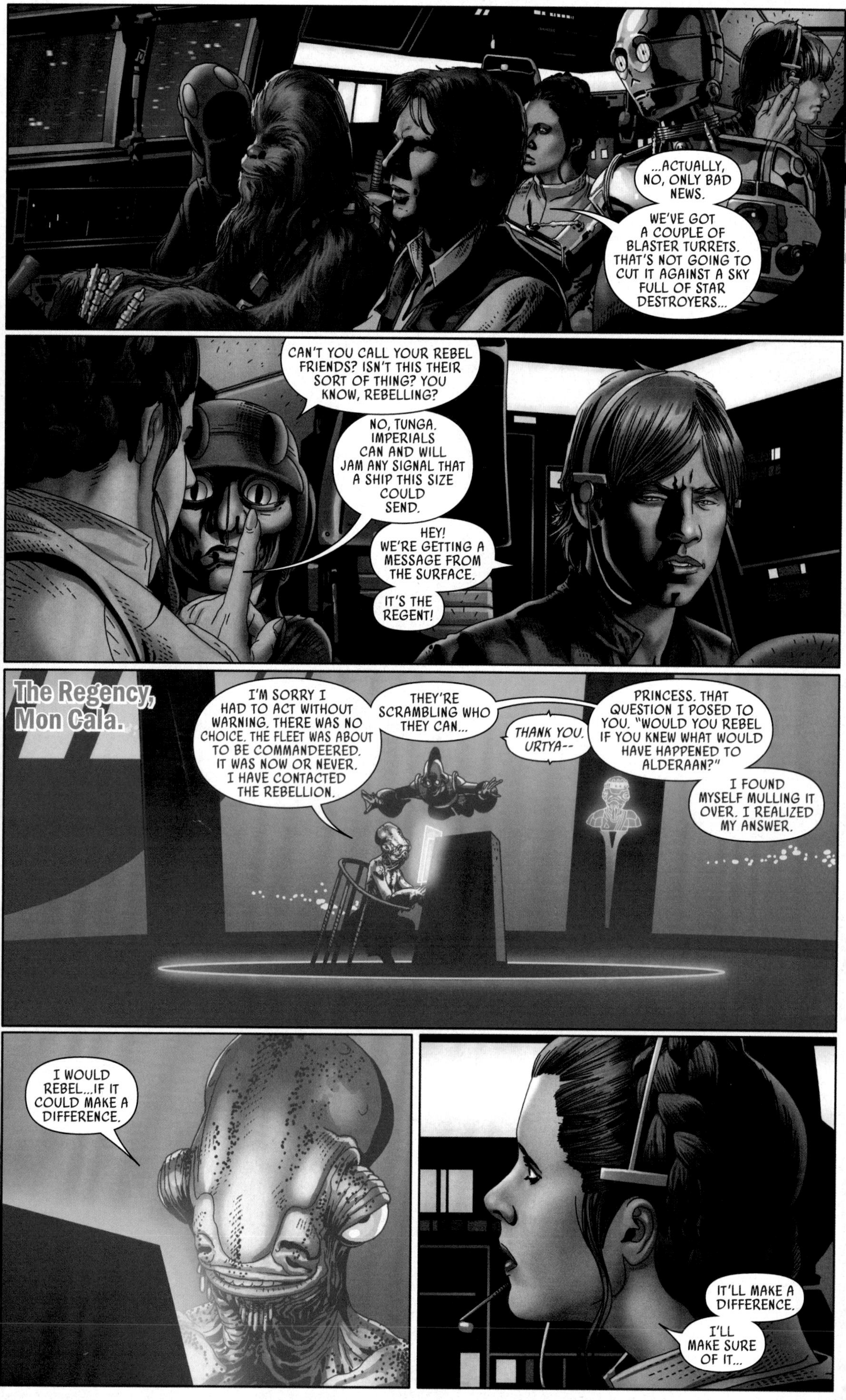
...ACTUALLY, NO, ONLY BAD NEWS.
WE'VE GOT A COUPLE OF BLASTER TURRETS. THAT'S NOT GOING TO CUT IT AGAINST A SKY FULL OF STAR DESTROYERS...
CAN'T YOU CALL YOUR REBEL FRIENDS? ISN'T THIS THEIR SORT OF THING? YOU KNOW, REBELLING?
NO, TUNGA. IMPERIALS CAN AND WILL JAM ANY SIGNAL THAT A SHIP THIS SIZE COULD SEND.
HEY! WE'RE GETTING A MESSAGE FROM THE SURFACE.
IT'S THE REGENT!
The Regency, Mon Cala.
I'M SORRY I HAD TO ACT WITHOUT WARNING. THERE WAS NO CHOICE. THE FLEET WAS ABOUT TO BE COMMANDEERED. IT WAS NOW OR NEVER. I HAVE CONTACTED THE REBELLION.
THEY'RE SCRAMBLING WHO THEY CAN...
THANK YOU, URTYA--
PRINCESS. THAT QUESTION I POSED TO YOU. "WOULD YOU REBEL IF YOU KNEW WHAT WOULD HAVE HAPPENED TO ALDERAAN?"
I FOUND MYSELF MULLING IT OVER. I REALIZED MY ANSWER.
I WOULD REBEL...IF IT COULD MAKE A DIFFERENCE.
IT'LL MAKE A DIFFERENCE.
I'LL MAKE SURE OF IT...

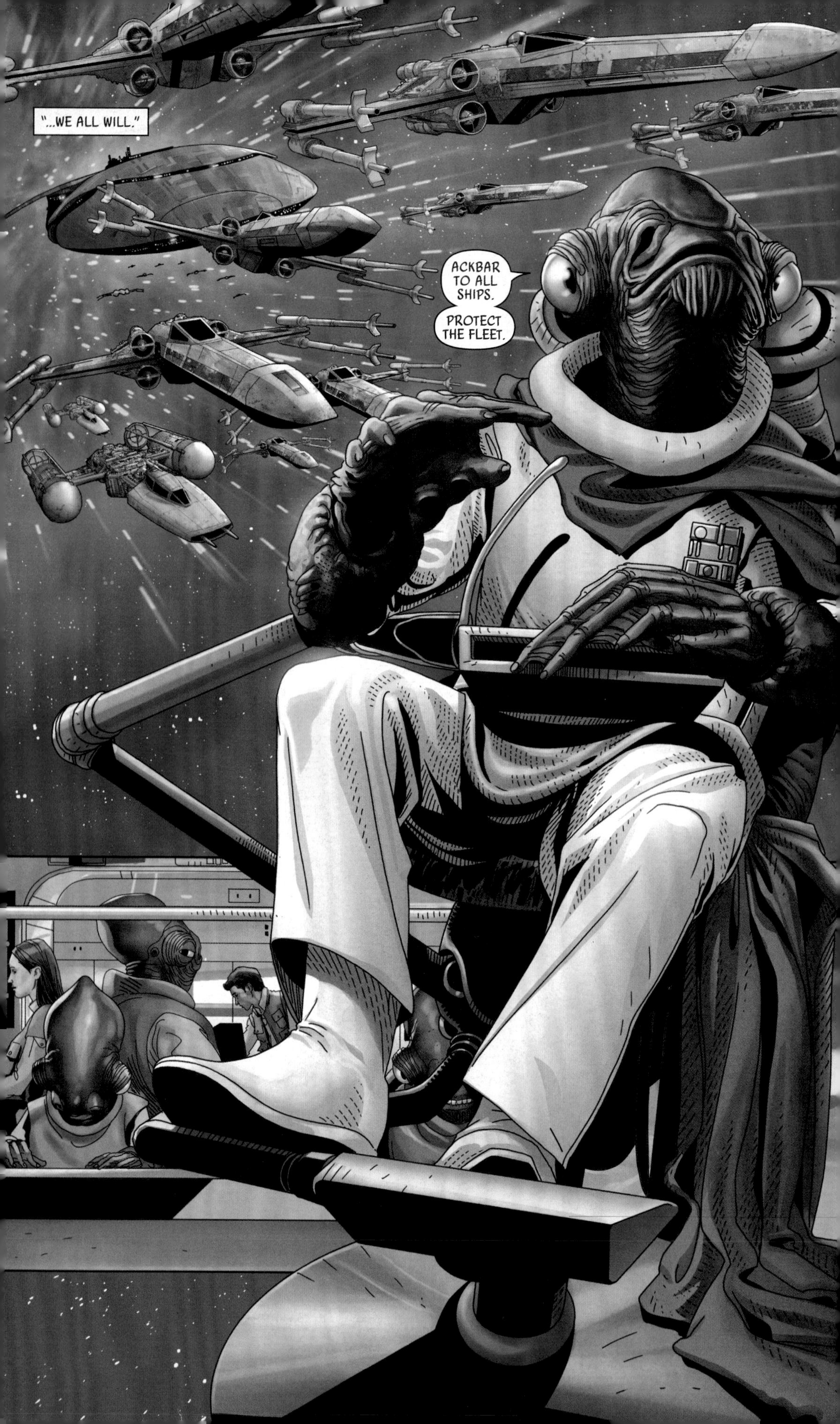
"...WE ALL WILL."
ACKBAR TO ALL SHIPS.
PROTECT THE FLEET.

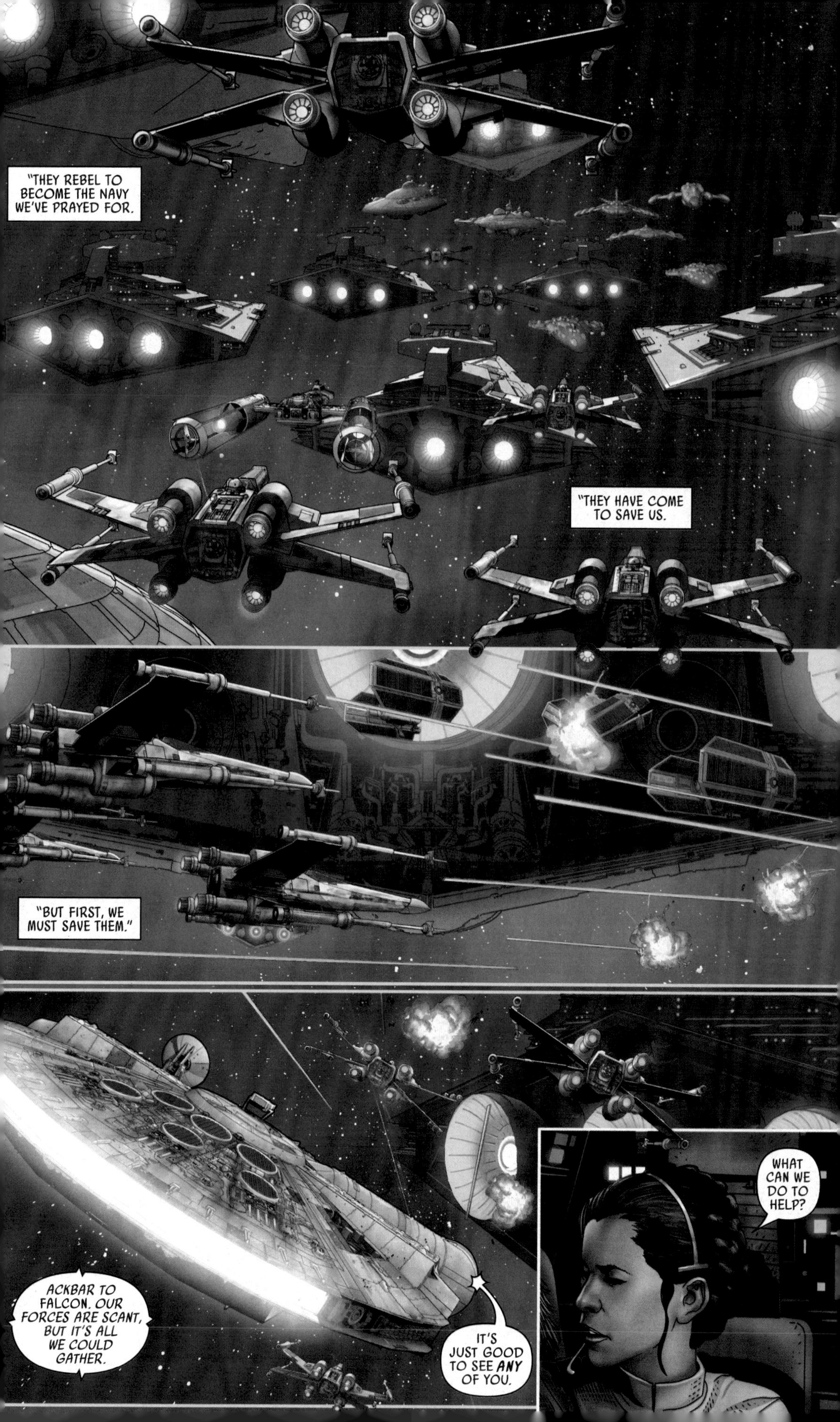
"THEY REBEL TO BECOME THE NAVY WE'VE PRAYED FOR.
"THEY HAVE COME TO SAVE US.
"BUT FIRST, WE MUST SAVE THEM."
ACKBAR TO FALCON. OUR FORCES ARE SCANT, BUT IT'S ALL WE COULD GATHER.
IT'S JUST GOOD TO SEE ANY OF YOU.
WHAT CAN WE DO TO HELP?

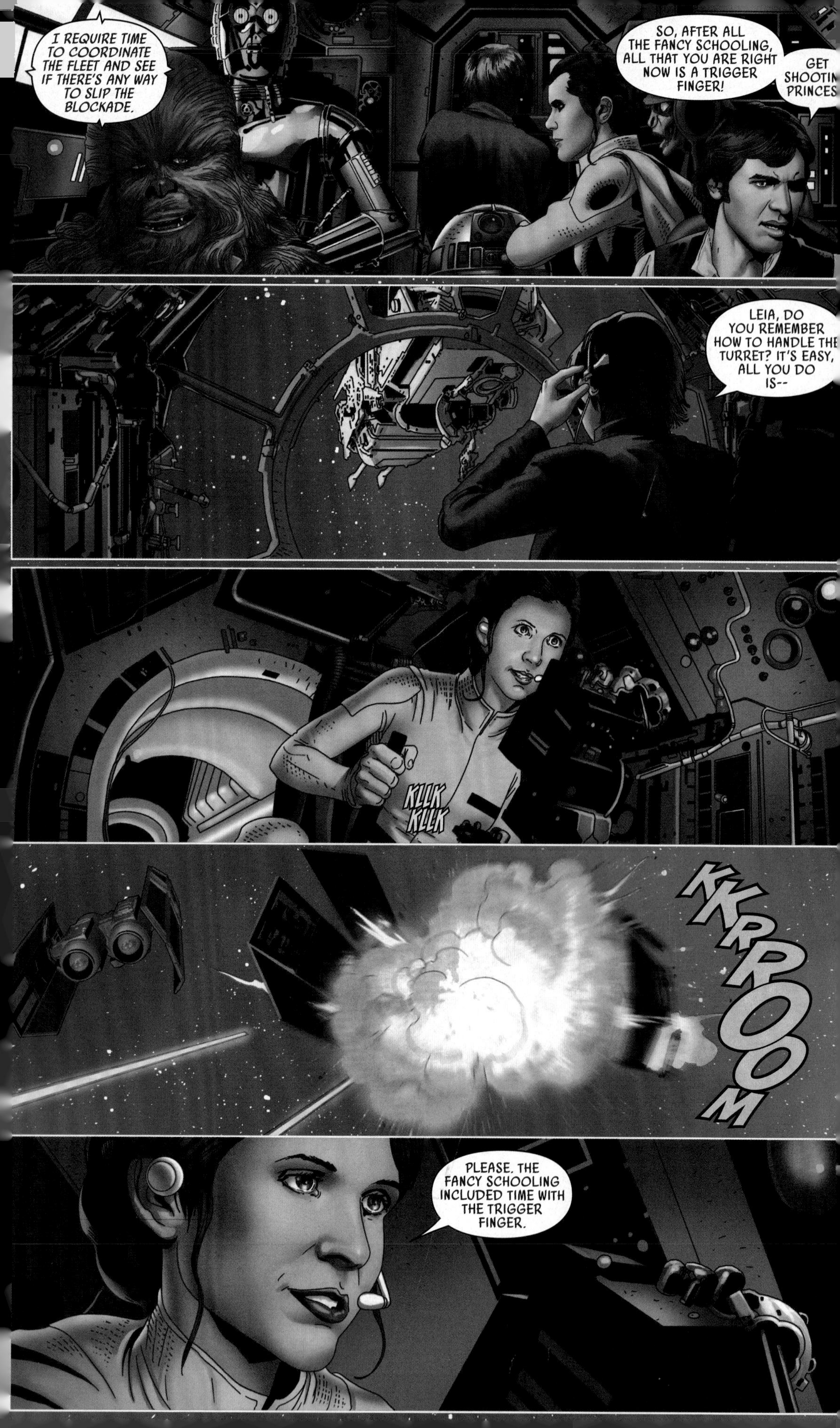
I REQUIRE TIME TO COORDINATE THE FLEET AND SEE IF THERE'S ANY WAY TO SLIP THE BLOCKADE.
SO, AFTER ALL THE FANCY SCHOOLING, ALL THAT YOU ARE RIGHT NOW IS A TRIGGER FINGER!
GET SHOOTIN PRINCES
LEIA, DO YOU REMEMBER HOW TO HANDLE THE TURRET? IT'S EASY, ALL YOU DO IS--
KLLK KLLK
KKRROOOM
PLEASE. THE FANCY SCHOOLING INCLUDED TIME WITH THE TRIGGER FINGER.

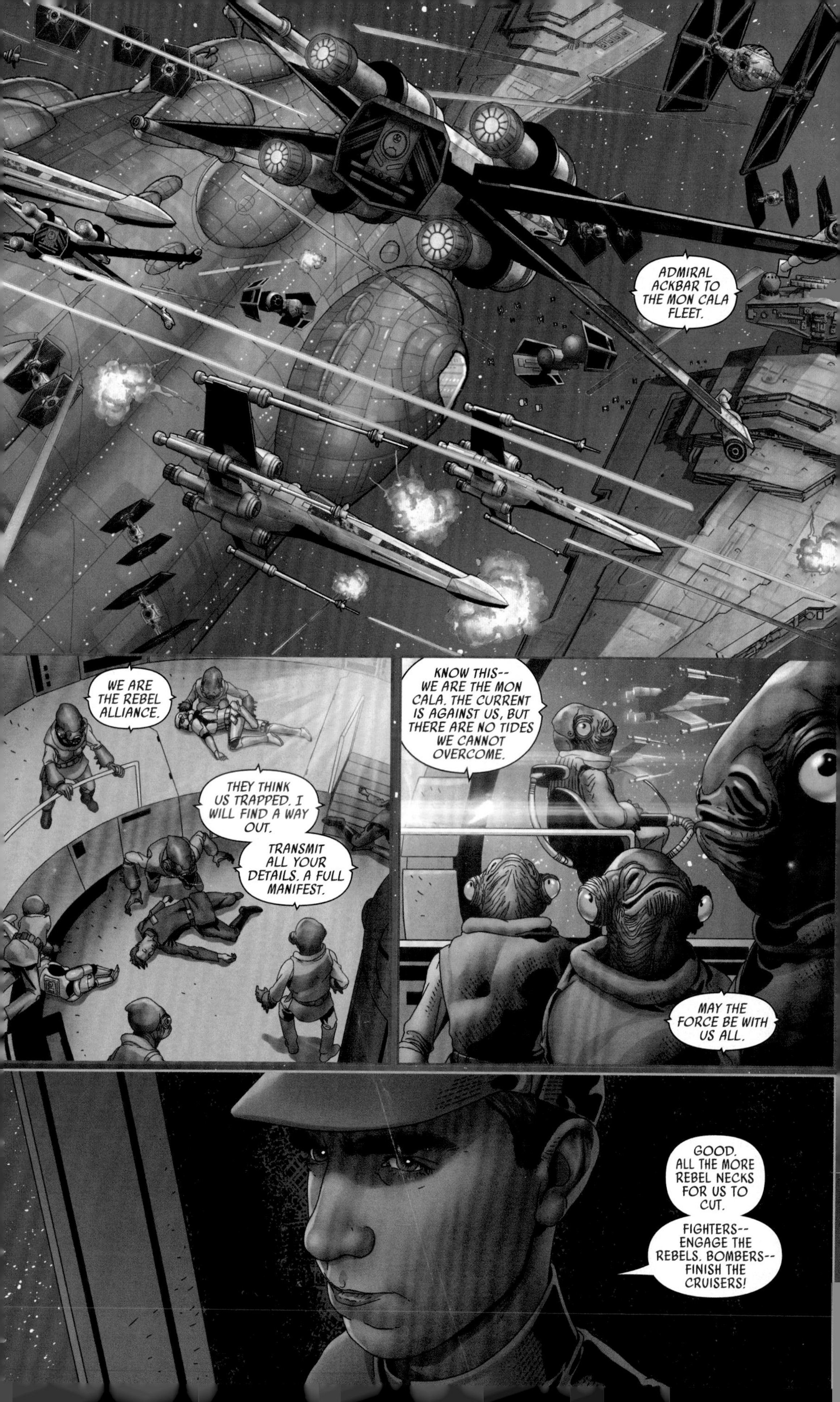
ADMIRAL ACKBAR TO THE MON CALA FLEET.
WE ARE THE REBEL ALLIANCE.
THEY THINK US TRAPPED. I WILL FIND A WAY OUT.
TRANSMIT ALL YOUR DETAILS. A FULL MANIFEST.
KNOW THIS-- WE ARE THE MON CALA. THE CURRENT IS AGAINST US, BUT THERE ARE NO TIDES WE CANNOT OVERCOME.
MAY THE FORCE BE WITH US ALL.
GOOD. ALL THE MORE REBEL NECKS FOR US TO CUT.
FIGHTERS-- ENGAGE THE REBELS. BOMBERS-- FINISH THE CRUISERS!

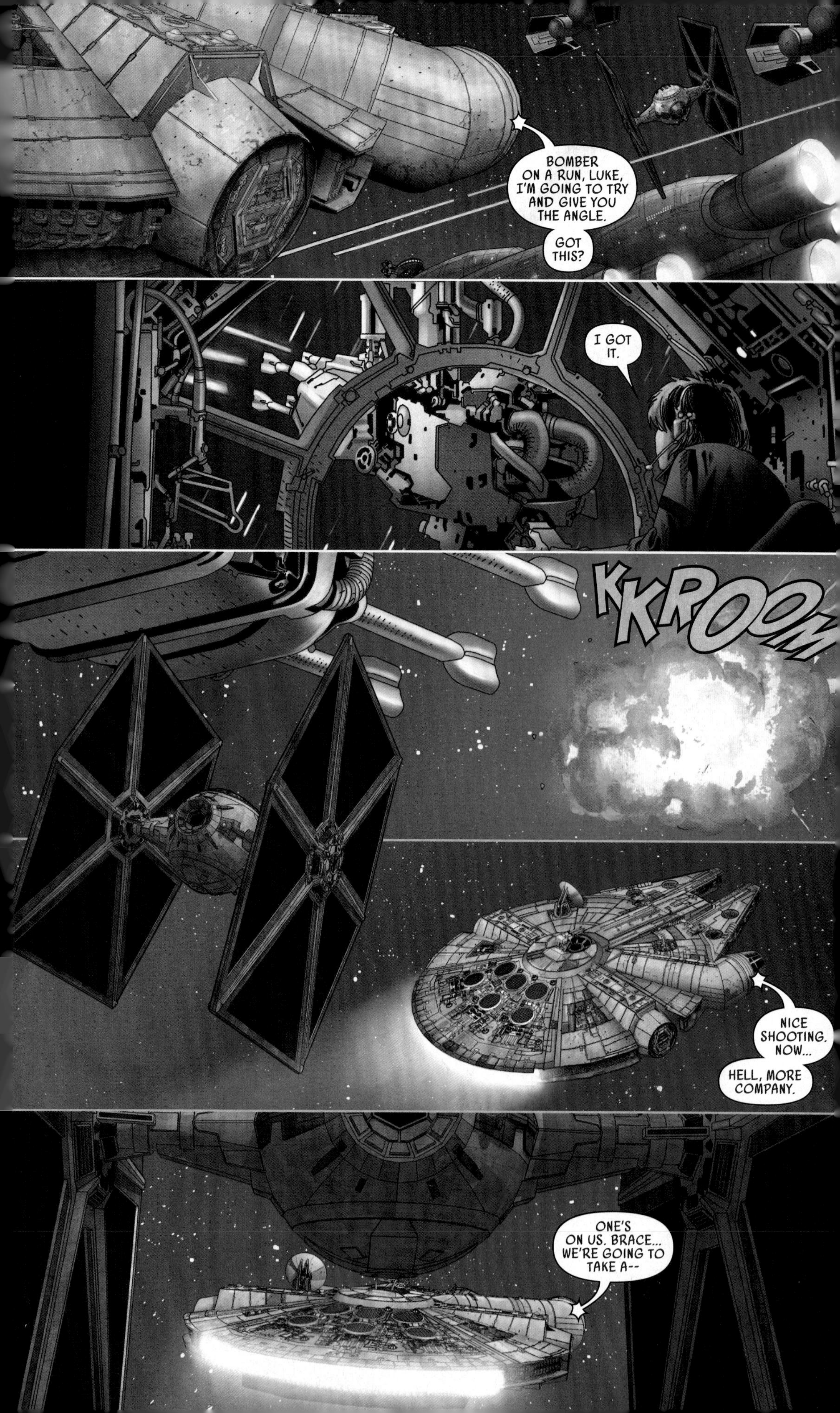
BOMBER ON A RUN, LUKE, I'M GOING TO TRY AND GIVE YOU THE ANGLE.
GOT THIS?
I GOT IT.
KKROOOM
NICE SHOOTING. NOW...
HELL, MORE COMPANY.
ONE'S ON US. BRACE... WE'RE GOING TO TAKE A--

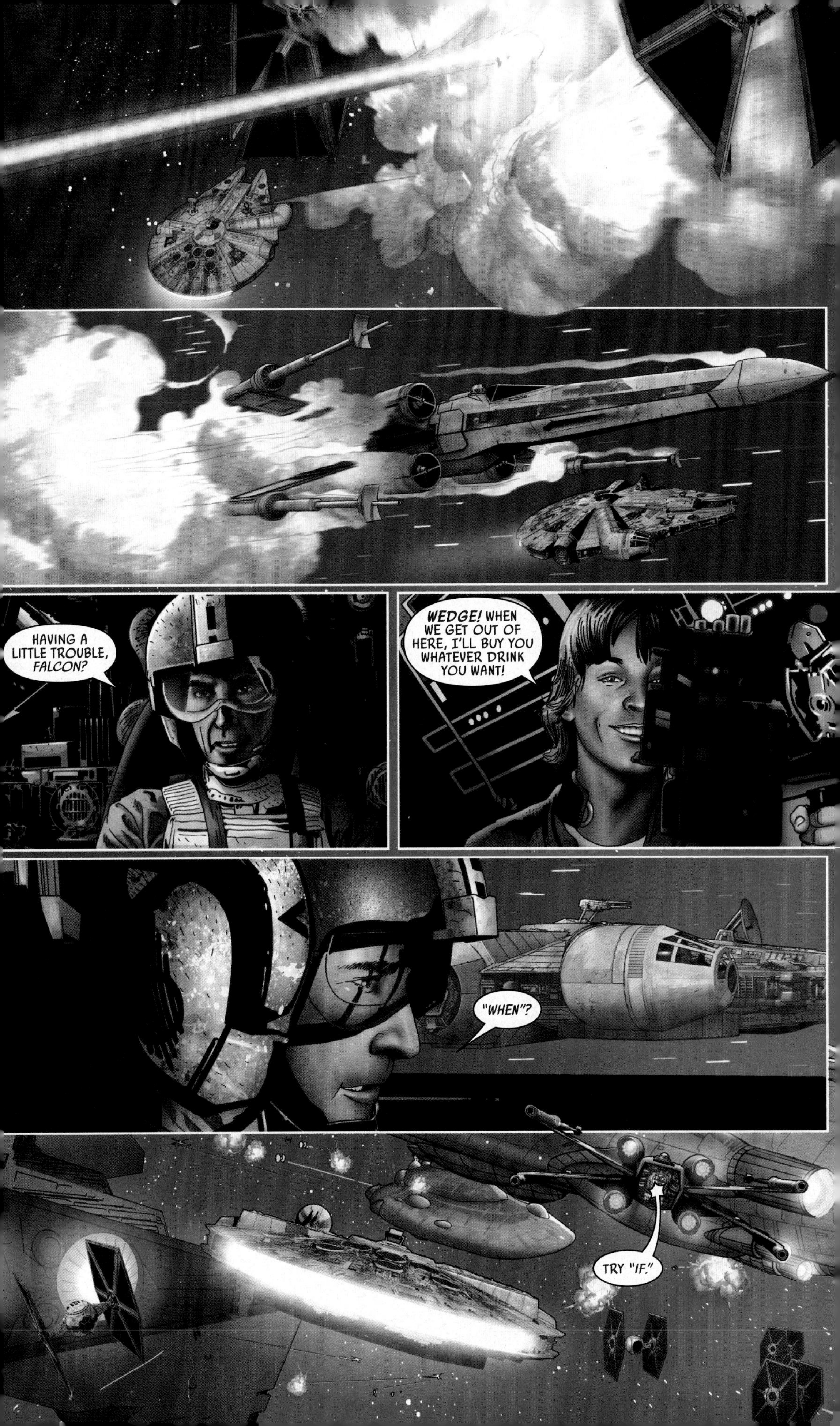
HAVING A LITTLE TROUBLE, FALCON?
WEDGE! WHEN WE GET OUT OF HERE, I'LL BUY YOU WHATEVER DRINK YOU WANT!
"WHEN"?
TRY "IF."

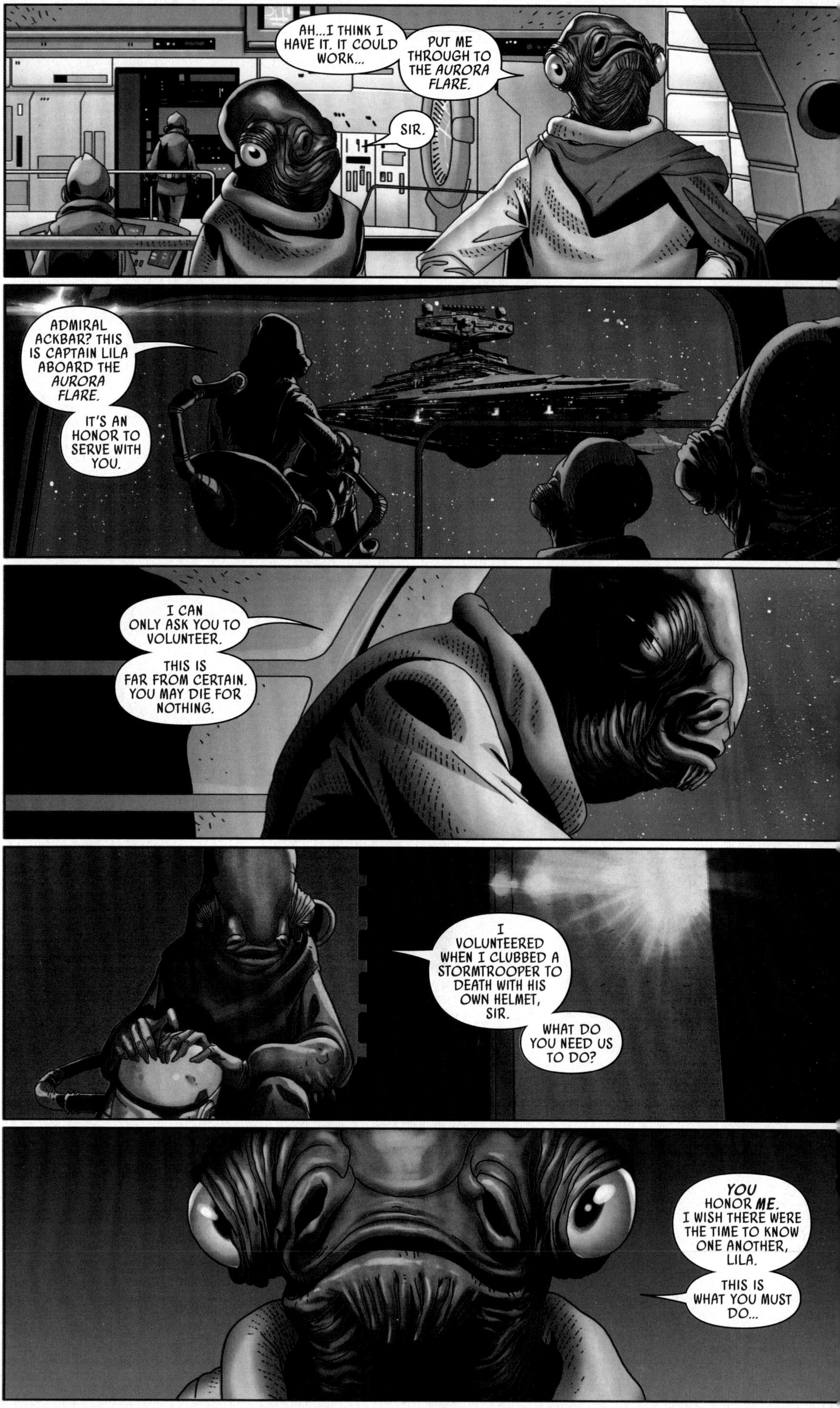

AH...I THINK I HAVE IT. IT COULD WORK...
PUT ME THROUGH TO THE *AURORA FLARE.*
SIR.
ADMIRAL ACKBAR? THIS IS CAPTAIN LILA ABOARD THE *AURORA FLARE.*
IT'S AN HONOR TO SERVE WITH YOU.
I CAN ONLY ASK YOU TO VOLUNTEER.
THIS IS FAR FROM CERTAIN. YOU MAY DIE FOR NOTHING.
I VOLUNTEERED WHEN I CLUBBED A STORMTROOPER TO DEATH WITH HIS OWN HELMET, SIR.
WHAT DO YOU NEED US TO DO?
YOU HONOR ***ME.*** I WISH THERE WERE THE TIME TO KNOW ONE ANOTHER, LILA.
THIS IS WHAT YOU MUST DO...

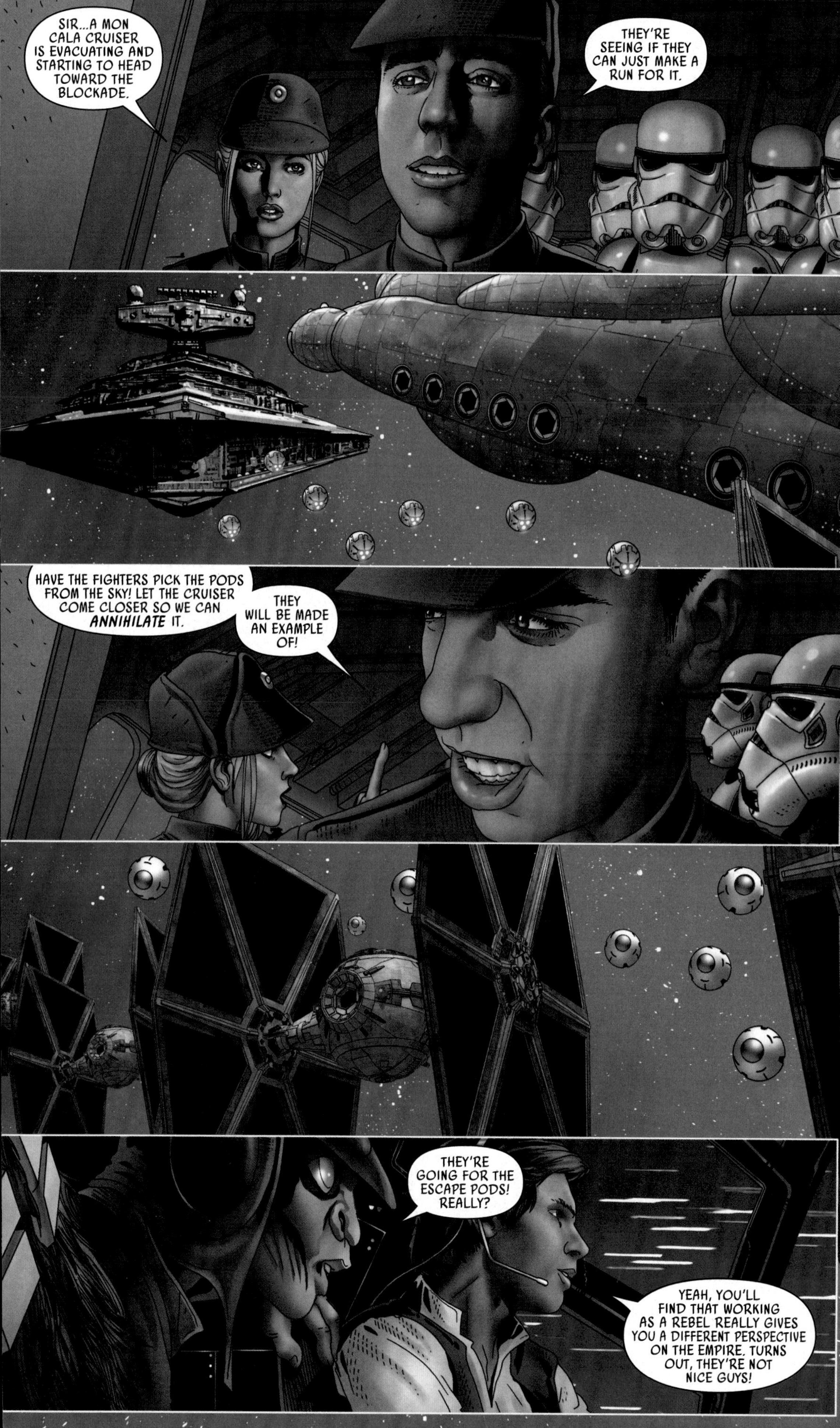
SIR...A MON CALA CRUISER IS EVACUATING AND STARTING TO HEAD TOWARD THE BLOCKADE.
THEY'RE SEEING IF THEY CAN JUST MAKE A RUN FOR IT.
HAVE THE FIGHTERS PICK THE PODS FROM THE SKY! LET THE CRUISER COME CLOSER SO WE CAN ANNIHILATE IT.
THEY WILL BE MADE AN EXAMPLE OF!
THEY'RE GOING FOR THE ESCAPE PODS! REALLY?
YEAH, YOU'LL FIND THAT WORKING AS A REBEL REALLY GIVES YOU A DIFFERENT PERSPECTIVE ON THE EMPIRE. TURNS OUT, THEY'RE NOT NICE GUYS!

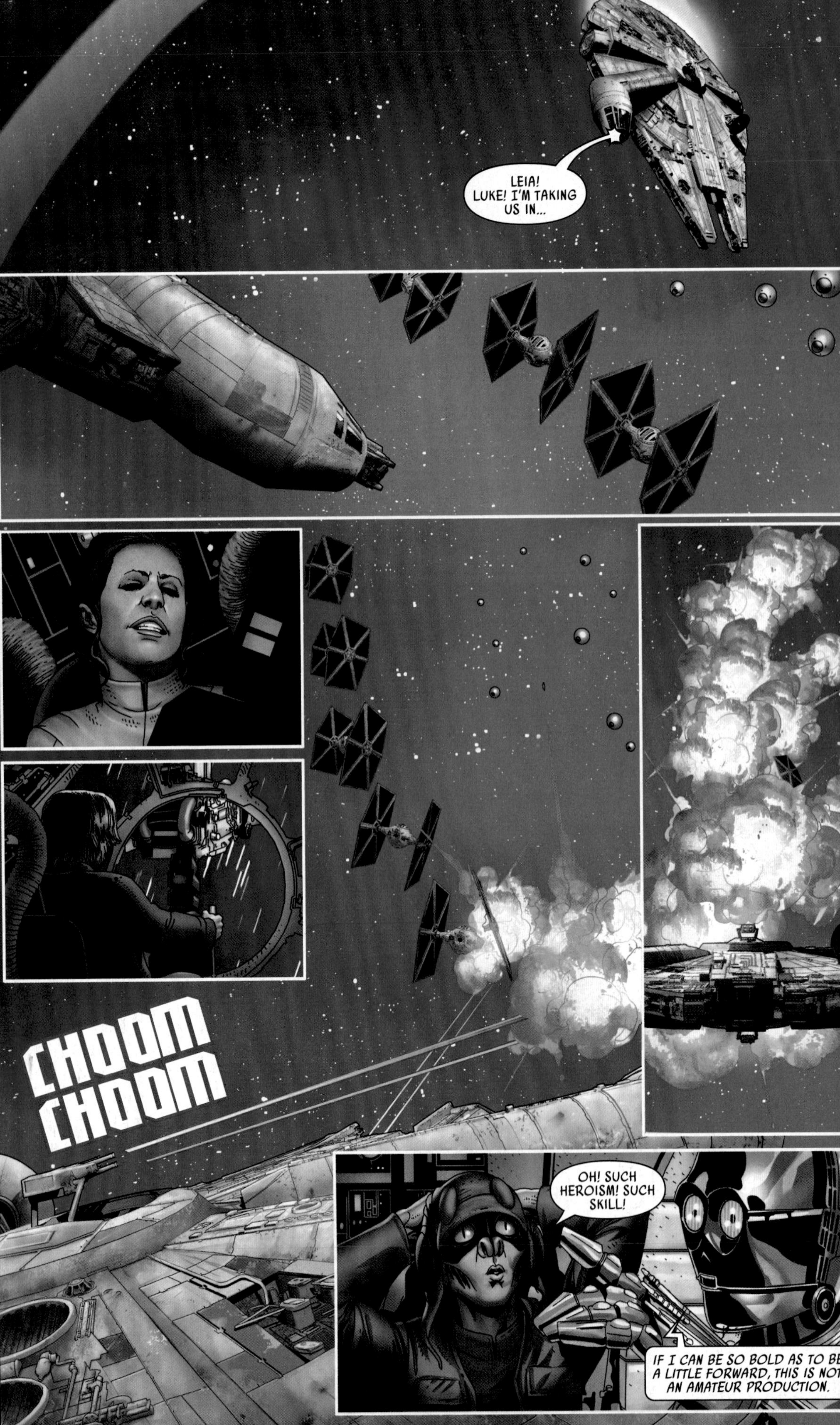
LEIA!
LUKE! I'M TAKING
US IN...
CHOOM
CHOOM
OH! SUCH
HEROISM! SUCH
SKILL!
IF I CAN BE SO BOLD AS TO BE
A LITTLE FORWARD, THIS IS NOT
AN AMATEUR PRODUCTION.

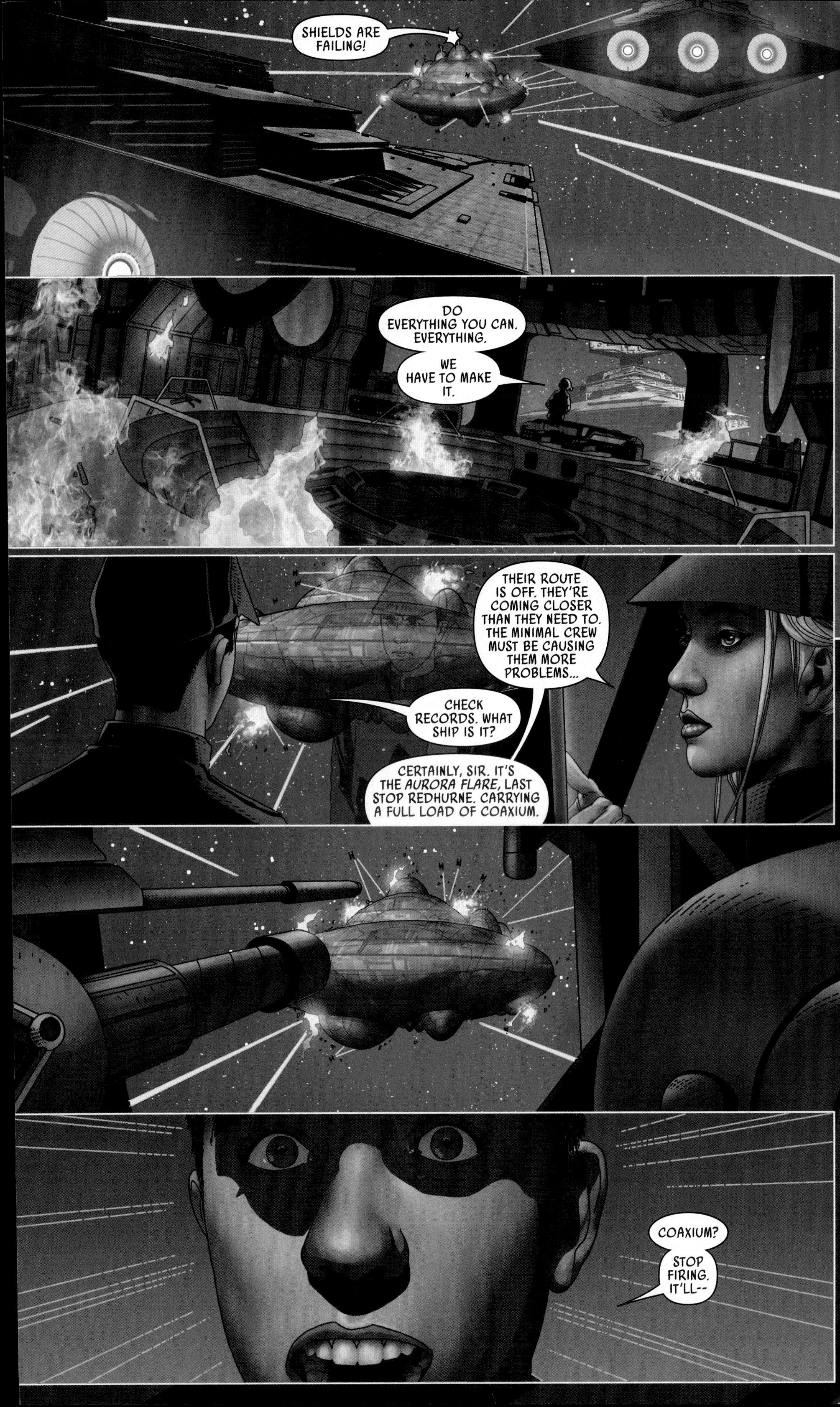

SHIELDS ARE FAILING!
DO EVERYTHING YOU CAN. EVERYTHING.
WE HAVE TO MAKE IT.
THEIR ROUTE IS OFF. THEY'RE COMING CLOSER THAN THEY NEED TO. THE MINIMAL CREW MUST BE CAUSING THEM MORE PROBLEMS...
CHECK RECORDS. WHAT SHIP IS IT?
CERTAINLY, SIR. IT'S THE *AURORA FLARE*, LAST STOP REDHURNE. CARRYING A FULL LOAD OF COAXIUM.
COAXIUM?
STOP FIRING. IT'LL--

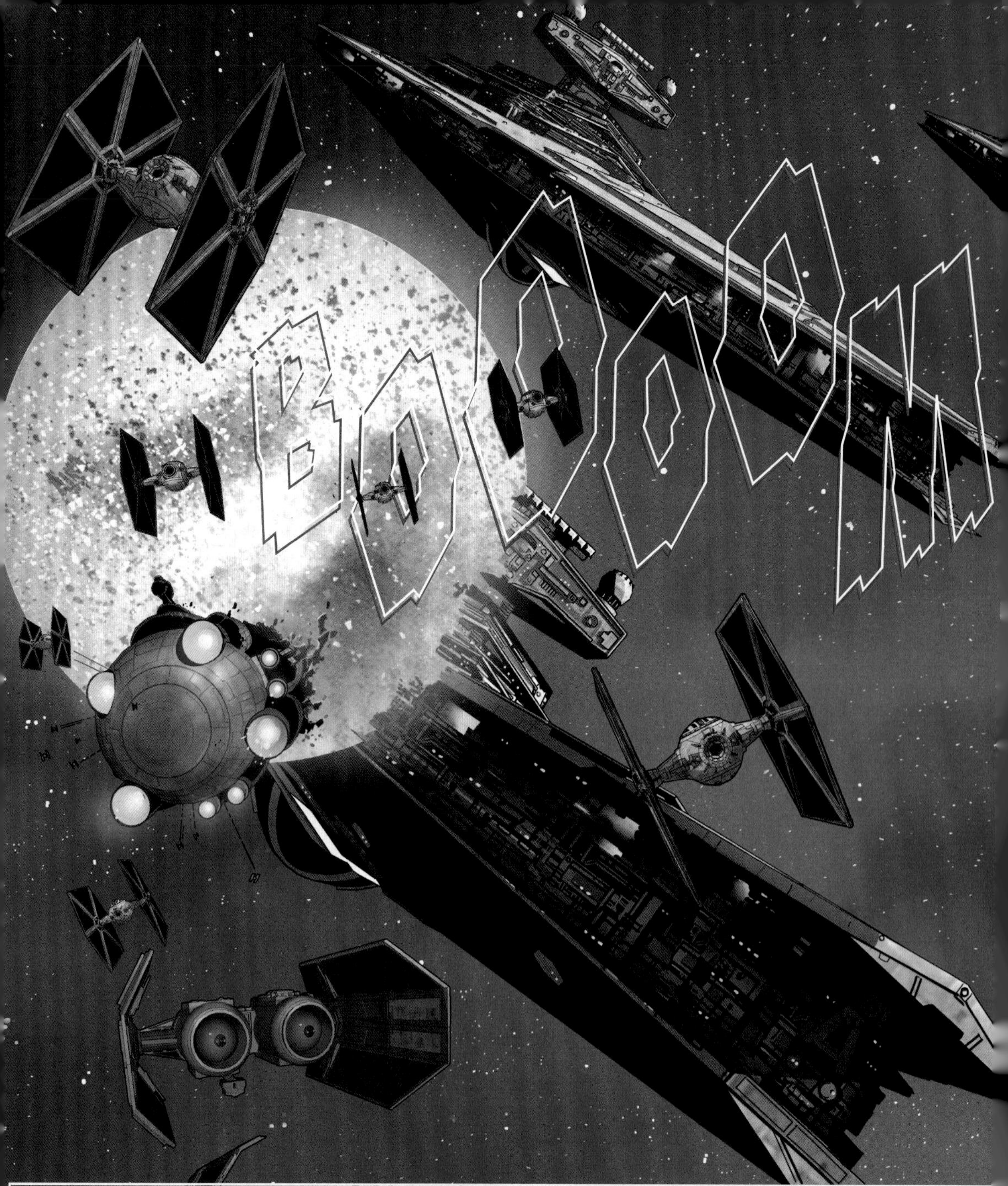
BOOOOM

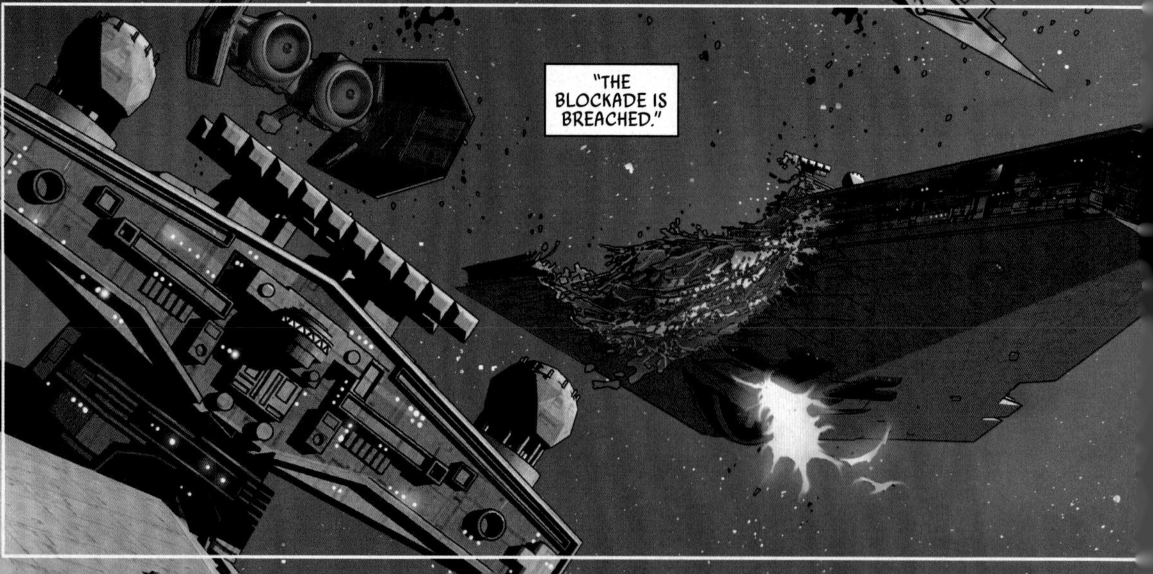
"THE BLOCKADE IS BREACHED."

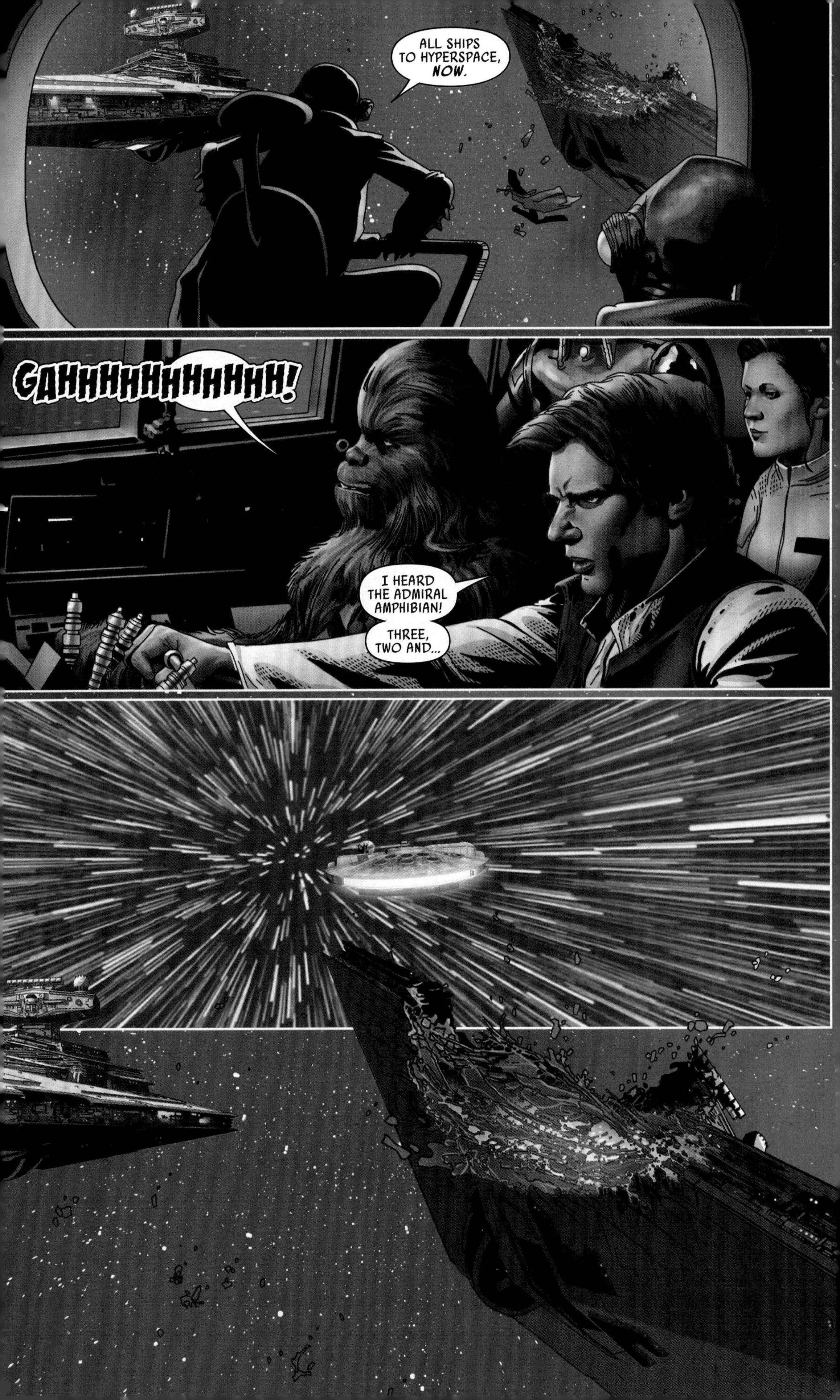
ALL SHIPS TO HYPERSPACE, NOW.
GAHHHHHHHHHHH!
I HEARD THE ADMIRAL AMPHIBIAN!
THREE, TWO AND...

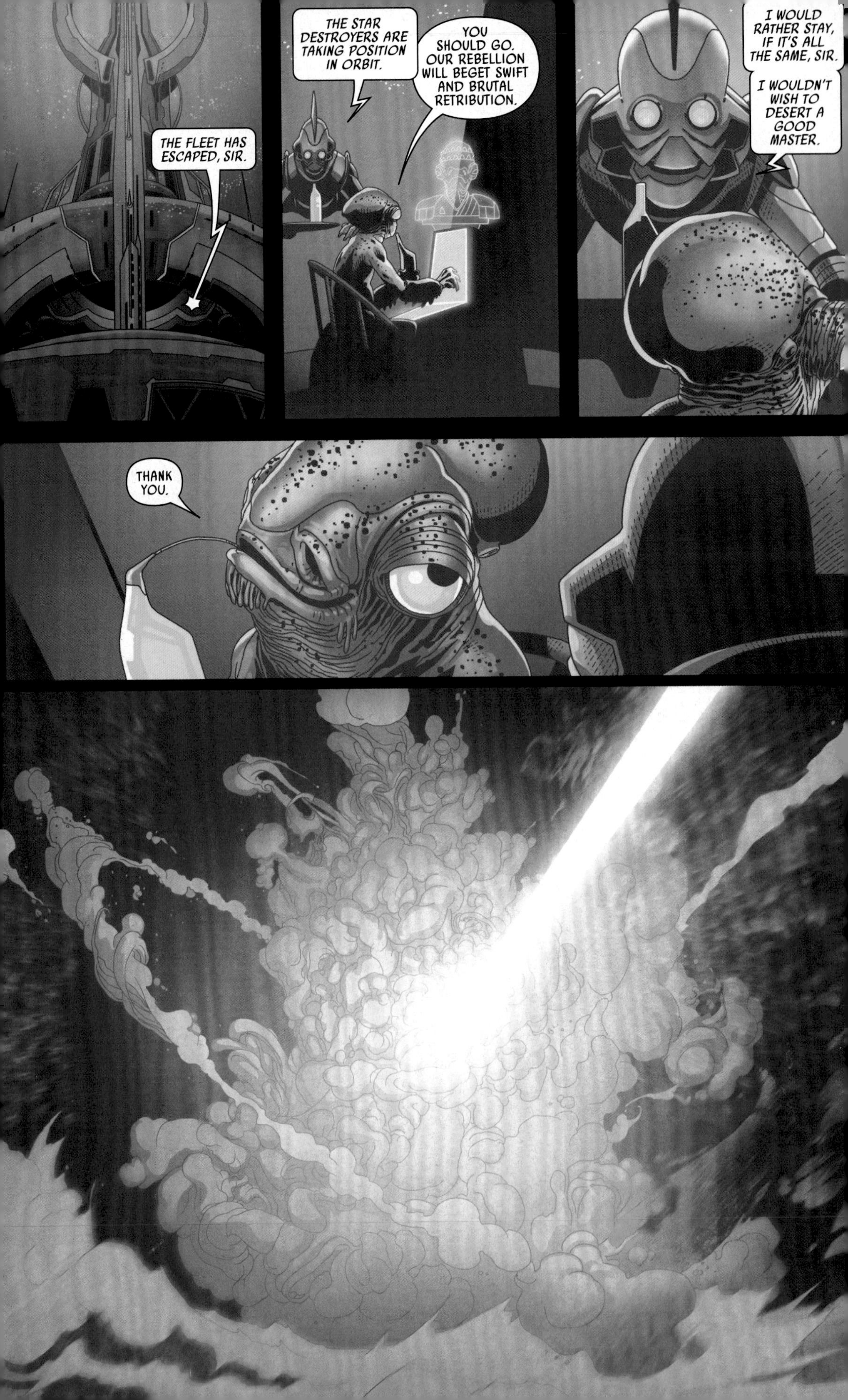
THE FLEET HAS ESCAPED, SIR.
THE STAR DESTROYERS ARE TAKING POSITION IN ORBIT.
YOU SHOULD GO. OUR REBELLION WILL BEGET SWIFT AND BRUTAL RETRIBUTION.
I WOULD RATHER STAY, IF IT'S ALL THE SAME, SIR.
I WOULDN'T WISH TO DESERT A GOOD MASTER.
THANK YOU.

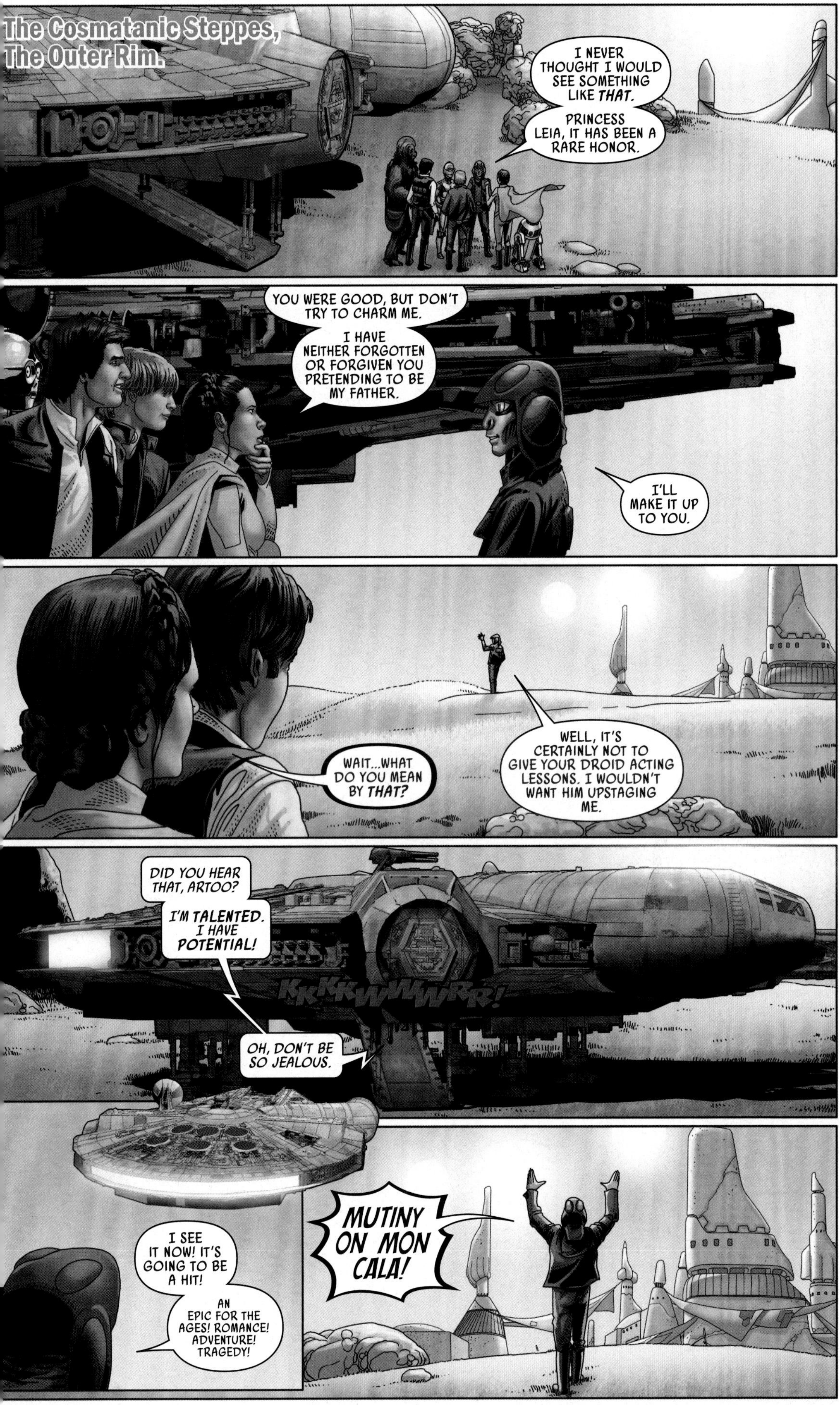
The Cosmatanic Steppes, The Outer Rim.
I NEVER THOUGHT I WOULD SEE SOMETHING LIKE *THAT*.
PRINCESS LEIA, IT HAS BEEN A RARE HONOR.
YOU WERE GOOD, BUT DON'T TRY TO CHARM ME.
I HAVE NEITHER FORGOTTEN OR FORGIVEN YOU PRETENDING TO BE MY FATHER.
I'LL MAKE IT UP TO YOU.
WAIT...WHAT DO YOU MEAN BY *THAT?*
WELL, IT'S CERTAINLY NOT TO GIVE YOUR DROID ACTING LESSONS. I WOULDN'T WANT HIM UPSTAGING ME.
DID YOU HEAR THAT, ARTOO?
I'M **TALENTED**. I HAVE **POTENTIAL!**
KKKKWWWWRR!
OH, DON'T BE SO JEALOUS.
I SEE IT NOW! IT'S GOING TO BE A HIT!
AN EPIC FOR THE AGES! ROMANCE! ADVENTURE! TRAGEDY!
MUTINY ON MON CALA!

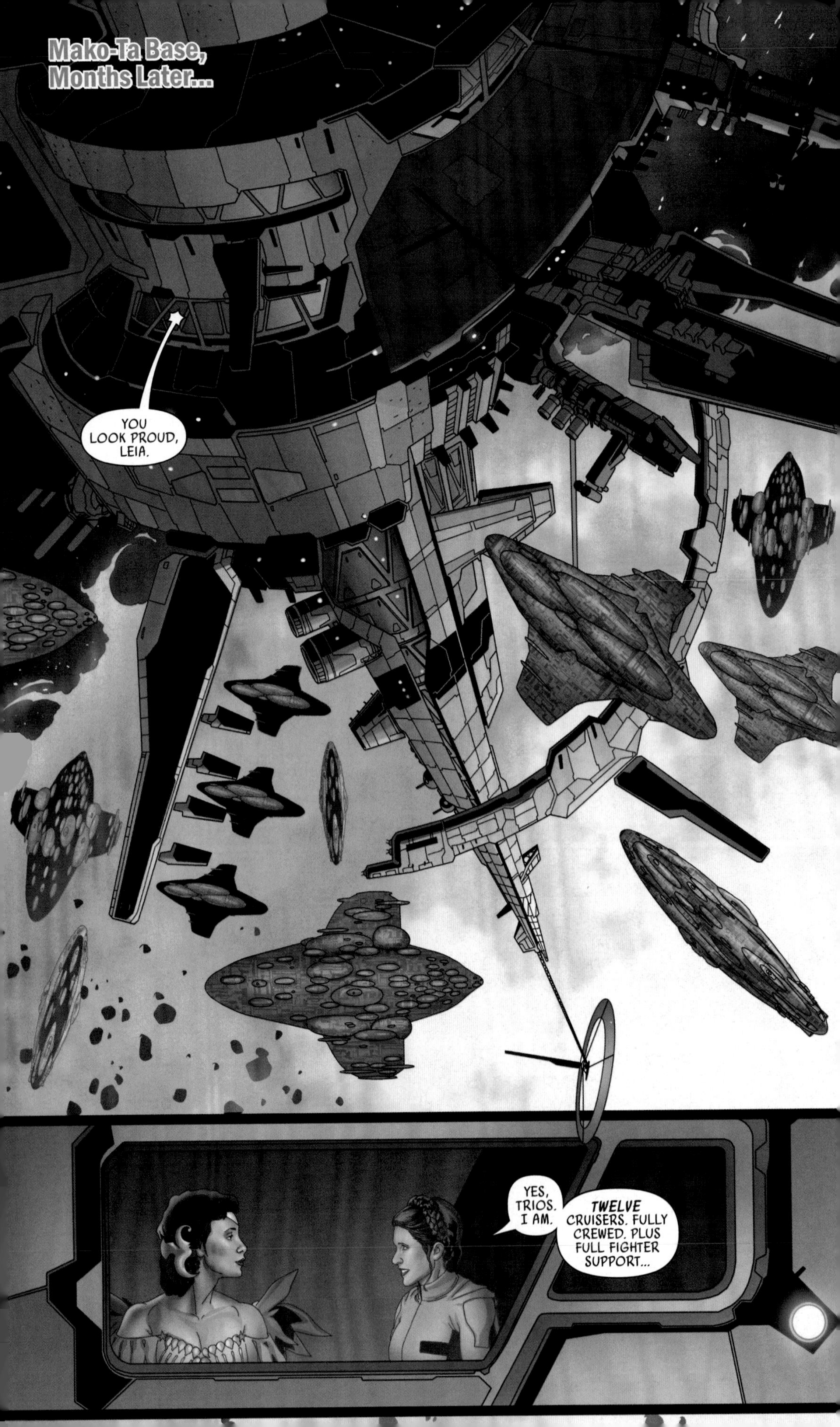
Mako-Ta Base, Months Later...
YOU LOOK PROUD, LEIA.
YES, TRIOS. I AM.
TWELVE CRUISERS. FULLY CREWED. PLUS FULL FIGHTER SUPPORT...

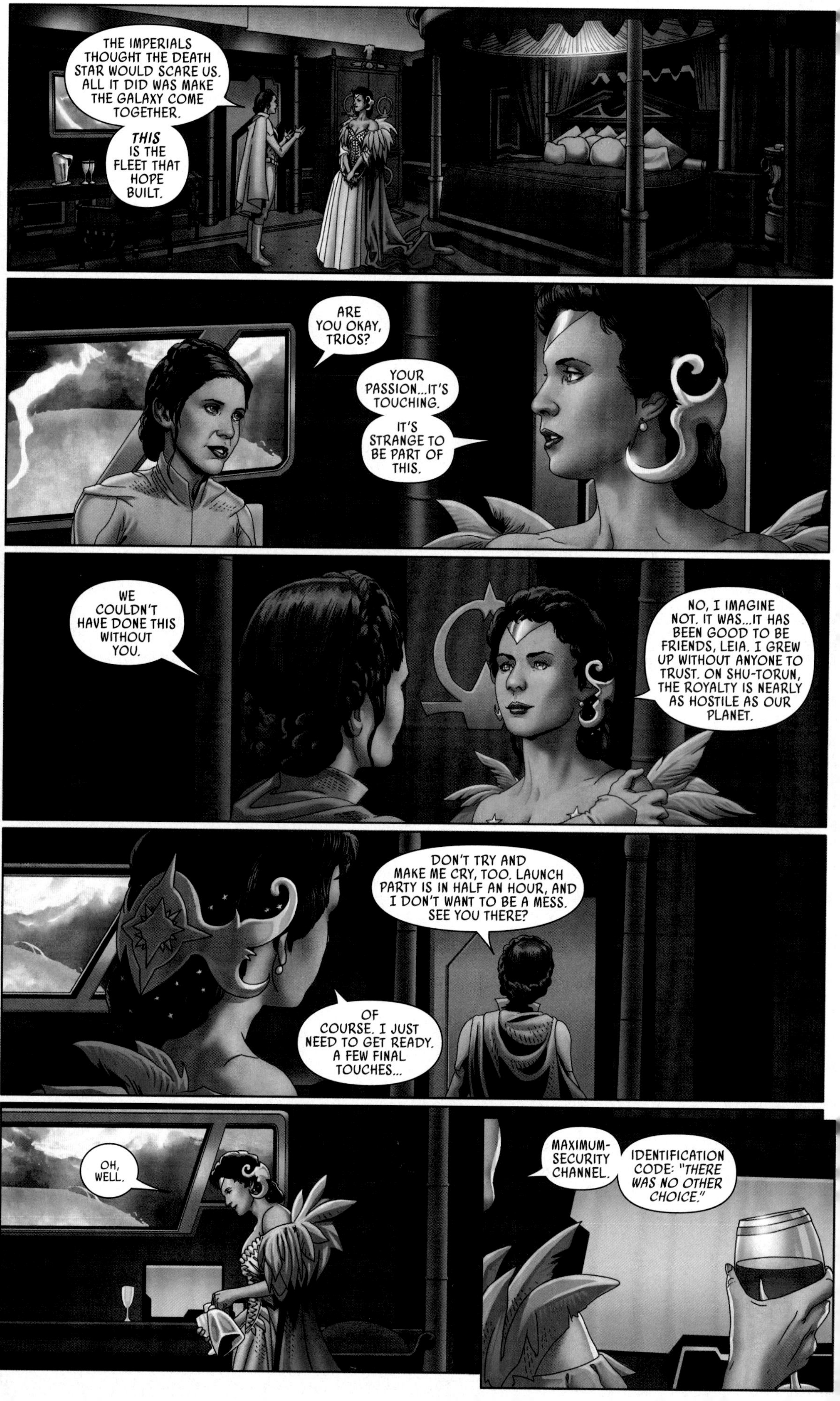
THE IMPERIALS THOUGHT THE DEATH STAR WOULD SCARE US. ALL IT DID WAS MAKE THE GALAXY COME TOGETHER.
THIS IS THE FLEET THAT HOPE BUILT.
ARE YOU OKAY, TRIOS?
YOUR PASSION...IT'S TOUCHING.
IT'S STRANGE TO BE PART OF THIS.
WE COULDN'T HAVE DONE THIS WITHOUT YOU.
NO, I IMAGINE NOT. IT WAS...IT HAS BEEN GOOD TO BE FRIENDS, LEIA. I GREW UP WITHOUT ANYONE TO TRUST. ON SHU-TORUN, THE ROYALTY IS NEARLY AS HOSTILE AS OUR PLANET.
DON'T TRY AND MAKE ME CRY, TOO. LAUNCH PARTY IS IN HALF AN HOUR, AND I DON'T WANT TO BE A MESS. SEE YOU THERE?
OF COURSE. I JUST NEED TO GET READY. A FEW FINAL TOUCHES...
OH, WELL.
MAXIMUM-SECURITY CHANNEL.
IDENTIFICATION CODE: "*THERE WAS NO OTHER CHOICE.*"

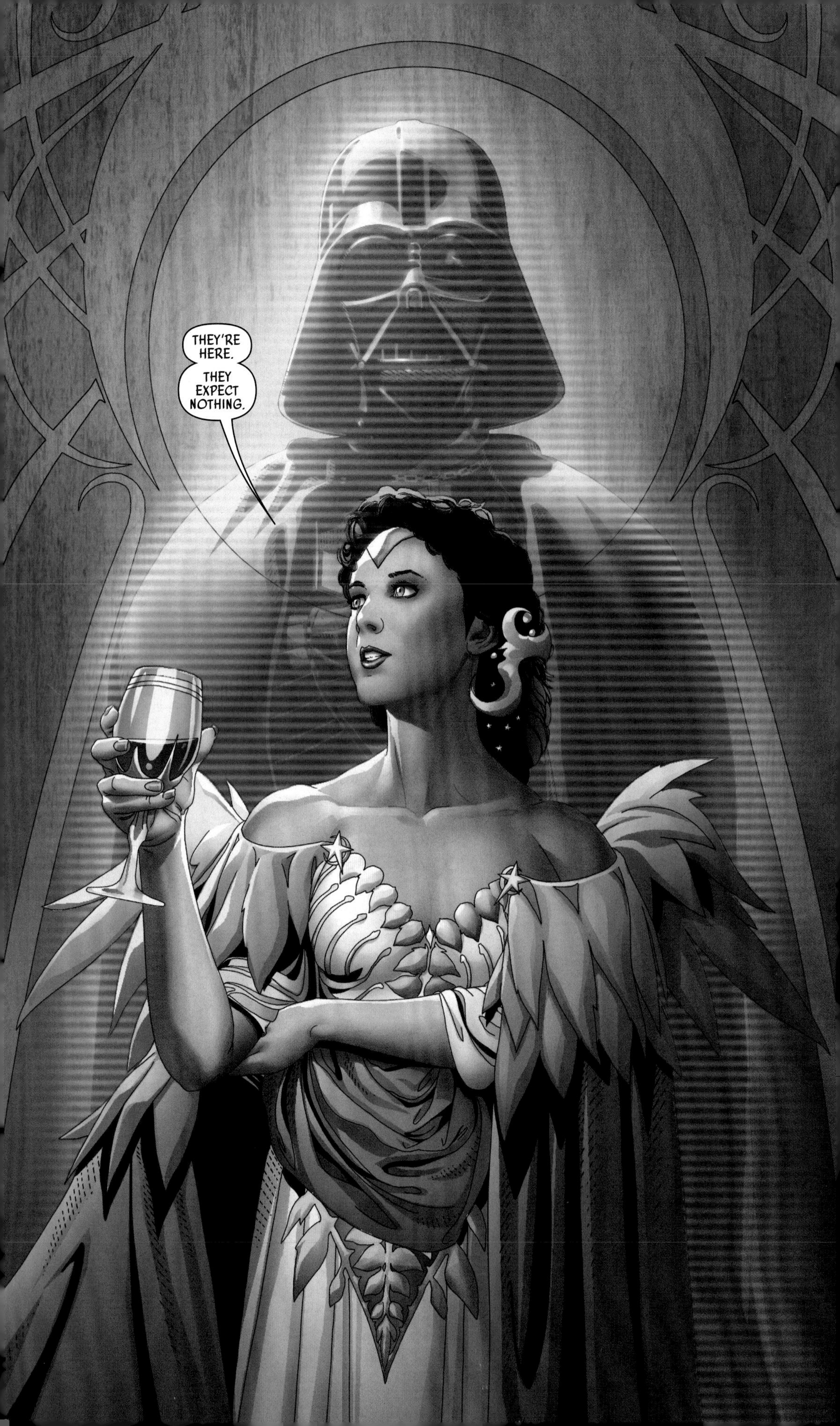
THEY'RE HERE.
THEY EXPECT NOTHING.

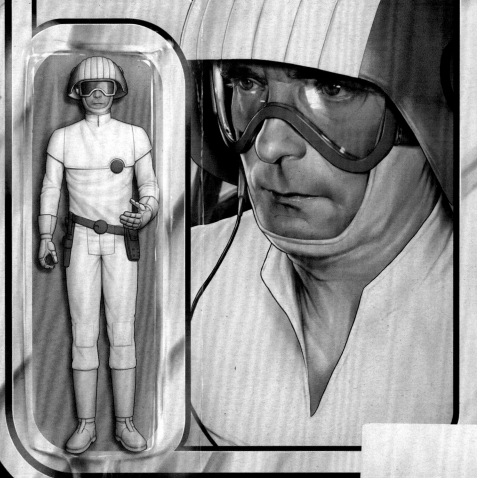

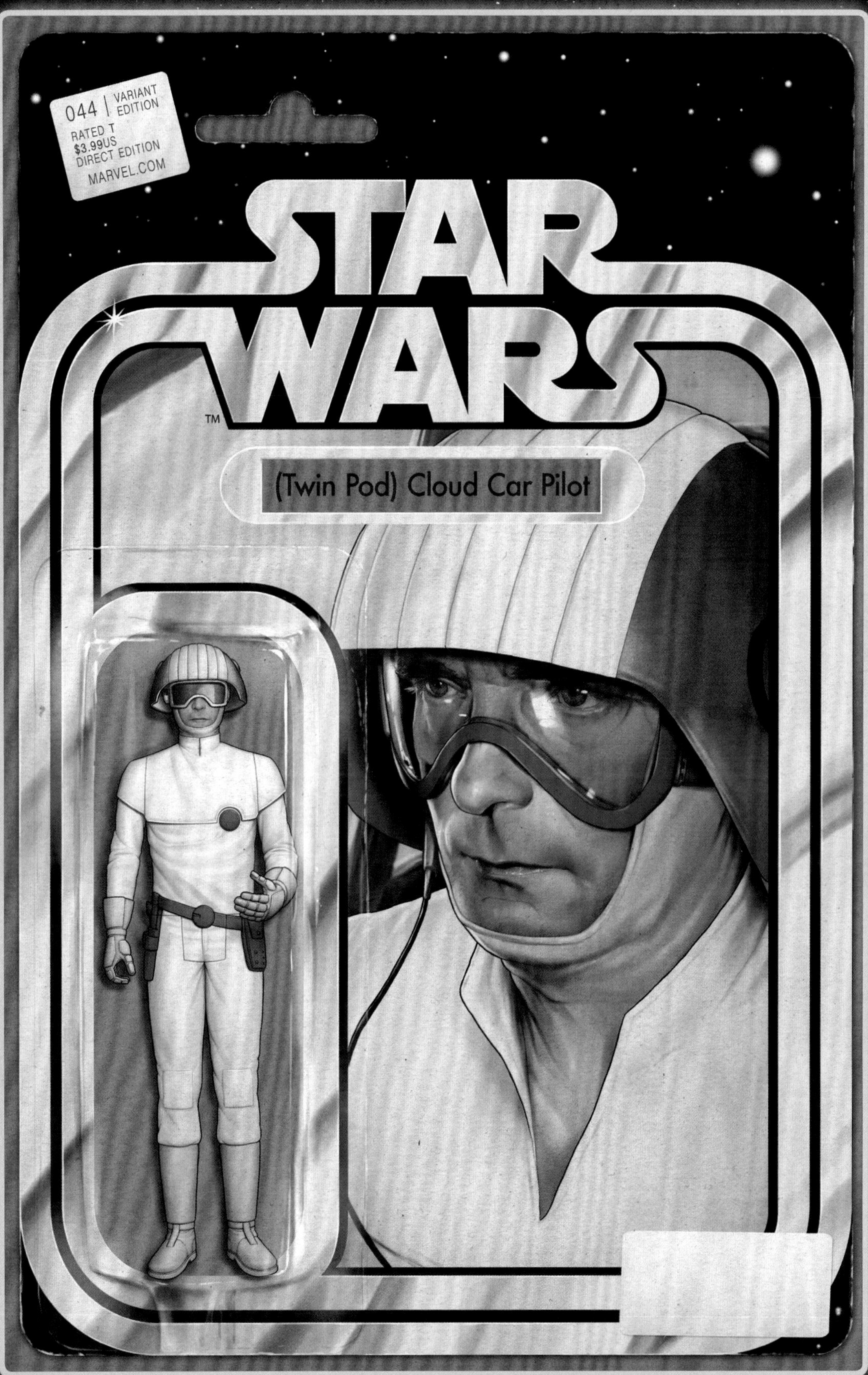

044 | VARIANT EDITION

RATED T
$3.99US
DIRECT EDITION
MARVEL.COM

STAR WARS

(Twin Pod) Cloud Car Pilot

TM

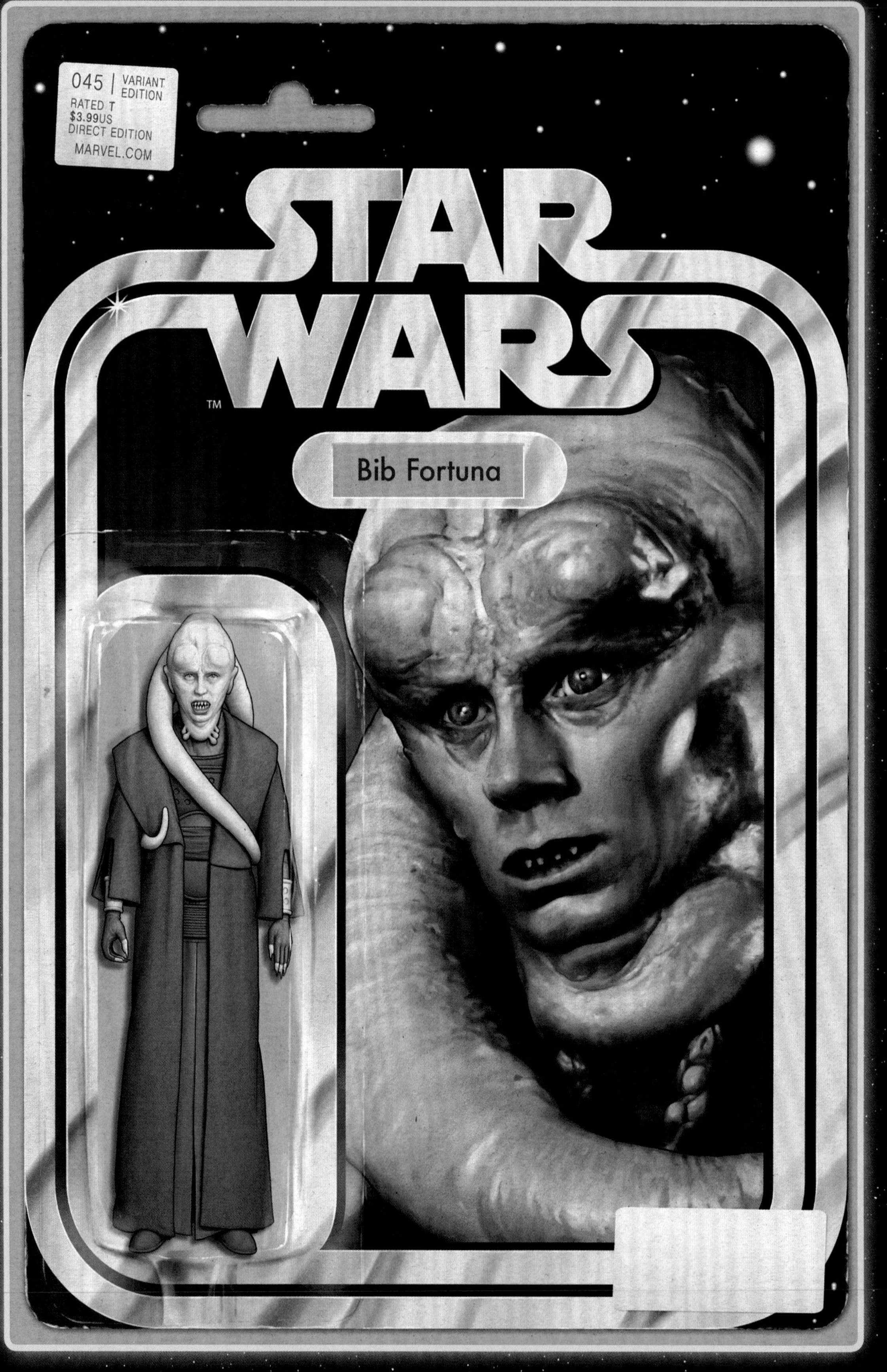
045 | VARIANT EDITION
RATED T
$3.99US
DIRECT EDITION
MARVEL.COM
STAR WARS
TM
Bib Fortuna

STAR WARS 45 Action Figure Variant by

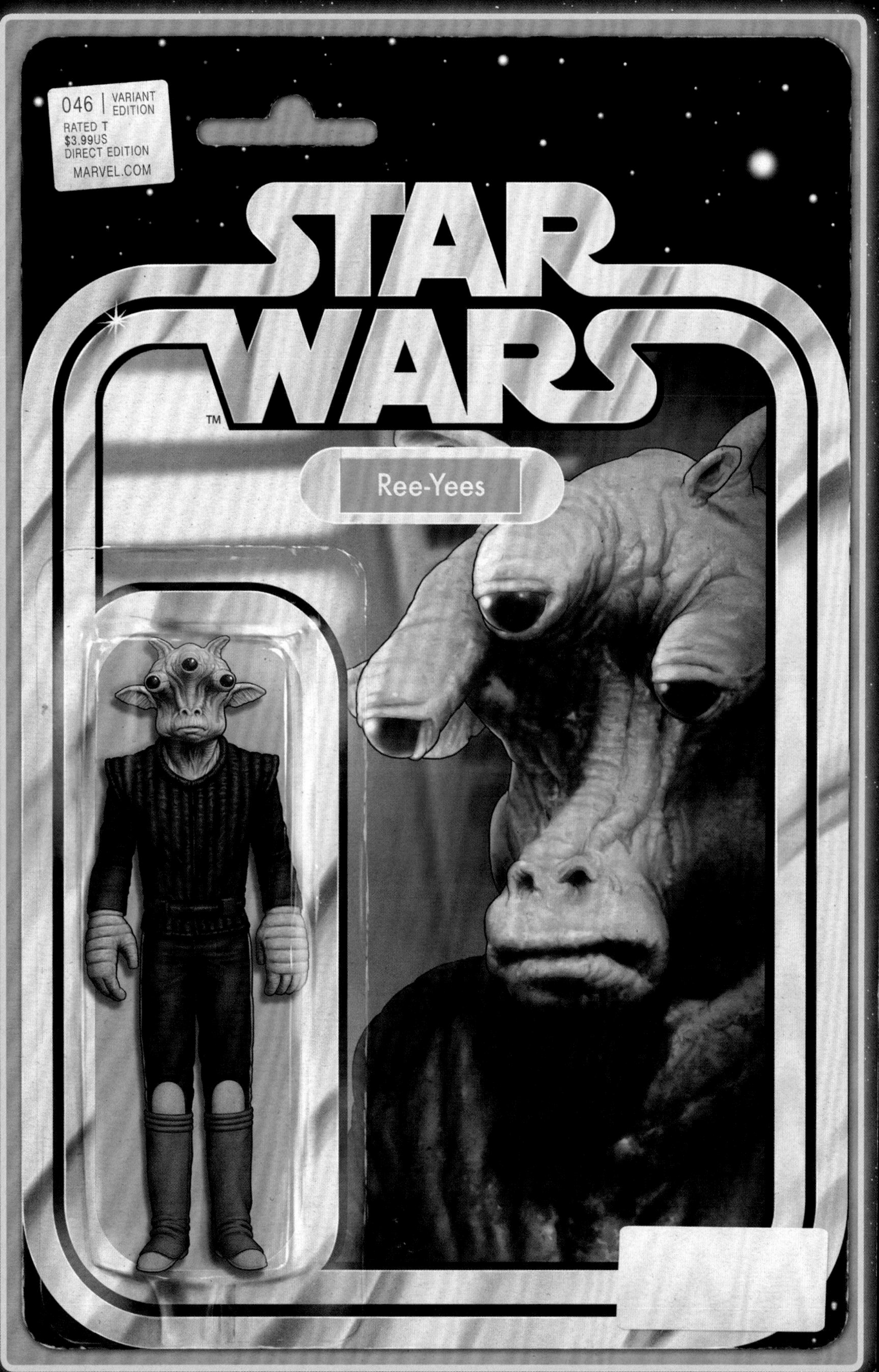

046 | VARIANT EDITION
RATED T
$3.99US
DIRECT EDITION
MARVEL.COM
STAR WARS
™
Ree-Yees

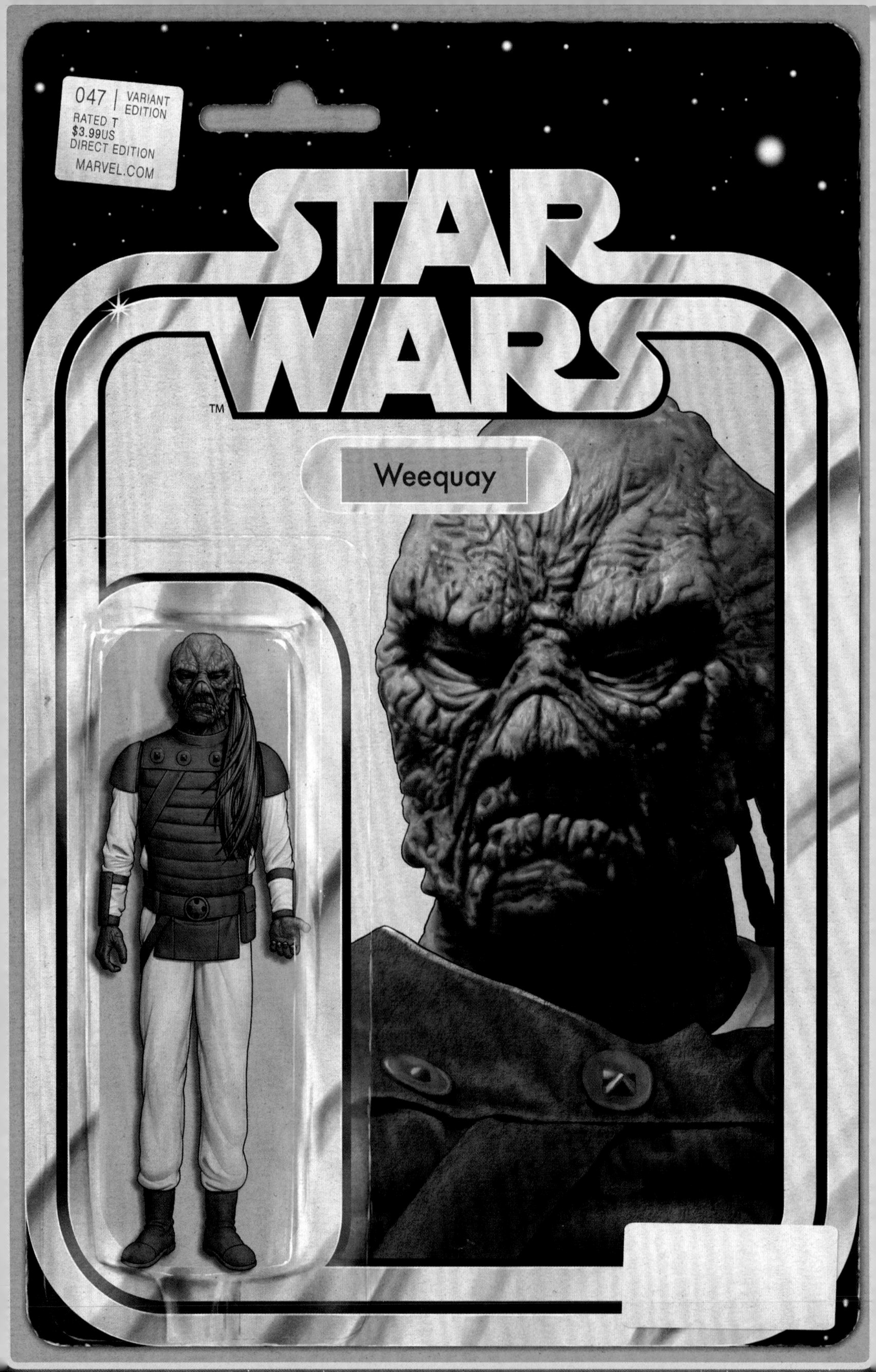
047 | VARIANT EDITION
RATED T
$3.99US
DIRECT EDITION
MARVEL.COM
STAR WARS
TM
Weequay

***STAR WARS* 47 Action Figure Variant by**
JOHN TYLER CHRISTOPHER

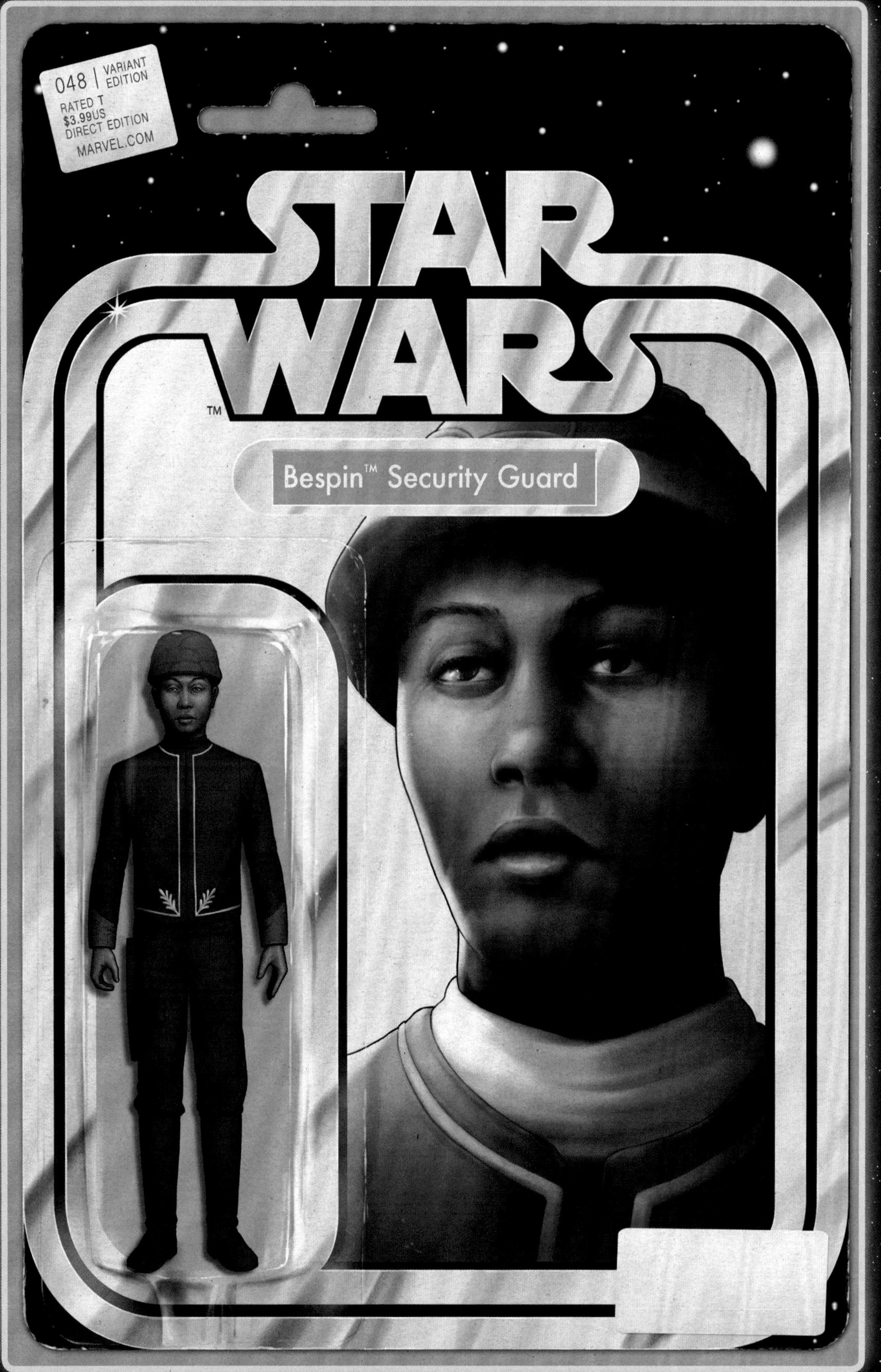
048 | VARIANT EDITION
RATED T
$3.99US
DIRECT EDITION
MARVEL.COM
STAR WARS™
Bespin™ Security Guard

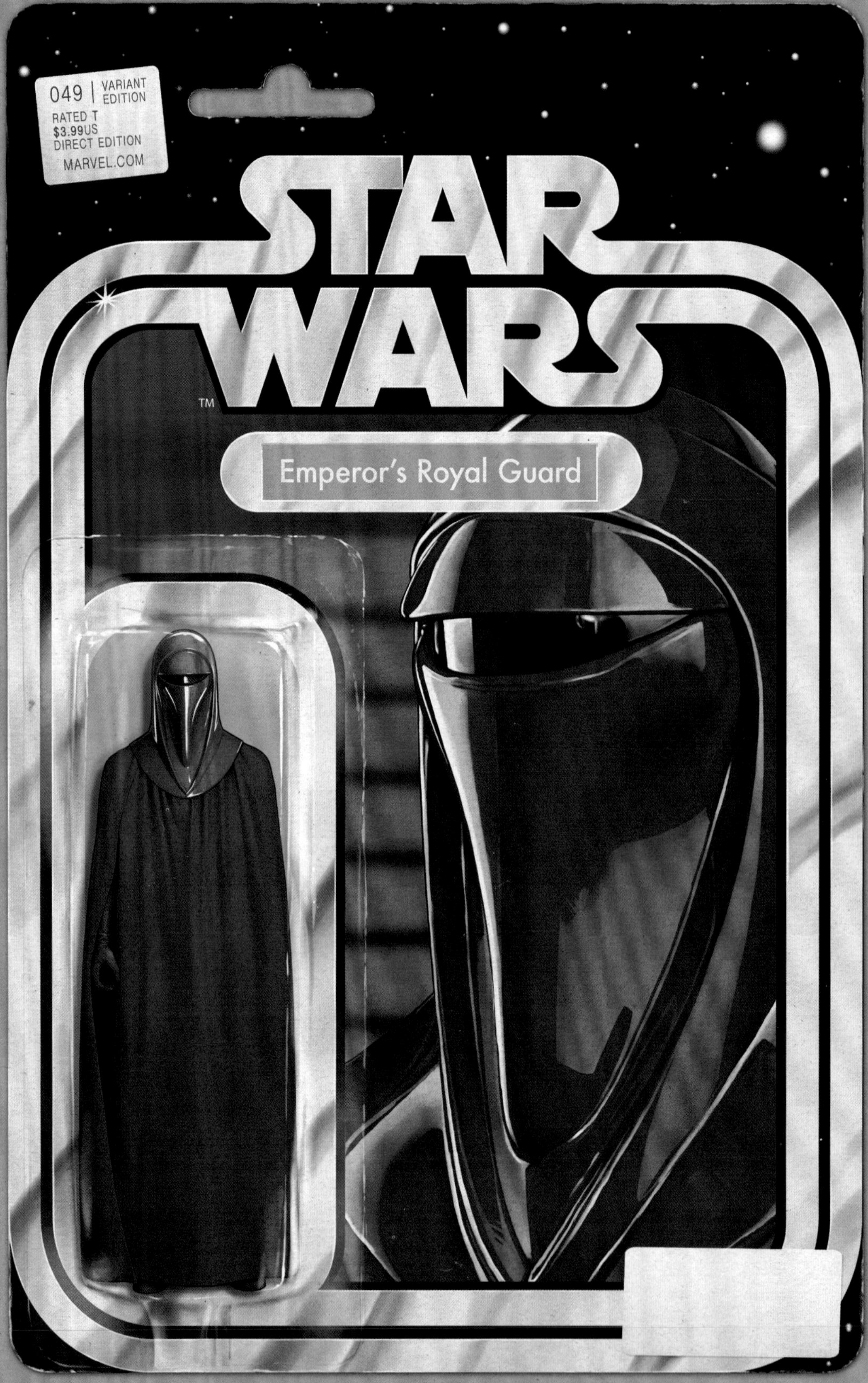

049 | VARIANT EDITION
RATED T
$3.99US
DIRECT EDITION
MARVEL.COM
STAR WARS
TM
Emperor's Royal Guard

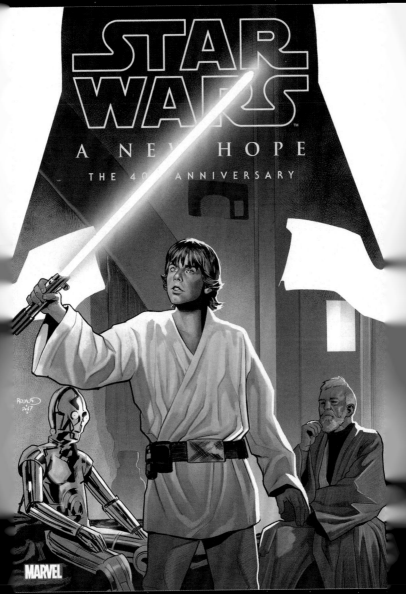

HAN AND CHEWIE IN A RACE AGAINST TIME, THE EMPIRE AND THE FASTEST SHIPS IN THE GALAXY!

STAR WARS: HAN SOLO HC
978-1302912109

ON SALE NOW

AVAILABLE IN PRINT AND DIGITAL WHEREVER BOOKS ARE SOLD

TO FIND A COMIC SHOP NEAR YOU, VISIT COMICSHOPLOCATOR.COM

AFTER BARELY ESCAPING DARTH VADER WITH HER LIFE, DOCTOR APHRA SETS OFF IN SEARCH OF RARE AND DEADLY ARTIFACTS!

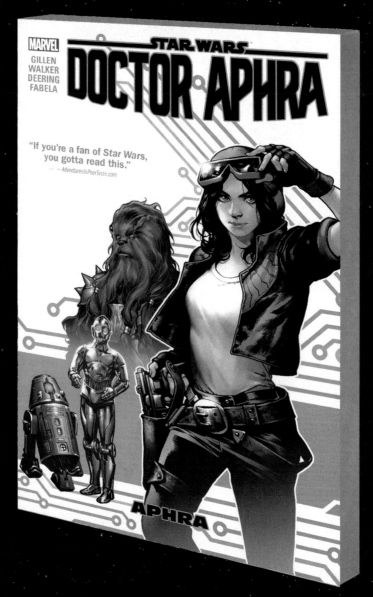

ACE PILOT POE DAMERON AND HIS BLACK SQUADRON TAKE ON THE FIRST ORDER!

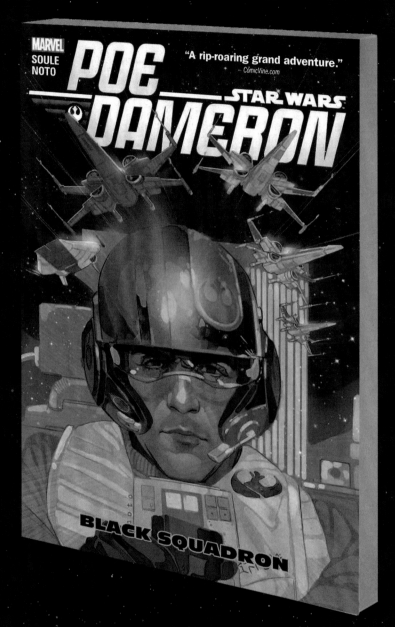

STAR WARS: POE DAMERON VOL. 1 — BLACK SQUADRON TPB
978-1302901103

ON SALE NOW

AVAILABLE IN PRINT AND DIGITAL WHEREVER BOOKS ARE SOLD

TO FIND A COMIC SHOP NEAR YOU, VISIT COMICSHOPLOCATOR.COM

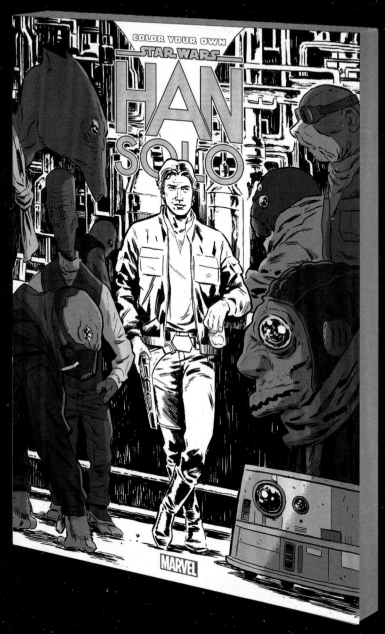

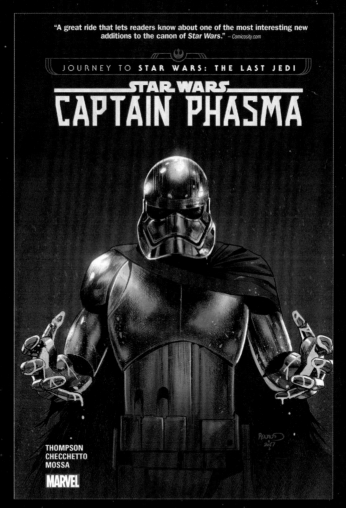

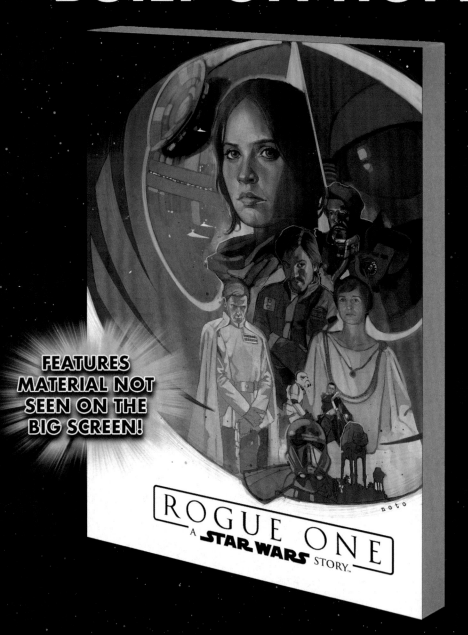